AN ITALIAN RENAISSA
SIX TALES IN HISTORIC _____ _____

Lauro Martines
Translated by Murtha Baca

This collection of six tales offers enticing views into the history of
Renaissance Italy, with fiction and fictional modes becoming gate-
ways to a real, historical world. All written between 1400 and
1500—among them a rare gem by Lorenzo the Magnificent and a
famous account featuring Filippo Brunelleschi—the stories are
presented here in lively translations.

As engaging and high-spirited as those in Boccaccio's *Decameron*, the tales deal with marriage, deception, rural manners,
gender relations, social ambitions, adultery, homosexuality, and the
demands of individual identity. Each is accompanied by an essay
in which Lauro Martines situates the story in its temporal context,
transforming it into an outright historical document. The stories
and essays focus mainly on people from the ordinary and middling
ranks of society, as they go about their daily lives, under the pressure of a highly practical, conformist, pleasure-loving (but often
cruel) urban culture. A fascinating historical work with a combined
anthropological, demographic, and cultural slant, this volume provides unique insight into Italian Renaissance society.

(The Lorenzo Da Ponte Italian Library)

Lauro Martines, former Professor of European History, University of
California, Los Angeles, has written extensively on the Italian
Renaissance. He resides in London and is also the author of a
recent novel, *Loredana: A Venetian Tale*.

Murtha Baca is head of the Standards and Vocabulary Programs at
the Getty Research Institute.

AN ITALIAN RENAISSANCE SEXTET

Six Tales in Historical Context

by

LAURO MARTINES

Translations by Murtha Baca

UNIVERSITY OF TORONTO PRESS
Toronto Buffalo London

ISBN 0-8020-8993-3 (cloth)
ISBN 0-8020-8650-0 (paper)

This book was first published by Marsilio Publishers in 1994.

Printed on acid-free paper

The Lorenzo Da Ponte Italian Library

An Italian Renaissance sextet : six tales in historical context / by Lauro
Martines ; translations by Murtha Baca.

(Lorenzo da Ponte Italian Library)
Translated from Italian.
ISBN 0-8020-8993-3

1. Italian fiction – 15th century – Translations into English. 2. Short stories,
Italian – Translations into English. I. Martines, Lauro
II. Baca, Murtha III. Series.

PQ4253.A44E5 2004   853'.0108   C2004-902096-X

This volume is published under the aegis and with the financial assistance of:
Fondazione Cassamarca, Treviso; Ministero degli Affari Esteri, Direzione Generale
per la Promozione e la Cooperazione Culturale; Ministero per i Beni e le Attività
Culturali, Direzione Generale per i Beni Librari e gli Istituti Culturali, Servizio
per la promozione del libro e della lettura.

Publication of this volume is assisted by the Istituto Italiano di Cultura, Toronto.

University of Toronto Press acknowledges the financial assistance to its publishing
program of the Canada Council for the Arts and the Ontario Arts Council.

University of Toronto Press acknowledges the financial support for its publishing
activities of the Government of Canada through the Book Publishing Industry
Development Program (BPIDP).

CONTENTS

for Lucien, *amico e figlio*

ACKNOWLEDGEMENTS

Fifteenth-century Italian prose is routinely ambiguous, repetitive, under-punctuated, and rich in obscure expression. My thanks therefore must go first to Murtha Baca, of the Getty Center in Los Angeles, for producing admirable translations of the six tales. I went over her renditions with an eye for fifteenth-century meanings, as well as for a certain register and style. My wife, the novelist and translator Julia O'Faolain, then stepped in to help lend grace and immediacy to the translations.

The six essays, each of them appearing after its tale, owe a debt to recent historical scholarship on Renaissance Italy. All the creditors are named in the bibliographic discussion at the end of the book.

I want to thank former colleagues in Paris, at the École des Hautes Études en Sciences Sociales, where I offered seminars, in the spring of 1992, on the subject of love in the Italian Renaissance. The ritual language of this surprisingly historical topic turns up insistently in several of the tales.

A word of thanks finally to an old friend, Luigi Ballerini, who originally invited me to do a book for the New York series in which the present volume first appeared. The invitation led me to the idea of working with a medley of tales, each of which would serve as an entrée to the history of Renaissance Italy.

Although the first edition of *An Italian Renaissance Sextet* appeared ten years ago, the need to find the face of history in fiction, and to trace what is truly devious (*l'imaginaire*) in times past, has never seemed to me more urgent. Historical work must be incomplete when it ignores the windings between reality and fiction.

Lauro Martines
London
2004

FOREWORD

1. *Purpose*

This book aims to use six tales as decoys for enticing readers into the history of Renaissance Italy. Fiction and fictional modes are to be our entry to a real historical world.

Twenty years ago historians were not prepared to read fiction as historical documentation. Even today such work is rare, two notable exceptions being the remarkable book by Emmanuel Le Roy Ladurie, *L'argent, l'amour et la mort en pays d'oc* (1980), and Stephen Kern's recent *The Culture of Love: Victorians to Moderns* (1992). Most other historical studies of narrative turn out to be preoccupations with the artful retailing of events either by witnesses, such as in a courtroom, or by later historians. Reality in poetry and fiction is still the undiscovered country in the study of history.

The Italian tales here presented in translation were all written in the fifteenth century, except the first, *Ricciarda*, which was penned probably in the 1390s but possibly later. The last tale, Antonio Manetti's *The Fat Woodcarver*, produced in the 1480s, had behind it a lively oral tradition. In the six essays, each appearing after the appropriate translation, I situate the tales in their historical context. Lest it be inferred that my enterprise is a venture in what might be called the historical sociology of literature, let me say at once that it is not. Admittedly, in attempting to explain how exactly the tales fit into their time and place, I seek to throw a socio-cultural searchlight on them. In the course of the analysis, however, there is a metamorphosis: the tales are imperceptibly turned into outright historical documents. The nature of this transformation, in the light of theory and method, is beset with problems. I hope that no one knows this better than I. But I broach no part of that in this book, because I have already treated the larger question—and the particular problems are surprisingly similar—in a theoretical book on poetry as historical documentation: *Society and History in English Renaissance Verse* (1985). The six essays, then, are applied practical exercises, seeking no more and no less than to take hold of the tales as history.

Emphasis on the presence of history in fiction does not deny the process of individual literary creation. In society, history and the individual are indissolubly married. But the historian is not called upon to run a check on individual creativity; she or he may leave such concerns to the literary critic and psycho-biographer. In this connection, it should be noted that the oral tradition of story-telling, as a source for Renaissance writers, will come into play at several points in the essays. Despite their realistic patina or submerged realism, four of the tales may be counted as fiction: *Ricciarda*, *Scopone*, *Friar and Priest*, and *Giacoppo*, although some scholars suspect that *Scopone* contains the traces of a historical incident. But the other two, *Bianco Alfani* and *The Fat Woodcarver*, are, I maintain, accounts of real incidents; they draw upon circulating oral testimony and reportage; and so I consistently refer to them as stories rather than tales. No doubt they contain elements of fiction. However, in the quest for historical under-standing, we must beware of any easy identifying of fiction with falsehood. Invention may hold more historical realism than a legion of quirky incidents.

Since the approach to history by way of fiction cannot involve historical analysis of a conventional sort, the reader of the essays should expect no measured movement through time, no reliance on chronologies or on major events as guideposts. Instead, the analysis will touch upon marriage, ritual, age, gender, sexuality, love, family ideals, clerical misconduct, personal social identities, small groups, links between town and country, and the invasive-ness of the public face of neighborhood and urban space. The tales and essays have to do mainly with people from the ordinary and middling ranks of society. We observe individuals in the daily give-and-take of city life: in conversation, groups, solitude, stress, pranks, and under the pressure of a practical, conformist, plea-sure-loving, but also tough—and often cruel—urban society.

Professional historians will recognize that the foregoing themes belong to the most searching and novel historical work of the past twenty years: scholarship with a combined demographic, anthro-pological, and cultural slant. *An Italian Renaissance Sextet* can thus claim to be an introduction to current historical practice.

2. *Tales*

As we know from the *Novellino* and *Book of the Seven Sages*, the Italian tale makes its first appearance in the late thirteenth century, and takes most of its anecdotes from a variety of earlier sources: classical, Latin medieval, biblical, Indian, Byzantine, and French. The hundred tales of the *Novellino* are short and crisp and carry a moral message. Here emperors, kings, lords, knights, wise men, and other outstanding figures usually hold the narrative stage; but there are also anecdotes about lesser folk and women. The lessons imparted often share a neatly delineated morality with the anecdotes of homilies and of the most able fourteenth-century preachers, who based the lessons of their narrative *exempla* on notions of a preordained moral and social order.

Insofar as the early tale was a borrowed and more-or-less fixed form, intended to edify and please the energetic classes of citizens at Florence, Bologna, Venice, and elsewhere, we may say that it had to be broken or opened up in order to satisfy the needs of ever-increasing numbers of listeners and readers. Even the early tale has occasional characters and adaptations that bespeak the pressure and input of living audiences, looking for entertainment and tuition more in line with their own historical experience. But not until Boccaccio's *Decameron*, in the 1350s, do we encounter a new Italian form, a genre which had received no recognition or treatment in the scatter of medieval treatises on rhetoric.

Boccaccio's charmingly mendacious claim, in his preface to the *Decameron*, that he had composed his hundred tales "for the ladies, but only for those who are in love," was a tribute paid to "love," that is, to pleasure and worldly experience. Hence the first aim of his story-telling marathon was to delight readers and listeners; but to do so, he had to touch them in their everyday doings, ideals, and reveries. Consequently, his well-wrought "tales or fables or parables or historiettes," as he calls them, were the perfection of a genre which was plastic and adaptable enough to take in the stuff of his primary audience, namely, contemporary urban experience. To take it in, to realign, condense, and make it risible, astonishing, or pathetic, and to give it back again in meaningful form.

The standard set by Boccaccio was not matched in the following century, not at least when the *Decameron* is viewed as a chain of tales held skillfully together by the author's company of seven young women and three young men, who are both the listeners and story-tellers. But in entertainment, inventiveness, and sheer energy, a number of individual stories from the fifteenth century, such as *Giacoppo* and *The Fat Woodcarver*, equal or surpass some of the better tales in the *Decameron*.

Like Boccaccio's and other fourteenth-century fictions, the fifteenth-century tale retains an axiomatic view of life: that is to say, the narrator affects to know life so well that it may be grasped by means of axioms or self-evident truths. Thus action and character are linked not only so as to provide reading or listening pleasure, but also to convey moral and social lessons. Such condensed knowingness (since our topic is the short tale) was fostered by the strongly pragmatic, here-and-now daily outlook of urban life in Renaissance Italy, with its concomitant and balancing emphasis on God and eternity. This dual stress on God and practicality went to help fashion a world where the means and ends of life were assumed to be clearly set forth as generally accepted truths, and where people believed that individuals departed from these at their peril. We are therefore dealing with a somewhat closed system of ideals and values: with the finite mental world which answered to the political, social, and economic fixities of urban life. That great civilizing ideal of the humanists, classical antiquity, did not alter the accepted ends of life, nor change the ways in which people earned their daily bread and confronted rampant disease. All Italian cities in the fifteenth century were under oligarchic or princely rule; and the attendant social structures were relatively inflexible, though more so, to be sure, in some cities than in others. Among the more inflexible in their anatomies of social command and obedience were aristocratic Venice and the princely capitals, say Milan and Ferrara; among the least inflexible were the Tuscan cities, above all Florence. And this may be why Tuscany, with its strong oral traditions, gave rise to the most energetic and fertile line of story-telling, as seen, for instance, in Franco Sacchetti (Florence), Giovanni Sercambi (Lucca), Gentile Sermini (Siena), and a dozen or so other authors of individual tales. Limited though it was, the incidence of vertical social movement in Tuscany, and particularly in Florence, fired ambitions, stirred up dreams, loosened tongues, and made for more diversity. But these, in turn, raised sharply critical voices against the people who stepped out of line or who appeared to be impractical. Nonconformity and impracticality: here was material for infinite joking, gossip, censure, pranks, tales, and prejudice; and here, too, in this spectrum of activity, which includes tales and stories, was a return to the axioms and mental world of Italian Renaissance cities, where ways and means, like ideals, were taken to be clear lines and points on the familiar charts of urban existence.

TALES

AND

HISTORICAL ESSAYS

ONE

1.

RICCIARDA

by Giovanni Gherardi da Prato

Trained in law, the poet and writer Giovanni Gherardi da Prato (ca. 1360–ca. 1445) spent most of his life in Florence, where he gave public lectures on Dante's Divine Comedy *from 1417 to 1425 and knew most of the city's men of letters.* Ricciarda *is drawn from his literary and fictional miscellany,* Il Paradiso degli Alberti, *written sometime after 1389, doubtless over a period of years. The title of the miscellany was given by Alessandro Wesselofsky, Gherardi's nineteenth-century editor.*

∞

Not long ago there lived in this glorious city of ours [Florence] a very beautiful young woman named Ricciarda, who was no less endowed with virtue than with beauty. This lady was given in marriage by her father to a most handsome, virtuous, and rich young man called Michele Pilestri, who died young, leaving her a widow with two small sons and a girl a little older. Looking after them with great prudence, rectitude, and modesty, Ricciarda had no other thought but to bring up her family to be worthy of praise.

And as she had much judgment, she took especially great care of her daughter, always keeping her nearby and under a vigilant eye, never letting her go to parties or other amusements anywhere except in her own company. The girl therefore had great respect for her mother and stood quite in awe of her. When at last the girl reached the age of marriage, with the advice and help of her relations, the able young woman married her to a most handsome and charming young man from a very old family, Lippozzo Greci.

As the time approached to have the wedding and consummate the marriage, the girl was instructed again and again by her mother never to think or desire to do or say anything but that which would please Lippozzo, nor was she ever to depart from his will; and after she had been thus instructed, the marriage took place.

Now when the young man was in the bedchamber with his bride, he began to kiss and embrace her, and she, obedient and quiet, made no resistance; and when her husband commanded her to undress and get into bed, she quickly did so. Whereupon the two were promptly in bed together, and as this seemed astonishing to the young man, he began to suspect her honor and honesty. Being in bed now, he told her to embrace and kiss him, and she did so without a word; then he added: "Now take pleasure in what I do, and without my saying anything more, let me know that you do." Then he drew her to him and set about consummating the marriage, and the girl, who was very ripe, began to taste the sweetness of it. Thus, feeling herself drawn by pleasure, moving her body in a thousand pleasant ways, much like a swallow or a wagtail when in love, and warmly clasping her husband as if she had been with him for years, she seemed to swoon.

Being an immoderately suspicious man, this behavior seemed to him to befit more the actions of a dishonorable woman than of a

maiden, and so Lippozzo at once concluded that she must have
led a promiscuous life. Displeased, he decided not to touch her
again, nor ever again to go near her; and pulling away, without
speaking to her, he waited for daybreak. And when morning came,
he arose very early and left the bedchamber and, saying nothing,
remained plunged in melancholy. After thus passing the whole
day, when evening came and he went to sleep again in the same
bed with her, he said nothing. The girl marveled greatly at all this,
but out of modesty, and fearing to do anything that might displease
her husband, said nothing.

And when the next morning came, both Lippozzo and the girl
got up very early, and having eaten a good meal, the girl returned
to her mother's house, as is still the practice, and there, being
received with great rejoicing, she remained for several days, as
custom requires. Then the time came when her husband was
meant to send for her, and when he failed to do so, Ricciarda was
stricken with amazement. Finally, after she had questioned her
daughter closely, again and again, about her every move and
action, and the daughter had told her everything, Ricciarda realized what Lippozzo had to be thinking, knowing well that he was
very suspicious by nature. And quickly making a wise plan, she
determined to go with her daughter to an estate of hers called
Carcherelli, located not many miles from Florence, beyond the
city gate of San Frediano. Having been there for some days, she
thought it time to carry out her plan, and so she sent word to
Lippozzo, requesting that for a good reason he please come out on
the next morning and have luncheon with her.

When Lippozzo received her message, he decided to go,
despite the difficulty of the matter, because he held Ricciarda in
great esteem on account of her surpassing virtue. And so he set

out, and when he arrived at Carcherelli, he was received by Ricciarda with the greatest rejoicing; and having conversed with him about many things, the admirable woman finally led him to a window whence the whole estate could be seen. While the two of them were standing there, speaking of the pleasures of the place and especially of the fine wide moats that surrounded it, a maid-servant came in and said: "Lady, do you know that the baby ducks have been born and that they're the sweetest little things in the world?" To which Ricciarda immediately replied: "Go, bring them here a while, so that we may see them." The servant quickly went off and brought them back in a little cape of hers, and as she showed them to the two, the lady and the young man began to speak about nature and about how many beautiful things she made, and how she gave to each thing its own properties. Speaking thus, Ricciarda, who had been holding the ducklings in her hand, suddenly flung them into the moat. Seeing this, Lippozzo was astonished and said: "Lady, what are you doing? Do you want them to die? Pray, do not do this!" Ricciarda laughed and said: "You shall soon see."

When the ducklings landed in the moat, they began to beat their wings and keep themselves afloat in the water, so that they swam to the edge of the ditch without any difficulty. The young man was greatly amazed, for what he had seen seemed impossible to him, and he said to Ricciarda: "Certainly, I would never have believed this if I hadn't seen it, and surely it is a great thing to think how nature instructs and teaches us." To which Ricciarda replied: "Lippozzo, I shall speak to you as I would to a dear, good son, and I pray you to listen to me as to a loving mother, and don't take it amiss if I speak to you with great frankness, for it shall be only for your own good, profit, and honor. Oh, how unreasonable and foolish is your assumption! Looking into the matter carefully, can't you see with what folly you are besmirching your own honor and mine and that of your wife? Do you not see that you are turning your back on your own good, with the most awful shame for yourself and for me, and with disgrace for your wife, who is the most inexperienced of girls? And don't you see how you are preparing such a grievous life for yourself and for me and for her, on account of your oh, so false suspicions? You marvel that my little girl, your immaculate bride, who is old enough to feel the power that nature gives, has felt pleasure in doing something that delights both you and her. Don't you see how much power nature has in every living thing, and especially when it comes to procreation? Aren't men and women born by nature already greatly disposed to reproduce, giving us pleasure in body as well as in spirit? Ah, you fool! And you wonder that my daughter, who has never heard or seen anything but what is virtuous, and who was instructed by me to please you in all things, was most chastely aroused by nature and did everything she thought would give you pleasure, to her own delight! Wake up now, leave off these crazy notions of yours, and consider that if my daughter had lived a dishonorable life, she would have gone to great lengths to appear pure to you. Aren't you old enough by now to know this, and to value the simplicity and purity and obedience of the girl? Go now and repent what you have done, and resolve to abide with your bride, as is right and proper. For as you see, it is difficult to suppress natural impulses, since they come forth without teacher or training. Who taught the ducklings to swim or the other birds to make nests, lay eggs, feed their chicks, if not nature? Go, for I swear to you by God's Cross that you have brought me such heartache and melancholy by your stupidity that I thought I would die; and were it not for the inordinate and kind love I bear you, I would not feel appeased until I had strangled you with my own hands, whatever the consequences afterwards. But I can only love you above every other creature, both out of respect for you and because you are and should be the master, guide, and perfect example for my dear daughter, your lawful wife." And here she put an end to her words.

Lippozzo, who was listening with shame, said nothing; or rather, having considered the woman's prudence for a moment, he was struck with wonder, and awakening from his error, made only this reply: "Lady, you are right, and I cannot excuse myself. But by the grace of God, I believe that from now on I shall act so as to make amends for the wrong I have done, and I shall always be most ready to obey whatever you say and command, begging you to forgive my failing."

When Ricciarda heard this, she called the girl and told her to speak to Lippozzo, which she did, to the great pleasure of each of them. And when the table was laid, they ate with much laughter and joking, and then Lippozzo went for a very long noonday rest with his bride, giving the greatest satisfaction, pleasure, and joy to everyone, especially to the most worthy lady. And thus was Lippozzo's error corrected so prudently and in a pleasant, irreproachable way by the wise lady Ricciarda.

2.

The Real in the Imaginary: *Ricciarda*

This little tale sparkles with touches of realism, beginning with the arranged marriages of the first paragraph and ending with the girl's blind obedience in the first sentence of the last one. Indeed, the entire narrative floats in the realities of Renaissance gender relations, at all events as attested in Florence.

The heart of the tale, Ricciarda, seems to be a fiction. Sketched in her bare though idealized essentials, she is a literary commonplace of the times, to be found in Boccaccio's *Decameron*, Renaissance love poetry, and a variety of fifteenth-century tales, such as Enea Silvio Piccolomini's 1440s *A Tale of Two Lovers*. Ricciarda is the beautiful, virtuous, well-born, well-mannered woman: wise, poised, strong-minded, and exceptionally articulate. Oddly, however, while appearing to be a woman of the world, a worldly woman who knows its ways, she was evidently reared much like her own daughter: to be chaste, to be supremely concerned about her honor (at once an individual and a tribal or family virtue), and to be obedient to her elders, above all to the men nearest her, father and husband.

In the middle and upper classes of Florence about 1400, girls (*ipso facto* virgins) and young widows were closely protected and watched, because their sexuality and supposed latent irresponsibility were seen as posing threats to family honor, name, and access to the range of desirable marriages. Hence, where and how had Ricciarda acquired her worldliness? Without mentioning the Greek philosopher by name, she could even talk about Aristotelian views of nature: knowledge in the currency of only the educated men of her day, such as physicians, humanists, lawyers, and certain clerics. Nowhere does the author account for the suggested breadth of Ricciarda's experience, nor is there any need to; she is a literary datum. Yet there is a concealed historical element at work here, as we shall see at the end of this analysis.

The anecdote is simplicity itself. Ricciarda brings her daughter up in a condition of such monitored purity (inexperience) and reverent obedience, that on the night of the marriage, in compliance with her husband's wishes, the girl shows pleasure and abandon in bed, which she assumes is also obedience to him. He silently concludes, instead, that she has had previous sexual experience and sees her, in effect, as a loose young woman. Accordingly, after the girl's customary return home, he refuses to fetch her back at the expected time; and Ricciarda then has to teach the young man the lesson of nature's power by flinging newborn ducklings into a moat. In short, a virgin who is ripe for love-making naturally makes love with keen pleasure, but the seal of marriage is what guarantees that she is "most chastely aroused [to make love] by nature" (*purissimamente incitata dalla natura*).

Can the tale be suggesting that it is a mistake for girls to be unquestioningly obedient to their new spouses? Not at all, for this would undermine the whole moral structure of a tale which is keyed to Florentine household ideals around 1400: that is, the obedience of wives to husbands, arranged marriage (which presupposes the obedience of young people), the virginity and chastity of women (thus their worldly inexperience), and the cardinal importance of family honor. The last of these was semiotic capital which, as a major aspect of social standing, touched directly on possible marriage alliances, business dealings, neighborhood social interaction, and even political status when the important families were involved.

Although she is a standard fictional character, Ricciarda also incarnates, as mother and former wife, the ideals of chastity, honor, and household care which underpinned the values of the great urban bourgeoisie of cities such as Florence, Siena, Bologna, Lucca, and Venice. Here the transmission of property to legitimate heirs was assumed to have fundamental importance. What was an eminent family without its imposing material and semiotic accumulations? And how could these be honorably or legitimately passed on, if not by means of the fidelity, obedience, and chastity of the women involved? So to read the tale as a subtle plea for less obedience would be to misread it and to get Ricciarda wrong. In the society of Renaissance Italy, obedience was not taught as action to be rendered by degrees. The admirable Ricciarda rears a daughter who entertains a mixture of great fear, apprehension, and reverence for her, as indicated by the noun *timore* (*di lei con grandissimo timore stava*). These are the trained emotions of a thoroughly pliable child, who would then agreeably and dutifully carry out every order issued by her husband. She was not even "to think . . . anything but that which would please Lippozzo." In short, the property and gender structures of Renaissance society imposed a corresponding framework of feeling. Now other troubling items in the tale also find their place in a pattern which is at once literary and ideological.

The girl is a phantom presence. Her name is not given and she never speaks; she is there to do as she is told. All the business is between mother-in-law and son-in-law, a man and the tale's authority figure. At the moment of peripety ("I swear to you by God's Cross"), the point when events peak and must turn, Ricciarda declares: "were it not for the inordinate and kind love I bear you, I would not feel appeased until I had strangled you with my own hands." The beautiful and wise woman of the world suddenly turns savage. Far from being out of character, this flash of rage is altogether appropriate. Her two sons are still under age, say about eleven and thirteen, being somewhat younger than their sister, who would be about fifteen or sixteen years old, if we see her as marrying a little younger than the average in the city's demographic profile. As widow and sole parent, Ricciarda exercises the power of the father, the emotional *patria potestas*, over her two sons and daughter; and Lippozzo, by his terrible assumption, has challenged the honor of her family and all that she is, all that she has. No wonder, then, that she thought she would die of a gloom bordering on violent anger (*maninconia*), a man's anger. For in the world of the upper class, Lippozzo's challenge threatened to be so destructive that, unless he took the girl back, only a blood feud and his likely death could bring satisfaction. The chronicle of fourteenth- and fifteenth-century Florence resounds with violent cases of feud among some of the leading lineages; and the Florentine government was often ready to see such quarrels privately and bloodily settled. Appropriately, therefore, Ricciarda's outburst, "I would not feel appeased" (etc.), turns on a revealing past participle, *apagata* (*io non mi terrei apagata*), which also carries the sense of payment or acquittance. Only by strangling him with her own hands could just *payment* be made to her. In a mercantile society, the word betokened action which must have seemed all the more just.

The tale has two settings, urban and rural. Evidently the duckling episode and the rhythms of the fiction call for a change of scene.

Yet we have no reason to assume that Ricciarda's ingenuity was limited to her use of resources in the country. As a model of worldly wisdom, she could no doubt have found other ways to illustrate her lesson within the city walls of Florence. The change of scene, therefore, has more to it than ducklings and literary grace. Here again we return to our historical ground in the themes of family honor and possible vendetta.

In Florence, as in other Italian Renaissance cities, all families of substance tended to own land and houses in the surrounding countryside, sometimes as far as twenty and even thirty miles into the hinterland. Rich families usually had large estates, including farms, villas (*case da signore*), streams, and timberland. When in an altercation with a tenant farmer, sharecropper, or lessee, Florentines would isolate the man—if they were utilizing the shrewdest practice—by summoning him into the city, into the midst of its intimidating ways, so as to bully and persuade him. Ricciarda reverses this practice and invites the young man into the country, not of course because she supposes that she will be able to bully him there. He is himself rich, comes from an old family, and also knows the country. Her design is another. Lippozzo's challenge and grievous insult have been given in the city, that great walled-in arena where the eyes of all neighbors are fixed on the actions and events that make or break families; it is an arena where all eminent lineages occupy, in a sense, a completely public space. Ricciarda therefore has to take precautions against Lippozzo's possible spurning of her lesson and entreaties. No violent, outlandish, or noisy scene can be allowed to erupt in the city. The young husband himself, struck by "the difficulty of the matter" (*come che duro li paresse*), does not look forward to the confrontation. She thereupon removes it to her big house in the country, where in fact Lippozzo too, if he is wise, must prefer that it take place. For as she emphasizes to him, the threatened scandal, if he should persist, would also dishonor him, to his own injury and enormous shame. Moreover, having drawn him in isolation out into the country, if he is unmoved by her plea, who knows what other measures she might have in mind? His rejection of the girl verges on being, in symbolic terms, a kind of capital crime: he threatens to strip an honorable family of its indispensable semiotic capital. In these circumstances, any manner of vendetta, however extreme, would appear justifiable. Ricciarda has to be concerned about her sons too, about their future marriages. After all, how would rumors of their sister's sexual promiscuity affect their status and marriageability in the city? As for the girl, the wife spurned, unless Lippozzo relented, her destiny—however large her dowry—would either be confinement in a convent or a "base" and shameful marriage beneath her own social class. Among the humbler social strata, and especially in the rural expanses outside the city, a substantial dowry could always overcome a woman's sexual lapses.

Nameless and wordless, save in the body language of her supposed sinning, Ricciarda's daughter functions, albeit by her silence or near absence, to help focus the tale on mother-in-law and son-in-law. Her low profile also suggests much about the obedience of the maiden and young bride. She is more to be seen than heard; and only years hence, as widow or *matrona*, may she come fully into her own as a decision-maker and, in this sense, a person.

We know nothing of Ricciarda's natal family name. The near quibble on her first name, suggesting moral riches, must suffice. Pilestri and Greci are the only surnames given, and they belong to her husband and son-in-law. Quite unconsciously, I suspect, the author is thus underlining patrilineages, in perfect harmony with the society's patriarchal structures. In kinship here, the family line of the father is the one which chiefly counts. But Pilestri and Greci are not eminent Florentine names; and if they are not pure fictions, they seem made-up, unlike many real family names in the stories of Boccaccio, Sacchetti, Sercambi, and fifteenth-century writers. In this feature, accordingly, the author distances his narrative from everyday Florentine realities. Yet the tale is trapped, as we have seen, in the social world of its day, and rightly so even for literary purposes, or how could contemporaries have seen it as answering to voices in their own experience? Ricciarda had been "given in marriage . . . to a most handsome, virtuous, and rich young man," and she marries her daughter to an exceedingly "handsome and charming young man from a very old family." The impact of these general formulae depended on what they excluded, on absences: that is to say, on how contemporaries pared them down to make something of them in particular. Just as in our time the expression "rock star" eliminates all but the image of a musical celebrity who travels continually, has flashy or costly properties, dresses loudly or defiantly, perhaps takes drugs, has bodyguards, and keeps a certain musical and sexual style, so in Florence, in the early fifteenth century, the epithets "handsome, rich, charming, and from an ancient lineage" could only refer to people of the highest political and social standing, with estates in the country, powerful friends and relatives, and possible major investments in banking or a luxury trade such as the silk industry. I make this point in order to emphasize the realistic visage of formulae which may wrongly strike us as having about them a pinch of the stuff of fairy tales.

Ricciarda herself, the duckling episode, Lippozzo's near worship of Ricciarda, and one or two other touches may be unreal; but the whole web of ideals and expectations in the tale is drawn directly from the city's pragmatic mental world.

During roughly the first half of the fifteenth century, the average age of marriage in Florence was about thirty years for men and nearly eighteen for women, though there were often gaps, of course, of fifteen, twenty, or more years between spouses. That both Ricciarda and her daughter were married to "young" men, say in their mid-twenties, was perfectly possible—young, but not nearly as young as their wives. And this brings us to the question of Lippozzo's sexual experience. Since male virgins are likely to be as maladroit as their female counterparts, why is it that he knew exactly how to deflower the girl? And where had he got the experience to judge the movements of her body in the act of love-making? Here again the story knows something which historians usually know from other sources. Florentine youths of the middle and upper classes not infrequently had sexual relations with female servants, household slaves, and prostitutes to be found in streets, taverns, and brothels. Many youths also had homosexual encounters, as recent study has demonstrated. Unremarkably, therefore, Lippozzo was experienced enough to initiate his young bride straightway into the pleasures of love-making. Yet there is another puzzling silence here. Ricciarda's daughter was a virgin, so there must have been some bloodletting and conceivably a modicum of pain on the night of the marriage. Could this have escaped the notice of the watchful Lippozzo? The tale cannot but be silent about this, or there would be no tale. Giovanni Gherardi must rely on his storytelling powers to keep his listeners and readers from detecting this sleight of hand.

There remains the tale's primary silence: how may we explain the widow Ricciarda's worldliness? Since Florentine demography reveals that girls born into the governing class were married earlier by a year or two than the city-wide average, our beautiful young widow is likely to be in her very early thirties—still an appetizing age for the city's upper-class lechers. We gather from the *novellieri* (short-story writers) that good-looking widows—presumably skilled in, but now denied, the enjoyments of sex—were particularly singled out and courted by men; but they were also the ones most spied upon, most vulnerable to rumor and gossip. Like the *novellieri*, San Bernardino of Siena and other preachers were especially tough in their attitudes toward them. Nevertheless, although brought up, presumably, like her own daughter, who had never seen or heard "anything but what is virtuous," Ricciarda had managed both to acquire worldly wisdom and to retain an immaculate reputation. This is the pleasing invention, the unreal core, of the tale; for at Florence about 1400, it must have been all but impossible to unite chastity and a sophisticated knowledge of the "sinful" world in the body of a beautiful young widow. Chastity— and what is more, a reputation for it—could belong in name to such a woman only if she was protected and supervised, as, for instance, in an orderly convent, in a religious establishment for pious ladies (*pinzochere*), or in the midst of watchful in-laws and close male relatives, who could keep a check on her movements. Ricciarda consults relatives about her daughter's marriage, but where are they at the critical moment of her confrontation with Lippozzo, who does not seem to fear them when he goes out to Carcherelli? Whatever their future role in a possible vendetta against the young husband, they are not at the villa. Having acted, it appears, in secrecy, Ricciarda is not under the probing eyes of relatives, nor even—in the country—of neighbors. In order for her to shine as a model of worldly sagacity, the tale requires her to be on her own—another touch of unreality.

One side of Ricciarda, the strict and chaste mother, is fused with upper-class family honor, and is hence about arranged (utilitarian) marriages, lineage preservation, and the decorous transmission of property. The other, her male side, is about *savoir-faire*, verbal ease, and mental vigor. As I noted earlier, she partakes of a *topos* or literary commonplace to be found, above all, in the lyric love poetry of the period, where her likes and variants appear as the beloved lady—a combination of beauty, half saint, worldly-wise woman, and harsh reprover. How, therefore, shall we relate Ricciarda's particular unreality—her mix of strict virtue and worldliness—to the real world of quattrocento Florence? In that male-dominated, patrilineal society, where the requirements of virginity and chastity sharply restricted the activities and operational space of women, and where real property (lands and buildings) clung chiefly to the masculine line, Ricciarda—like all her literary variants—is a projection of the male imagination in a world where no woman could normally be the equal of men. The male author, like his male readers and listeners, seeks to recover in Ricciarda the female as social partner and equal. In the devious need to rectify the great gender imbalance, the projection always goes too far, because the gendered social structures of everyday life overshadow perception and imagination. Consequently, again like all her equivalents in the love poetry and pertinent tales of the fifteenth century, Ricciarda is cast as a model of moral and social perfection, so as *more* than the equal of men. In this new inequality, the disproportionate gender divide of daily existence is again fully reproduced, but now turned upside down in an imagined reconstruction. Ricciarda equals chastity and is therefore—by semiotic extension—subordinate wife, daughter, sister, and mother; yet in this virtuous perfection, she rather intimidates Lippozzo. She is also her other (male) half, worldliness: the side of her which would be the equal of men in conversation and public life; and in this incarnation, too, she is more than the equal of the young man.

One might, to be sure, propose a psychoanalytic reading of this tale. Since all the give-and-take is between son-in-law and mother-in-law, and in view of her formidable qualities, Ricciarda looks much like the mother figure of the Oedipal triangle. There is even the hint of a possible flirtatiousness between the two. In the tale's final paragraph, when the young man returns to making love with his new wife, the pleasure seems to be mainly Ricciarda's. Moreover, in characteristic psychoanalytic reasoning, we might even say that in imagining Lippozzo's situation, the author splits the mother figure into the idealized Ricciarda on the one side and on the other the sexy, subordinate, nameless girl. Any ambivalence in the young husband is thus easily explained. However, this predictable interpretation of the proceedings lifts the tale out of time and place, takes it out of history, and submits it to a universal, psychoanalytic anthropology. Here social structures, property and gender relations are all brushed aside. The approach is non-historical. Critics and readers who reason this way would seem to know the truth about "human nature," psychodynamics, and the like. I hold that historical analysis cannot and should not claim to be so knowing.

TWO

1.

SCOPONE

by Gentile Sermini

Scopone *(my shortened title) is from the forty* Novelle *(no. III) of the Sienese writer, Gentile Sermini, who collected his tales shortly after 1424. Nothing else is known about him, apart from what we are able to discern in the tales regarding his views and tastes.*

☙

How Bartolomeo Buonsignori turned a prickly briar[1] into a supple willow.

Among the ranks of its citizens, the magnificent city of Siena had a noble young man named Bartolomeo, who hailed from the Buonsignori house; and he was wise, wealthy, generous, well-mannered and loved by everyone. Left fatherless at the age of twenty-five, Bartolomeo delighted greatly in hunting, falconry, and fishing, all the more so as he owned Monteantico, a place very well

1. Prickly briar: *scopone*, also the name of the peasant.

39

suited to the occupations he enjoyed. So he left Siena, and maintaining an honorable way of life in the country, keeping horses, servants, dogs, falcons, and hunting nets of all sorts, he led a very pleasant life. All the local men who liked hunting used to gather at Monteantico, and groups of young men would often come out from Siena as well, to pass the time pleasantly with him. Since Bartolomeo was extremely rich, he received everyone handsomely; and having an able steward who tended carefully to things, he had a large income from his pasture lands, tenant farms, and livestock. Bartolomeo knew well that his income was far greater than his expenses, and he resolved to live in this manner as long as he was young. Thus he had a universal reputation for generous hospitality.

Now, Bartolomeo had a local man there, a peasant of uncouth appearance: miserly, loutish, ignorant, ungrateful, and all for himself; niggardly with his own things, but very liberal with the things of others, which he was glad to grab whenever he got the chance. He was grasping in other people's houses, where he disdained to drink water and looked down on wine if there wasn't enough. I won't even speak about meat, for once he threw himself upon it, he went at it like a wolf. He was fat and ungainly, a marvel of barnyard ugliness, coarse in appearance, ill dressed, and with an aquiline nose of such dimensions that it could have held up a pair of baskets for spectacles. No winter was ever so cold that he would wear stockings or a doublet; he was always covered with bits of earth; and he hated to wash his hands and face, so that he was covered with a crust of dirt, and his breeches were mended with rushes. Now this man was one of Bartolomeo Buonsignori's tenant farmers; and having started out with nothing, thanks to Bartolomeo's generosity, the dishonest Scopone had managed to acquire his own house, vineyard, and land. And considering himself to be a rich man, he had little regard for Bartolomeo and even less for other men. But this did not prevent him from turning to Bartolomeo now and then, when he needed something, for he found it sweet to beg favors and irksome to return them. And since, generally, when his fellow peasants are able to put three coins together, they immediately put on asses' ears[2] and begin to strut about, scorning all men, so too did Scopone. And as Bartolomeo was always kind and favorably disposed, he could deny Scopone nothing, thinking that at some point this would lead the man to a more civil way of life. Indeed, he had already shown him such favor that Scopone was indebted to him for a hundred florins; and Scopone, stubborn ass that he was, reckoned on never returning a single one. And behaving very badly, he was overly familiar with Bartolomeo, often jesting and joking with him; and concealing his wickedness with jests, he would call him by his first name, as he had done when Bartolomeo was a boy. And although Bartolomeo was always ready to serve him, he could never get a good turn out of Scopone.

Now Scopone had a good dog, and on holidays he always went off alone with it, hunting for martens and laying snares in the woods, and he laid a good many. This was his occupation on the days when he didn't work, and sometimes he would go to the river with his fishing poles; and whatever he caught he would take to Bagno a Petriuolo [a local spa] to sell on the sly, so that Bartolomeo would not find out; for Scopone feared lest on some occasion Bartolomeo's humane generosity win him away from his customary avarice. Nor was Bartolomeo ever able, even once, to get any help from Scopone or the use of his dog for his own hunting.

2. i.e., act uppity.

Now it happened that six young men from Siena decided to do some hunting and pass the time with Bartolomeo at Monteantico, so they sent along a letter beforehand, letting him know that they were coming, and saying that they wanted to hunt during Holy Week, and requesting that he provide some good game for them. And on reaching Bagno a Petriuolo, where many people were staying, they were kept there for the evening by friends.

Having received the letter and wishing to welcome his friends handsomely, Bartolomeo summoned Scopone, as well as other helpers, told him of the six friends, and requested that he provide some fish, that he inspect all his nets and lines, and promised to take everything Scopone caught and to pay him well for it. Scopone replied that he would do so, and departed; and being a mean, suspicious fellow, from fear that someone else might get there first, he went straight off to check all his equipment and found he had caught some fifty pounds of fish. And after he got the fish home, he took it promptly to Bagno a Petriuolo to sell, telling them at home to say nothing about it. His wife, who was expecting a child, begged him for the love of God to leave four fish for her. But cruel Scopone, with a jerk of his head, went off without giving her even one; and he hurried away with all his fish to Bagno a Petriuolo, saying to himself: "If Bartolomeo wants fish, let him go get it himself as I do, and a pox on him. What am I, his slave? And if he has no fish, let him give his guests nuts, the sort of thing I eat." When he arrived at Bagno a Petriuolo, he went to the market to sell his fish, and when he was asked how much he wanted, the lout barely answered, as if he cared little about selling it; but in a low voice, without looking anyone in the face, he said: "I want five *soldi* per pound." And when several people tried to bargain with him, Scopone, becoming more and more loutish and uncouth, simply said: "I won't take less." Since everyone saw what a churl he was, two men then went to the Lord of the Baths (for it was customary to choose one during holiday times), a fun-loving young man from the Malavolti family, and accused Scopone of having come with fish to starve the company of folk who were staying at Bagno a Petriuolo.

After hearing their complaint, the lord went to Scopone, accompanied by a band of young men, and when he asked the price of the fish, Scopone, more churlishly than before, continued to insist on five *soldi* per pound. Immediately recognizing the man to be a base peasant, the lord consulted with his attendants about what to do with him, and all agreed that he should get what he deserved. Whereupon Scopone was instantly seized, his fish taken from him and sent off to be cooked. They then tied him to a column in the village square with his hands behind his back, and the lord at once summoned his secretary, Ugo Malescotti, a young man blessed by nature with many talents. Ugo was a master at singing and playing every instrument—a savant, historian, and perfect orator; and so merry, that he kept everyone at the baths amused. Moreover, he improvised as a singer better than anyone else. So the lord called for Ugo and ordered him to read the malefactor's punishment. When he got a look at Scopone, Ugo took up a large hoe, instead of a piece of paper, and on it he began to read out, in a fine manner, the penalties to be imposed on the criminal. All the bathing crowd were in the square, where they watched Ugo, standing up on a bench, ceremoniously read the man's punishment as if from the hoe; and the sentence ruled that Scopone was to wear a fool's cap and be beaten with brooms[3] throughout the town, as punishment for wanting to starve them and for having always falsified his

3. Beaten with brooms, *scopato*, with a pun on the peasant's name.

accounts with a spade and hoe, not with a pen. And finally, Ugo added on his own that Scopone was to be beaten with the handles of brooms for having falsely defamed his noble lord, Bartolomeo Buonsignori, when, at the moment of being seized, he had exclaimed: "Take the fish? Don't touch it, for it belongs to Bartolomeo Buonsignori, who sent me here to sell it." Scopone had placed more value on the fish than on the honor of his master. So Ugo made this little addition to Scopone's punishment, to compensate for his slandering such a gracious, noble young man. And having given the order, along came a lovely little fool's cap and two hefty brooms, and Scopone's shoulders were bared—and now Ugo willingly went from being a secretary to a public executioner. He took the heavy brooms by the brushes and began to strike Scopone vigorously. And continuing to do so all the way down the street, Ugo carried out the sentence so well that everyone was laughing hilariously—for, his clothing aside, anyone seeing Ugo for the first time would have thought that he was none other than the executioner and that he had never known any other calling. And after beating Scopone in all the usual places [of public punishment], they returned to the main square, where Scopone was again tied to the same column, and a table was quickly brought, laden with goblets and flasks of different wines, and bread, lemons and salt, and Scopone's fish, now all fried, were set before him. And when everything was ready, the lord and all his company washed their hands and laughingly began to eat in front of Scopone. I'll not tell of all the taunting and scorn, by word and gesture, that they heaped on Scopone as they ate his fish. One would say: "Take a bite, Scopone," and another, "Oh, what good fish this is! Oh, how right you were to bring it to us!" And another would hold some fish right up to Scopone's mouth as if to make him break his fast, and then pop it into his own

44

mouth, saying: "Did you like it?" Some teased and others pretended to pity him, but then treated him worse than the rest. A few
wiped their hands on his clothes, while others taunted him in other
ways. And this went on until they ate up everything right before his
eyes. And that fish seemed as good to Scopone as it had to his
pregnant wife, to whom the brute hadn't seen fit to leave even one.
Once the whole company had finished eating, the merry Ugo said:
"Scopone, you're a real savage. What, you wouldn't eat a bite with
this company, who invited you so many times? But I suppose you
were expecting, as usual, to eat afterwards with the servants. Now
come, you shall eat." And he untied Scopone from the column, and
with the rope around his neck led him to the bridge at Farma, with
the whole company following. And there he released him, saying:
"Go, Scopone, and sin no more."

As soon as Scopone was released, numerous children and
adults, as prearranged, their aprons full of stones, gave him such
an escort that he returned to Monteantico with his shoulders
flayed by brooms and his legs battered by stones. And when he
arrived at home he got into bed and stayed there for ten days,
although many others would have stayed there for a year after
such a trouncing. And wishing to keep what had happened a
secret, lest Bartolomeo or others come to know of it, Scopone gave
out the story that he had fallen from a walnut tree. But as fate
would have it, the six youths from Siena had been at Bagno a
Petriuolo, had joined the company in eating the fish, and had seen
everything. Wanting to set out for Monteantico, they took their
leave of the lord of Bagno. And when Ugo saw them about to ride
off, he said: "I want to go with you," and with a lute and a fine lyre
around his servant's neck, he took leave of the lord and rode off
with them. Soon they all arrived at Monteantico, where they were

joyfully received by Bartolomeo. And when the dogs and horses had been seen to, they were treated to a generous supper. When the fruit came around, Ugo, as arranged, took his lute, got up on a bench, and improvised forty stanzas. It was marvelously sweet to hear him sing. And in his song he told the story of Scopone from beginning to end, for he was a master at improvising songs and playing the lute. All the company, including Bartolomeo, took great pleasure in the story. And because Bartolomeo hadn't known about the goings-on at Bagno a Petriuolo, when Ugo sat down, he asked to hear it again in prose, from start to finish; and thus they remained all evening, feasting and amusing themselves. Now, although Bartolomeo was secretly outraged with Scopone, he didn't let on, but kept it all in mind. And when the hour to sleep came, they all went to bed.

In the morning Bartolomeo had arranged for fishermen to lay their nets, so when everyone had risen and breakfasted, they headed for the river, where they caught a great deal of fish. And to make a long story short, they enjoyed themselves greatly, fishing and pursuing many other pastimes and diversions until Palm Sunday, when Bartolomeo invited twenty youths, all good hunters, for the whole of Holy Week, and they all gladly accepted, agreeing that in the morning they would all be there with their spears, dogs, and snares.

Now Scopone was present at all this. And when Bartolomeo saw him and asked what was wrong with him, Scopone replied that he was all bruised and battered because he had fallen from a walnut tree. Bartolomeo then motioned to the wily Ugo, who immediately did what needed to be done to bring shame on Scopone. So getting to his feet, he said: "Bartolomeo, I want to tell you a story. This good man saying that he fell from a walnut tree reminds me that I recently fell out of an almond tree and went to Bagno a Petriuolo to be healed; and because my legs and shoulders were all battered and torn, I saw some doctors there. And since their unguents are rather hard to take, they tied my hands behind me and then brushed certain ointments of theirs on my shoulders, repeating the applications,[4] much to my discomfort. And since my head was hot they removed my cap and gave me a paper hat with carrots painted on it, which looked neither like a hood nor a cowl with lappets, because it had tails hanging behind the ears; so that in a way I looked like a bishop without a staff or benefice. To stimulate my appetite, they ate in front of me at my expense; and to make me really hungry they kept offering me food, holding morsels up to my mouth and then eating these themselves. And in the end they said to me: 'Now come, you shall eat with the servants now that you've worked up a good appetite.' They took me to the bridge at Farma, where I found a table all laid out, and many sergeants bearing rampions, ice, and marble cheeses,[5] with which they gave me such a pleasant escort that I'll never go back there again." At this he turned to Scopone, as if he believed the story about his falling from the tree, and said: "Brother, if you want to recover from your fall from the walnut tree, go to Bagno and you shall be healed as I was healed after my fall from the almond tree." Then turning to Bartolomeo with a compassionate look on his face, he said: "Truly, they play some nasty tricks on you in that place."

Aside from Bartolomeo and the six young men from Siena, all those present believed Ugo's story to be true. But knowing the real story, Bartolomeo and the young men were amused by two things: by such a well-told tale thought up on the spur of the moment, and

4. Much wordplay in the original text here.
5. More textual wordplay.

by the fact that the company believed it. Scopone was scowling by the time Ugo finished his story, which he well knew was meant for himself, and saying nothing he wended his way through the crowd and got the devil away from there. At this point the large company departed and the twenty hunters remained, had dinner, and while at table decided on the hunting order for the coming week and where the hunt would take place. Thus on the Monday morning they began to hunt, continuing so every day until Good Friday. And on Holy Saturday Bartolomeo and all the others, with ten loads of game, went on to Siena. And when they had distributed the game to their friends, relatives, and comrades, they all celebrated Easter together; and after Easter Bartolomeo returned to Monteantico.

Some days later, unable to forget Scopone's effrontery, Bartolomeo said to himself: "I have always helped this man, and never have I had anything I wanted from him, nor does it seem that he has ever been grateful for anything I've done for him. And he has grown rich off me, and puts on airs, and now he has done me this act of villainy and as consolation defamed me by saying that I sent him to Bagno to sell the fish." In short, recognizing that Scopone was a bad sort, Bartolomeo decided to rid himself of the man once and for all, and having made this resolution, he sent for him. Then he ordered his steward to settle accounts with Scopone, and this done, it turned out that Scopone owed Bartolomeo 102 florins. In the presence of several of his men, Bartolomeo now said: "Scopone, you owe me 102 florins, isn't that true?" And Scopone answered yes. So Bartolomeo said to the steward: "Let him keep the two florins and demand that he pay the rest at once." Now finding himself in desperate straits, and believing that his usual fawning ways would help him as in the past, Scopone contrived in various ways to win Bartolomeo over, to no avail. So in the end he was forced to mortgage his vineyard and sell enough of his goods and chattels to enable him to pay 100 florins to Bartolomeo. This done, and now finding himself ruined, he returned home, a despondent and desperate man. Remaining thus for some days, thinking constantly about what had happened, he came to recognize the error of his ways and the cause of his troubles. And knowing Bartolomeo to be kind-hearted, and that he alone was the one who could help or hurt him, an amazing thing happened: seeing exactly where his own best interests lay, Scopone at once took a decision, and insofar as his own character allowed, he suddenly altered his own nature. For he determined to be the very opposite of what he had been, and thus he continued always. And holding firm to this resolution, one day when Bartolomeo had no business abroad and had remained at home by the fire, Scopone went to see him. When he arrived, Scopone threw himself down on his knees with his arms crossed over his breast and tears in his eyes, and said: "My lord, I have failed you in every way, and therefore deserve every ill from you. You always treated me well, and I was never grateful for it, so greatly did my sinful nature blind me. Now, thanks be to God, I have come to know myself, and have firmly determined to be a different man from now on, with a different character. My lord, I beg your forgiveness and promise you that in future I shall behave in such a manner that you shall love me better than any other servant you may have. I commend myself to you, praying you to have faith in what I say, for I say it more with my heart than with my tongue. And you can be sure that I have now come to hate the evil life I led before, and have become so resolute that I have altered my whole nature and condition; and you shall clearly see this by experience. Test me, by God, so that you may be certain of what I am telling you. And to conclude, I commend myself and my children to you."

With these and other fitting words, Scopone humbled himself so much that Bartolomeo, being sweet-natured, was rather moved by his words, and made this reply: "Scopone, stand up, and weep no more. I have heard you. Go home for tonight, and come back tomorrow and I shall give you my answer"—and Bartolomeo neither smiled nor frowned at him. Making no further reply, Scopone took his leave, and the next morning returned to Bartolomeo.

In the meantime, in order to make Scopone's case an example not only to himself but also to others, the wise Bartolomeo had arranged for four of his chief retainers to be there with him, under some pretext, when Scopone arrived early that morning; and when he humbly approached and saw the four men, he instinctively began to withdraw. Then Bartolomeo said: "Scopone, come forward. Have no fear of these men." Although he would have preferred to find Bartolomeo alone, Scopone came closer so as not to contradict him. Bartolomeo then said: "Have you come for my answer?" And he replied: "My lord, yes," and threw himself down on his knees. And Bartolomeo, making him get up, said: "Are you still firm in your resolution of last evening?" And he replied: "My lord, yes, and even more so, if that were possible." Now, although he was enjoying the scene of Scopone's humiliation, Bartolomeo still wanted to make him mend his ways and make an example of him for others; and in the presence of everyone, he said: "Scopone, you were too familiar with me, and keeping your own advantage ever in mind, you always played dishonestly. You know that I have always served and helped you, and you have always been impudent and ungrateful to me, nor did you ever take any trouble to please me. You always failed me when I needed you; you didn't care a fig about my honor, nor did you think of my shame. You know that I love hunting, and you know that I was never able to have you, not to speak of your dog, on any hunt with me. In short, for all the good I did you, I never had anything but harm from you. I took your shameful deed to heart more than you know; for in order to honor the young men I told you were coming from Siena, I prayed you to bring me the fish you caught and said that I would pay for it. And having no regard for me or for my shame, when the occasion came for you to serve me, you sneaked off to Bagno a Petriuolo to sell the fish. But fortune decided to take my revenge: for you got your payment by having the fish seized from you and eaten before your very eyes. Then you were crowned with a fool's cap, beaten through the streets, and finally driven from Bagno with a hail of stones—that's the walnut tree you fell from. You would have done better to sell the fish to me. But then you did even worse—you claimed that you were selling it for me, thus making me out to be a fishmonger, which I never was. These are the honors I have from you; so that in short—for I haven't said a quarter of what I could say—I determined to have nothing more to do with your insolence or bad behavior and to make you see the error of your ways by fair means, without doing any wrong to you. So, I decided that I wanted to be paid"—and looking intently at him, he said: "Is what I have said true or false?" Taking in all his words, Scopone, who had kept his head down, shamed, and with his arms crossed over his breast, replied: "My lord, I have failed you much more than you have said. I deserve every ill, and confess that I am a sinner, and ask your pardon for the love of God, firmly resolved to make up for every evil thing I've done, and to do good in the future." And weeping, he humbly commended himself to Bartolomeo. Knowing Scopone's bizarre, coarse behavior, the whole company was amazed to hear him speak this way. After Scopone had given his reply, Bartolomeo called him by his proper baptismal name—Neri—and said: "I have heard your reply, by which I understand, as you say, that you have changed your nature; and you were given the name Scopone on account of your bad, difficult character, and because you were always unbending. So having recognized what you were, I determined never to have anything more to do with your rough ways. Now that you are changed, as you say (for this is how I understand it), if you want to have anything to do with me, I want to change your name, as you have changed your demeanor. And seeing you become so humble, since you were called Scopone before, because you would never bend for anything, so now that you are bending like the willow, I wish henceforth to call you Salcione [Willow]. Thus I name you this morning, and thus do I want you to remain content." Scopone bowed his head and said: "I am content with whatever pleases you." Then Bartolomeo said: "The willow is by nature supple and pliant, and is used to bind other woods. Therefore, having changed from Briar to Willow, you have bound me; and I am pleased to forgive you and to treat you much better as Salcione than I did when you were Scopone. And let the name Salcione, along with my favor, be enough for you for as long as I shall hear that you are Salcione; for I warn you, a relapse is worse than falling ill for the first time. And if you should return to the ways of your former name, don't ever come back to me for favors or forgiveness. Now you have heard me."

If Scopone had tendered a good reply before, he now answered with twice the humility, reiterating what he had already said. Then Bartolomeo, having made him mend his ways, gave the order that he should henceforth always be called Salcione. Next he gave him reserved rights to the raising of horses and cows, so that in a short time Salcione was able to get back his vineyard, and rose to even more comfortable circumstances than before. And realizing that it was better to be like a willow than a briar, he came to hate his former life, and became humble, courteous, ready to serve, loving, amiable, grateful, and tactful with everyone, and above all with Bartolomeo, being ever at his side in moments of need, and striving to do things that would please him. Thus he became Bartolomeo's most faithful servant in all the world; nor was his name ever changed, for he was always deservedly called Willow.

* * *

I now hold for certain something I first heard some time ago, namely that since peasants know no law, nor any experience of tact, it does no good to become too familiar with them. Rather, if you want some good out of them, according to my wise man,[6] open neither your hand nor your purse to them, nor any secret of yours. They should be kept at a distance, and well in hand; and if they ask a favor of you, since you should waste nothing on them, grant it rarely and make them hanker for it. Show that you don't think much of them; don't smile at them; look at them rarely; and in dealings with them, do what is right, not what is wrong. Don't punish them with your own hands, but rather use the courts; don't pardon their failings, for this will make them cocky. Settle your accounts with them often and in the presence of witnesses; and make them pay what they owe you as promptly as possible. Don't

6. The author here refers to the speaker of a set of verses at the end of his thirty-eighth tale.

have them at table with you; don't jest or banter with them; don't let them take more than their due from you; and don't let them delay too long in giving you what is your due, otherwise they'll try to get out of it. If they come to your house, get rid of them quickly by giving them only one drink; keep them in fear of you, so as to make them respect and esteem you. Don't let them feel too secure with you, nor with the things that belong to you; keep them in check, keep them humble, and keep them poor. For if they feel the weight of three good coins in their pocket and are too sure of you, you'll never get any good out of them: vinegar made from fortified new wine is the worst vinegar there is. And for the little good you might get out of them, they will think that they deserve to have you doff your cap to them whenever they pass you on the road with their asses' ears[7]. I won't even speak of their colored skirts and tight-fitting hose and brand-new jerkins and seven-domed caps, the likes of which not even a nobleman from the court of Swabia would wear, and of how they roll their eyes, giving you savage looks, to show you that you should fear them and that you should greet them before they greet you. According to my teacher,[8] such people should not be allowed to reside in the city, as they would quickly make you regret it, for the life of the peasant is not consistent with that of the city dweller. And although many other things could be said about this, in order not to go on too long about it, I have decided to stop here.

7. See note 2 above.
8. See note 6 above.

2.

Ceremonies of Identity: *Scopone*

In the second half of the fourteenth century, epidemics of Black Plague so ravaged Siena, that its population fell from a peak of over 50,000 souls in the 1330s down to little more than 15,000 by the early 1400s. A textile and banking center, and the seat of a dwarf republic, Siena had once been surpassingly robust. Now it was governed by an oligarchy of five tiny political blocs. It was less verbal as a city, or at least less obviously literary, than neighboring Florence, and also more cautious and conservative in its general social, religious, and artistic outlook.

Siena's diminished size and energies had not cut the city's ties with the outlying rural expanses. If anything, scarcity and fear had invested those ties with a greater importance. Like Florence, Milan, Bologna, and other inland cities, Siena always lived in large part off the labor and agricultural produce of the surrounding countryside; and like them, too, it was home to a class of rich, absentee landlords who owned most of the Sienese hinterland.

Rumor and word-of-mouth stories coursed their way speedily along the narrow, winding streets of diminished Siena. Sermini's tale reveals the imprint of the resultant oral culture, doing so partly in its medley of voices (Scopone, Bartolomeo, Ugo, and the moralizing narrator), but above all in having about it a touch of the fairy tale, in its black-and-white characterizations, starkly laid-out ideals, and bluntly drawn lessons.

The concluding paragraph or coda, lying outside the narrative proper, is rather an amazing primer on how to treat sharecroppers and tenant farmers. In a plain-spoken, medieval preaching style, it encapsulates the near-proverbial "wisdom" of a ruling class in its attitudes towards a subject peasantry. This much, at any rate, of Sermini's tale is history, not fiction.

In the third quarter of the fourteenth century, Bartolomeo Buonsignori was the lord of Monteantico, a fortress near the meeting point of the Orcia and Ombrone rivers. And since name is identity at the crux of this tale, there can be nothing innocent about two of the principal names: Buonsignori (good lords) and Monteantico (ancient or long-standing mountain, i.e., in moral and social terms, the high standing of an ancient family). A leading expert on the period, the agrarian historian, Giovanni Cherubini, suspects that a real historical incident lies buried in the tale; and while this may be so, the overperfect names, Buonsignori and Monteantico, suggest that the real Scopone would have been connected with some other illustrious Sienese family, such as the Salimbeni or Malavolti. In any case, by the 1420s, even if it held a kernel of truth, the story had collected a thick veneer of unreality, already apparent in the opening sentence, where we find that Bartolomeo "was wise, wealthy, generous, well-mannered, and loved by everyone." Strung together in this fashion, four of these formulaic adjectives—*savio, cortese, costumato, amato*—belonged fully to the idealized and polished love verse of the fourteenth and fifteenth centuries. As a model of courteous, courtly, or humane generosity (*cortesia*), Bartolomeo is an ideal type, not a figure drawn from the real life around. Similarly his foil, Scopone, the picture of villainy, is also a type: the type of the coarse, filthy, stinking, selfish, ugly, thieving peasant.

We may be tempted to conclude, therefore, that they are caricatures, each an ideal or grotesque exaggeration, hence unrealities not to be taken seriously. But Bartolomeo and Scopone go beyond caricature because they represent powerful, shaping social ideals, that is, historical realities. In this emblematic function, or even, if we prefer, as caricatures, they hover close to the vital concerns of fifteenth-century Sienese readers and listeners. They incarnate interests and views—not always necessarily coherent—of such strength and importance that their decisive actions unfold, as we shall see, in a framework of ritual and rites of passage. In other words, in the emotional investment of the author and his readers or listeners, the feelings connected with the chief characters are so urgent and deeply felt, that only the fundamental language of ritual—a symbolic body code, or the language of gesture—can adequately handle the story's action. But there is urgency only because Bartolomeo and Scopone (later Salcione) impersonate essential social identities: namely, landlord-peasant, lord-servitor, and ruler-subject, while also broaching the whole question of right relations between town and country.

Writing out of a patriarchal society, Sermini immediately informs us that the young Bartolomeo was left fatherless at the age of twenty-five, in order to establish him fully as his own master and to make his confrontation with Scopone an affair of destiny. Then, having been presented with the earthiness (soil) and animality (wolf, barnyard, and donkey) of Scopone's person, we are ready for the city's visit to the country: the arrival of the six young men from Siena and the change of scene to the health and recreational baths at Bagno a Petriuolo, an urban oasis in the country because it was frequented by well-off people from Siena and from neighboring and more distant towns. Here is to take place

Scopone's first castigation (cleansing) by means of punishing brooms and jeering wordplay (Scopone: *scopa*—broom or briar, and *scopare*—to brush or beat), a cleansing at fashionable local baths and at the hands of gentlemen from the city. Tried, so to speak, by the Malavolti "lord" of the baths who also takes counsel from his advisors, Scopone is tied like a common criminal to the column in Bagno's main square and then subjected to the whole ritual of judicial punishment. The ceremonial office of hangman or executioner (*manigoldo*) is exercised by Malavolti's secretary, Ugo Malescotti: an amphibious figure, half bard and jester, and half learned courtier and functionary, who, like Bartolomeo's estate-manager (*fattore*), navigates back and forth between the lower world of subordinates and the upper world of those in command. Exactly as prescribed by penal codes almost everywhere in fifteenth-century Italy, the criminal, Scopone, is then paraded, while being beaten, up an down the few streets of the balneary village, in addition to being publicly thrashed "in all the usual places," a common expression in the Latin of the penal codes of the day. He is also crowned (*miterato*) with a bizarre and ludicrous cap, its drooping tails cut in imitation of a donkey's ears or tail, signaling the memory that such cap-wearing culprits were once mounted and paraded backwards, ridiculously, on a donkey—yet another touch referring to the gross animality of Scopone's person.

But the round of ritual activity does not end here. There now follows a banquet in celebration of the peasant's condign punishment, with his own fish mockingly thrust into his face and almost touching his mouth and nose. He is the focal point of the village square; and his humiliation, highlighted by the banquet of insults heaped publicly upon him, is a basic part of his chastisement. When, at the end of the banquet, he is finally untied from the column and told, "Go . . . and sin no more," we can scarcely fail to pick up an echo of Jesus's admonition to the adulteress, "Vade, et iam amplius noli peccare" (John 8: 11), after He had managed to keep her accusers from stoning her. This is then immediately followed by another biblical echo in ironic reversal, as Scopone is cast out of Bagno and stoned by a crowd. His worldly crimes are turned into outstanding sins and his ordeal is given a religious twist. The sentence was a brutal one, for in the penal customs of the age, expulsion from towns and cities was a fate normally reserved for thieves, lepers, and rebellious or malfeasant whores, and was often preceded, in the first and third cases, by branding or mutilation. Scopone's body would bear the ritual signs of his punishment for some time.

The next scene is introduced by the protean Ugo: bard, musician, orator, and functionary, who is also the moral voice and memory of the community, the maker of an oral tradition. He improvises forty stanzas, telling the whole story of Scopone's arraignment and punishment. That is to say, in a gesture of ironic mockery, the life of a vile rustic is raised to a literary status customarily reserved for heroic deeds; it is entered, so to speak, into the oral record of the community, as if to make it a permanent part of local history; and this is as much as to say that the community should not forget the crimes and punishment of Scopone, unworthy representative of rural society's lower orders. But Ugo's forty stanzas, by their effect on Bartolomeo, will also serve to complete Scopone's transformation of identity. Already half-dead, as it were, from the effects of his public beating and humiliation, he will be reborn as a new man. Moreover, the build-up or entrée to this metamorphosis is consciously framed against the backdrop of Holy Week, in an odd mix of ludicrous and lugubrious symbolism, wherein the ugly and squalid Scopone is in no way a Christ-like figure, though he is tied to a column and beaten, as in many fifteenth-century depictions of the flagellation of Christ, and though he is to die and be born again, even if the new and near-perfect man and servitor (Salcione) is born of a near animal (Scopone).

It may be well to keep in mind that although being a despised rustic, Scopone is not the lowest of the low. He is propertied; he has hunting and fishing rights; and he owns an exceptional hunting dog. But he is also ambitious. This is his great vice from the narrative viewpoint, which of course is skewed against him: his ambition is represented as ingratitude, avarice, and thievery. Bartolomeo Buonsignori, Scopone's *natural* lord, is the very opposite: in his landed wealth, he is generosity itself, as demonstrated by his extraordinary hospitality and the ten loads of game carted back to Siena, where it is all doled out to "friends, relatives, and comrades." Interestingly, no mention is made of anything set aside for charity, and the large-scale killing of animals peaks during Holy Week. The coming passion of Christ seems not to have got in the way of big hunting. But inasmuch as religious signs and occasions permeated so much of the common culture of the age, we must wonder whether or not any of the foregoing details holds a play of hidden lore, symbolism, or significance.

We come finally to the story's decisive ritual episodes. At his mock but pitiless trial, Scopone is laughingly accused of having falsified his accounts by means of spade and hoe. Though a mere peasant, he is here fleetingly represented as a sort of crooked tradesman. But the grand Bartolomeo, outraged by Scopone's making him seem a fishmonger, knows nothing of trade, nor, presumably, about keeping accurate accounts, as this might smack of avarice. This is the job of Bartolomeo's estate manager. Yet the nobleman knows exactly how to ruin (and reform) his man: he calls for immediate payment of the outstanding debt. Scopone is hereupon plunged into such a crisis of material desperation, which then galvanizes his entire personality, that the experience miraculously gives birth to a new man. At this peripetal point, the tale fairly ripples with ritual action.

Finding Bartolomeo at home one day, sitting by the fire (a symbolic reprise of the nobleman's warmth and light), Scopone "threw himself down on his knees with his arms crossed over his breast." The Italian expression, *colle braccia in croce* (with his arms in cross form) is more suggestive or reminiscent of the Cross. In that kneeling, humbled posture of prayer, Scopone's first words to Bartolomeo are, "My lord" (*signor mio*), the correct appellative when a man was addressing his natural lord; and in this case, for an instant, Bartolomeo would appear to be in the place of the Lord, especially as his supplicant will in a moment intone, "Lord, I beg your forgiveness," for in fifteenth-century society, when order prevailed, microstructures and macrostructures were assumed to be in complete consonance. In tears and for the first time ever, Scopone speaks to Bartolomeo with all the due respect. He also uses the proper status pronoun, *voi*, whereas previously he had always used the familiar and presumptuous form *tu* (thou); and henceforth it would always be thus and he would always be addressed familiarly as *tu* by Bartolomeo, in frank recognition of the unbridgeable social and political gap between the two. So then, kneeling, prayer by gesture, cross-armed pleading, weeping, the due nominatives, and doubtless a lowering of the head: here was the language of obedience and homage, the external expression of Scopone's internal metamorphosis. Most appropriately, his side of the interview ends with the standard (Renaissance) ritual expression from a client or servant to his patron or lord, "I commend [i.e., entrust] myself to you" (*vi raccomando me*); and for the first time too we see the new personality as a caring family man, for he also commends his children to Bartolomeo.

But the vows made in private must also be spoken and witnessed in public. Scopone's true identity is defined almost purely in terms of his relation to Bartolomeo; and this social bond is a community or public matter, hence rightly fit to stand as an example, as Bartolomeo concludes. The business between the two is not solely a private contract between individuals acting out of the sight of other men. Scopone must not merely be humble, he must be seen to be humble. Consequently, in the second interview, at first reluctantly but then whole-heartedly, Scopone enters into his right and proper public persona, that of grateful and faithful servant, in the ratifying presence of four of Bartolomeo's principal clients and servitors. Revealingly, meanwhile, Bartolomeo's gentle scolding of Scopone stresses not only the peasant's previous ingratitude and social sin of impudence, but also his brazen disregard for the public needs—honor and manifest largess—of the nobleman's identity as *seigneur*, an attitude which had culminated in the shaming and dishonoring of Bartolomeo as an alleged "fishmonger."

The ensuing ceremony, the creation of a new identity, is ritualized, indeed given the status of a rite of passage. Like nine out of ten rural Tuscans in the fifteenth century, Scopone had no family name. This custom and privilege was still largely restricted to the upper (and older) propertied classes. For the first and last time, but only so as to change it, Bartolomeo calls Scopone "by his proper baptismal name, Neri" (*suo nome proprio delle fonti, cioè Neri*), the community having long since renamed or nicknamed him Scopone. In his person as lord and patron, hence as maker, as one who could make the earthly fortunes of another, Bartolomeo now dubs him, "Salcione. Thus I name you this morning, and thus do I want you to remain content." Whereupon our peasant, who is changing from stubborn Briar to pliant Willow, bows his head in acceptance of his re-christening and replies, "I am content." Nor is the ceremony an empty one: for Bartolomeo at once rewards him with special privileges over livestock breeding, enabling the peasant to recover and even surpass his previous material fortunes.

These observations may seem to have moved us from history to literature, but such a neat distinction, here at all events, is perfectly arbitrary, as we shall see.

In the concluding sentence of the tale proper, just before the start of the coda, we again fleetingly enter a kind of never-never land, adumbrated by a string of six adjectives. We are told, in effect, that henceforth Salcione was to be ever "humble, courteous, ready to serve, loving, amiable, grateful, and tactful with everyone" ("*umile, cortese, inservigiato, amorevole, grazioso e conoscente e discreto con ogni persona*"). Linked thus—but especially *umile, cortese, amorevole*, and *grazioso*—these words belong to the lexicon of courtly love in Italy, specifically to Italian love verse of the fourteenth and fifteenth centuries; and because they were continually used in a variety of upper-class love contexts, they are among the most difficult words to translate. It is in the fifteenth century that the adjective *cortese*, for example, picks up the sense of being humane, of having a gentle ("noble") humanity; and *grazioso* may mean amiable, charming, pleasant, or even kind.

We are to believe, then, that refined amatory sentiment, of the sort praised and sung about at the courts and in the cultivated circles of "bourgeois" Florence and Bologna, reaches out into the Sienese countryside to redeem and transform the peasant, Scopone. In fact, something like this happens, and now the figure of Bartolomeo Buonsignori comes forth in all its power and authority. The tale's opening sentence offers us five adjectives that both define him—"he was wise, wealthy, generous (*cortese*), well-mannered and loved by everyone"—and make possible the seven adjectives for Salcione at the end. In his despair, Scopone sees that his true interest lies in serving his *seigneur*; but this perception is paired with his "knowing Bartolomeo to be kind-hearted" or "sweet-natured" (*di dolce sangue*), and this knowledge not only completes Scopone's profound transformation but also binds his loyalty. Thus the urban-courtly invasion of the Sienese countryside is accomplished entirely through the person of Bartolomeo. He is the real begetter or creator. He can make, break, and remake Scopone; so he is rightly the one to rebaptize him "Salcione."

In short, history and literature—social ideals and rhetorical possibilities—meet in the figure of Bartolomeo. He is the idealized avatar of his social class: nobleman, landlord, lordly, openhanded, and a natural ruler in whose service the working people of the country are best off. How far idealized we may see by edging over into Florentine territory and noticing the antics of a real nobleman, Bartolomeo di Rinaldo dei Donati, who seems to have kept mostly to his rural properties. In November of 1380, in Remole, on the western outskirts of Florence, he tried to rape the wife of a local peasant by simply breaking into their house. Rejected and in a rage, he gave her a violent beating, and when her husband suddenly arrived with three other men, he rushed away but only to return on horseback, bearing a boar spear. The peasant immediately fled for his life, whereupon the aggressor, spurring his horse, set off in hot pursuit, shouting furiously and hurling the spear at him time after time, until the terrified man somehow managed to get away. It is unlikely that the criminal complaint lodged in Florence against the nobleman brought any kind of redress, owing to Donati marriage connections in the city. No one can say how typical of noblemen such violent behavior was in Tuscany's valleys and highlands, but the haughty aspects of the incident were a common enough feature of the period.

In the tale, by contrast, our idealized nobleman, Bartolomeo Buonsignori, is seen to earn and merit the loyalty, service, and obedience of rural working folk because he is kind-hearted (*di dolce sangue*), that is, humane and generous (*cortese*). In this embodiment, intriguingly, he is in addition—as would have been instantly obvious to all fifteenth-century readers and listeners of a cultivated sort—the prototype of the "noble-hearted" lover, also to be found in Boccaccio's *Decameron*. There is a wisp of something feudal and chivalric in all this. But let us never forget that for all his hawking, hunting and fishing, his horses, dogs, and falcons, Bartolomeo is also, like his big-banker forebears, a quintessential urban man. His friends, relatives, and companions all reside in Siena. The primary audience for this tale of his life, even if it be a life indissolubly linked to his rural estates and servants (Scopone), is in propertied and upper-class Siena. One day he will marry a Sienese girl and take his place in the public life of that city.

Avatar of his social class? But so too, in his grotesque way, is Scopone. Whereas one, however, is an idealized, "loved-by-everyone" incarnation, the other is an ugly manifestation of that class of rustics —tenants and sharecroppers (*mezzadri*)—who labored on or tended the lands that belonged to the absentee prosperous merchants, urban noblemen, and to religious houses. And where the one again, in his civility and generosity, embodies the principle of community and is a harmonizing agent, the other, the peasant at his worst, is antisocial and a menace to the concordant community, because of his wild greed and selfishness. Scopone is, as a matter of fact, unworthy of his Christian name. Bartolomeo, accordingly, in the strained human traffic between town and country, with his inimitable social and moral qualities and his commitment (for the duration of his youth) to full-time residence on his lands, appears as a healing figure of love and amity. His contact transforms beastly rural folk into obliging, loyal, civil, contented, trustworthy servants. His fairness and goodness at the top render people at the bottom happy in their social stations. He is the maker of a utopia; and the story of his life—which is also Scopone's story, though from the other side—is at once a literary, historical, and ideological construct. It follows, therefore, that in its fifteenth-century setting, the tale was also bound to pick up a religious tincture. Scopone, the brute, is in effect the fallen Christian who denies food even to his pregnant wife. Hence there is something saintly about the forgiving Bartolomeo, the instrument of Scopone's salvation, though we need not give this any particular emphasis. For in view of the stark black-and-white contrasts in the tale, the religious culture of the age necessarily enters into the play of semiotic elements: it works Scopone toward the demonic and Bartolomeo Buonsignori toward the holy.

Sermini's coda, the concluding paragraph of the tale, poses a narrative problem only if we go at it with modern criteria; and at an early point in planning this book, I considered omitting it from the translation, with a view to offering a more perfect narrative. But while a literary argument—albeit anachronistic—could be

made for such a cut, I can find no historical grounds for it. The
tail sticks because the story is history *and* literature.

With its ruthless advice, the tail is a grim reminder of the anxious and suspicious relations between city and country, landlords
and peasants. Since the story is narrated from the viewpoint of the
possessing class, Scopone is depicted as a figure of gross or black
comedy. We are meant to despise him and to laugh approvingly at
the ferocious punishment meted out to him. The general tilt or
attitude here was far from being new in the fifteenth century.
Urban satire of the peasant in Italy went back to the early thirteenth century, to legal and to other Latin texts, where he already
appears as a *pauper superbus* or barely-human monster. The fourteenth century saw a rising taste for swingeing anti-peasant
proverbs. In the early sixteenth century, the rustic could still be
imagined as a creature born in excrement, overcome by the scent
of perfume, and revived by the smell of manure (Folengo). But
even outside this purview, there can be no denying the fierce element of class in the coda. For in translating it, although we put the
key noun of the paragraph (peasant) in the plural, Sermini uses
the pejorative singular, *villano*, with all its adjectival suggestions
regarding conduct which is villainous, vile, stubborn, coarse,
uncivil, and insulting. He is literally saying not "Beware of peasants" but rather, "Beware of the base peasant," of the whole bloc,
type, or class of them. Satire there may be in the body of the tale,
but not in the concluding prescription, which by the fifteenth century belongs—though it was seldom so tartly put—to a tradition of
advice for rich urban dwellers. The plagues of the fourteenth century had depopulated cities and their agrarian environs, making
for shortages of rural labor. As a result, tenant farmers, sharecroppers, and seasonal laborers had seen an era of relative prosperity.

But by the 1420s this was passing, and urban resentment against "uppity" peasants had, meanwhile, grown. Sermini's whole picture, including the final paragraph, catches a moment of this history, as well in its fleeting as in its more enduring lineaments. In this light, the tale ends with a remarkable claim: "such people [peasants] should not be allowed to reside in the city, as they would quickly make you regret it, for the life of the peasant is not consistent with that of the city dweller." There is a pinch of something almost ethnic here, as if the question involved two different races of men. To try to retrieve something of the original feeling in the quotation, we might recast it in contemporary terms: it isn't right for blacks to live among whites.

THREE

1.

FRIAR AND PRIEST

by Giovanni Sabadino degli Arienti

*Despite his polysyllabic surname, this poet and writer (ca. 1445–1510) was the son of a Bolognese barber. He studied contract law (*notaria*) at the University of Bologna, but then attached himself as secretary and writer to a leading member of the ruling Bentivoglio family, and subsequently had close contacts with the courts of Ferrara and Mantua. Friar and Priest (my summary title) comes from his collection of sixty-one tales (no. XII),* Le Porretane, *first printed at Bologna in 1483. Among his other works is a series of thirty-three short biographies in praise of women,* Gynevera de le clare donne, *obviously in imitation of Boccaccio's* De claris mulieribus.

∞

Most revered gentlemen, we were a group of young men from Arezzo,[1] all wellborn and debonair, who used to go out sometimes into our countryside to enjoy its coolness and amuse ourselves at local festivals. Accordingly, in mid-August we left Arezzo for Monte San Savino, where they celebrate the feast of the Queen of

1. The.supposed narrator of this tale is the Aretine, Cristoforo di Francuzzi.

Heaven and run a horse race, and after lunch the young men and damsels of that village and thereabouts dance in the beautiful square of the castle until nearly sunset. We brought with us one of our comrades, a priest about sixteen years of age, pleasant, virtuous, witty, and very comely, named Ser Francesco di Ludomero. Now, as this youth had such god-given beauty that all who beheld his face took him for a beautiful girl, we had a Florentine lady dress him up in a silk skirt, blouse, stockings, and headdress in the style of the ladies of Florence, so that, between his dress and his talking like a woman, he truly seemed to be a young lady come out of paradise. When he arrived with us, dressed in this fashion, at the place where they held the dancing, and made a charming curtsey to all the people of the company, he was immediately seated in a place of honor among the other women. And his beauty was so great, as you have heard, that the eyes of all the men and women at the fête were riveted on him as on a miraculous thing; and they could not get enough of gazing upon and contemplating his angelic visage, modest bearing, and noble manners. And several youths, being already in love with him, were vying to dance with him, all the more so since he danced in the Tuscan manner more gracefully than any woman there. Now in the square of this village there is a church where the Augustinian friars live. At that time the prior there was quite a gregarious fellow called Friar Puzzo, who had come to see the dancing. Whereupon seeing this comrade of ours so fair and comely, and believing him to be a woman, he immediately fell madly in love with him, for it seemed to him that never in his life had he seen a more beautiful thing in the world. And hearing that the young woman had come from Arezzo in the company of a group of young Aretines, one of whom he knew, the friar approached him and said: "Who is that young

Florentine woman dancing so gracefully?" And our friend replied: "Why do you ask this?" The friar said: "Because she is a very fair creature, and her manners please me greatly." Owing to the friar's question and his continual staring at the girl, our friend understood that he had lost his scapular [his head], and said: "She is one of our company; we brought her here from Arezzo to the festivities." When the friar asked if she was a relative of his, our comrade replied: "Enough, ask no more. If you want me to intercede for you with her, ask as if I were your son." The friar replied: "Thank you. But because I have always been very fond of you and have great faith in you, I shall speak to you as a true and close friend. The beauty of this young woman pleases me so much that I am all on fire with love for her, and all the more so since the habit I wear compels me to conceal this impetuous, consuming flame that is like a fiery furnace. So I know not what I should do, for on the one hand decency restrains me, but on the other the inescapable arrows of the son of Pluto[2] drive me to come to the aid of my own tortured heart and try my luck at this love that is so sweet and burns so brightly. Thus, goaded by so much power, which neither the mighty Samson nor the wise Solomon was able to resist, do not be scandalized, for God's sake, my dear brother, if I, a weak little friar, in no way comparable to those lofty men, confidentially reveal my lot to you. Help me; alas, I'm dying, I'm burning, I'm consumed by desire. With you as my go-between, I am eager that this young woman know of the great love I bear her; so if you would, since you have offered to help me, recommend me to her and take a letter to her for me. And I will be so grateful that I shall be your slave eternally."

2. Cupid was the son of Venus and Vulcan, not of Pluto.

This friend of ours, hearing such talk from the prior, was secretly enchanted by the prospect of the amusement that would come of it, and replied: "Sir, I shall do it. Write a little letter now, for we are about to leave, and I shall bring you a reply. And let me tell you that this young woman knows very well how to write and read." Rejoicing over this offer, the friar left the festivities without delay, and produced a note that went like this:

"I feel obliged to heaven, beautiful young lady, whom I love more dearly than anything else in the world, only because it has made me worthy of seeing your beauties, which are more heavenly than human, and which delight me as much as anything I ever saw in this world or believe exists in heaven. Neither you nor anyone else in the world should be at all surprised if, despite the fact that I am a friar and a monk, I am burning in the fire of my lofty love for you; for from the moment I saw you appear among the other fair ladies at the dance, it seemed to me that I saw a second sun rise from your beautiful face, blotting out the first, full of such sweetness and blessedness that my spirit was suddenly filled with tenderness and my heart and soul were flooded with thoughts of you, so that now, to the delight of my heart, I never cease to think of you and your noble virtues. And for the consolation of my amorous soul I have written you this affectionate little letter, a token of the fervent, heartfelt love that I bear you, in the firm hope that it will be graciously received, thanks to the kindness visible in your generous bearing. And if this is so, I fervently pray you to be content to be loved by me, who have elected you to be queen of my heart. For if you should do the contrary, you alone would be the cause of my imminent death, which I am sure (since you are human and not made of stone) would pain you always, although you may deem me to be a lover unworthy of your lofty value. So, dear young lady, since I cannot withstand the

amorous arrows, for God's sake, don't disdain my infinite love. I
conjure you to give me a favorable reply, which I await with surpassing desire; and to you, whence all my health and happiness proceed,
I give myself, and pray that the supreme God shall always keep you
safe and make you take pity on me."

When he had written this letter and sealed it with gold fila-
ments, he gave it to the young man, saying: "Most greatly do I
commend my suit to your prudence." And the young man, taking
the letter, said that he would do all he could, and returning to the
festivities and finding us, his comrades, he gave us an entertaining account of the friar's falling in love, to the delight of us all. So
we quickly got our damsel away from the fête, in order to carry on
with our amusement, and accompanied her with appropriate deco-
rum to the house of a dear friend of ours. And when we got there
and told the young priest about our prank and showed him the
love letter, he was extraordinarily delighted by it and said: "This
shall be the drollest thing we've ever done. But what do we do
now?" And we replied, laughing: "We must answer the letter,
telling him that you are not the sort of young woman to fall in love
but that you do not altogether dislike being loved by him, so that
he won't despair of your love. Indeed, by giving him a little hope,
for our own great pleasure, we shall make him wear a garland of
the god Cupid over his scapular." And thus, after much talk and
plenty of laughter, we composed the reply and the young priest
wrote it out in his own hand, and it read as follows:

"My dear sir,
If it were not that my age and position as a woman prevent me from
reprimanding you, a man worthy of reverence both for his years and

75

for his virtue, I should be most aggrieved, admonishing you that it is neither seemly nor praiseworthy for a man of your quality to fall in love and tempt decent young women away from those things that they should hold more dear than their own lives. But since it is fitting that I emulate the courteous tenor of the letter I have received from you, I shall take the whole matter in good part, forewarning you, however, that I am not, as you may believe, one of those flighty girls. It is true that one should hold dear the favor of men of virtue like yourself, because some good may always come of it, no matter how little intelligence and worth or even beauty I might possess, though you deem my beauty heavenly, and surely immoderate love deceives you in this. But however it may be, if from me alone your health and happiness proceed, I am very content to be loved by you, and I am, in accord with your choice, queen of your heart, though always saving my honor and integrity, which I commend to you above all things, and may merciful God protect you from all evil, and guide both you and me in the path of virtue forever."

Having written this reply, our friend brought it to the friar, who took and read and reread it with endless joy, kissing it a thousand times, not knowing what to do, and asking our friend if he believed that he could hope for mercy from his lady love. And answering yes and no, according to what the friar asked, but endeavoring to persuade him to persevere in this love, at last our friend said to him: "My lord prior, without wasting words, since I am your friend and believe it to be a work of mercy to help those who languish in the flames of love, whenever you wish, I am ready to bring her along with my companions to dine with you, and will find a way for us to leave her alone with you."

Hearing this welcome offer, the friar joyfully threw his arms around our friend's neck, saying to him: "You really must be my

God." And when the prior even offered him his heart, our friend said: "Well, we should serve our friends liberally. Tell me what I must do to bring her to you." And the friar replied: "Come along tomorrow, and go into the church and pretend to go around looking at the church and its paintings, and quickly come into my room, where I shall have ordered a meal to be served and some beautiful veils and money to be given to the young woman." Then leaving him and having been instructed as to what he should do, our friend returned and reported everything to us, which amused us vastly, and an hour seemed a thousand years to us before we could get on with our prank. And the next day, the meal awaiting us, we all went (for there were eight of us young Aretines) and our priest was of course dressed as a woman. And when we arrived at the church we looked at it and gazed at its paintings, and then entered the friar's chamber. He was waiting for us beside himself with joy; and when he saw us, he welcomed us graciously and had a fine, elegant meal served to us.

When we had eaten, one by one we slipped out of the room, leaving the young woman alone with the friar. And he, seeing that we had departed, very softly closed the door of the room, saying: "Lovely young lady, these veils are for you. And if they are not beautiful enough to be worthy of your noble charms, forgive me, for I gladly give them to you along with my soul, as I told you in my letter," and he tried to kiss her. And the young priest, finding himself alone and thus assaulted, not wanting to be kissed, began to say, as we had instructed him (and he was a very clever actor): "O, woe is me! Where have I been left, where have I been led? What an evil day when I came into the world! Alas! Poor me! Is this the way women are seduced? Has my brother-in-law left me here so that I might be disgraced?" And the friar, thinking to calm

77

her, kept saying: "My soul, do not be sad. Console yourself, if you wish me to live. Don't be afraid, you are in good hands. Look, take this money here, or anything else you want." And when the friar sought to take the young man's hand and touch his breast, which the young man did not want, he said, continuing his lament: "Woe is me! Sir, keep your hands to yourself. If my mother or brothers knew of this, I would be dead. Am I thus to lose my honor, which I so warmly commended to you when I replied to your letter?" Then the friar began to say: "What is this I hear, dear young lady, sweet hope of my amorous soul? You are not among wolves nor in a dark forest among wild beasts, but in a safe and pleasant place, near to me, who love you more than my life. What would you say to someone who hated you, if you make your delicate glance and angelic face so harsh to one who loves you immeasurably? Surely you complain without reason, on account of your ungrateful heart. Although your looks are charming, to compensate for your glorious beauty you are lacking in mercy for the love I bear you and shall bear you for as long as I live." And saying these words, he opened his arms to embrace him; and the young priest, drawing back, said piteously: "Sir, for the love of God, let me be, for I hold my honor too dear, as you also should, if you truly loved me. For if you will not rein in this lascivious desire of yours, I would rather be in a forest among wild beasts and be devoured than be here and lose my honor, for which I sweetly pray you to have a care, if you wish to be loved by me." And as the friar continued to beg the damsel to satisfy his love, and the young priest continued to refuse, the friar became all inflamed with desire. And unable to change his mind with prayers, gifts, and extravagant promises, he seized him and threw him on the bed. Now the young priest, finding himself on his back and thinking it was time to reveal his identity, suddenly changed his faked Florentine accent and spoke in the accent of Arezzo, saying: "My dear sir, don't overexert yourself, for I am more of a man than you are." Amazed and wanting an immediate explanation, the friar put out his hand and felt that the "young lady" was a very well-endowed young man. But seeing how handsome he was, feeling all aflame with desire, and determined to satisfy his unruly appetite, he said: "Very well! I like you no less as a man than as a woman." Then the young priest, rather alarmed by this, quickly pushed his feet against the friar's shameless breast, knocking him backward, and jumped off the bed, saying: "Friar, go hang yourself! O unbridled lust, o unruly friar's appetite, how worthy you are of eternal disgrace! Who would ever have believed that under that holy habit of yours, glory of the Christian religion, you had been led to such wickedness? Who would have believed that you, a teacher and preceptor in a monastery, would not only not repent your original desire, but that you actually tried to taste the abominable sin for which Sodom and Gomorrah were miraculously burned to ashes? O diabolical spirit, o profane heart, how could you bear to violate your holy vocation? How is it that the heavens do not move to punish your sacrilege so as to make you an image of suffering and an example of pain to other evil and villainous friars? But certainly, as soon as I am able, I shall make known this stinking appetite of yours, to your shame and detriment."

The rest of us were hanging about near the chamber of the mocked friar, and hearing the priest dressed as a woman speaking angrily, we rushed laughing into the room and said: "What is this? Sir prior, what's wrong with you?" All full of shame, he replied: "Since you have duped me, I pray you for the love of God to say nothing, and if there is anything you want from me, just ask for it."

We said we would do so gladly. But the moment we got outside the church, we would have split a gut if we had kept this joke a secret; so we told it openly to everyone in the village. And when it got out, to his great disgrace and shame the friar was immediately expelled from the monastery. And bursting with laughter and delight we returned to Arezzo, leaving a pleasant memory in Monte San Savino on account of the prank that we and the young priest had played. He is still living today—an excellent priest, witty, and a perfect chorister.

2.

A Ritual Cleansing: *Friar and Priest*

There is a good deal of unreality in the framework and setting of
this jocular tale. Putting it in the vicinity of Florence, Arienti
wants to turn to account the Florentine reputation for wit and
sophistication. But he actually makes neighboring Arezzo his
point of departure, a lesser city under Florentine rule, and has his
eight young bloods go out from there to a religious festival in the
village of Monte San Savino, an old fortress on the way to Siena.
This is the sort of burg which was often derided by members of the
urbane bourgeoisie of cities such as Florence, Bologna, and
Milan. Revealingly, however, country people as such are not at all
introduced into the narrative. Though a caricature, friar Puzzo is a
type of cleric who could have been found in any major Italian city.
In effect, Arienti clears his stage and gentrifies his countryside, so
as to make it more acceptable to his readers and to highlight the
trickery of his young Aretines, all of whom hail from an upper-
class urban background. Yet the air of superiority in their approach
to Monte San Savino is plainly evident: "we were a group of young
men from Arezzo, all wellborn (*gentili*) and debonair, who used to
go out sometimes into our countryside to enjoy its coolness and
amuse ourselves at local festivals." On this occasion, they go out
with a beautiful sixteen-year old priest, intending to play a trick
on the country bumpkins. Arienti, then, is offering us a subtle
mixture of idealization (fictional gentrification) and verifiable historical attitudes.

81

In Arezzo, the beautiful priest would have been recognized everywhere; not so, however, in the Aretine backcountry, where, though welcome, the party of eight would have been looked upon as strangers or even, if they affected a Florentine accent, as foreigners. The reverse was also true: men and women who came from outside a city, even if from just beyond its great walls, were legally considered foreigners (*forenses*) inside the city. This broaches another feature of the story's framework: a half-concealed, near ethnic element. Since in Tuscany and other parts of upper Italy, most of the countryside (*contado*) was owned by the rich urban nobility and bourgeoisie, and partly also by the Church, rural towns and villages had perforce to receive their urban visitors with good grace, as these were necessarily associated with the class of mighty absentee landlords. But the reverse was not the case: no Tuscan or other North Italian city would have offered an honorable reception to eight rustics from a neighboring hamlet. Accordingly, we should imagine the arrival of the young Aretines in Monte San Savino as they would have been imagined by Arienti's audience: an arrival that was a vestigial, symbolic, or ritualized invasion, however graceful, with some degree of strutting and acting, especially as one of them at least, the young priest, pretends by his accent to be from Florence. This added importance and authority to their arrival.

If we are to understand the essential business of *Friar and Priest*, we must fix its setting and circumstances, as in the preceding comments. For Arienti has a given audience in mind and he is aiming his tale at their particular attitudes. Who were his most likely readers?

Born in Bologna about 1445, the son of a prosperous barber who was also a follower and client of the Bentivoglio faction,

Arienti managed to study the rudiments of law (*notaria*) at the University of Bologna and was matriculated in the guild of attorneys (*notai*), but seems never to have practiced. Instead, following his father's lead, he became a servitor to the Bentivoglio—Bologna's *de facto* ruling family in the later fifteenth century—and for twenty years (1471–1491) worked as a private secretary to the count Andrea Bentivoglio. Driven by persisting financial need and a yearning for recognition, he entered into contact with other important personalities, including duke Ercole d'Este of Ferrara, to whom in fact he dedicated, in 1478, the sixty-one tales of *Le Porretane*, where our account of friar Puzzo first appeared. As an audience and narrative setting for *Le Porretane*, Arienti imagines a small group listeners at the baths of Porretta in the Apennine Mountains near Bologna. Here, he pretends, over the space of five days in 1475, the group retailed the sixty-one (mainly comic) stories. His own vital milieu in Bologna included lawyers and other *literati*, but especially the courtly Bentivoglio and their satellites. Hence his auditors and readers were the city's fashionable people: the well-educated (some of whom were poets and prose writers), friends and relatives of the Bentivoglio, who were always in search of amusement, probably certain priests, as well as others of a similar sort from abroad, such as correspondents of his at Ferrara, Mantua, and Milan. This audience thrived on gossip and needed no introduction to lubricious clerics, anti-clericalism, town-and-country relations, male homosexuality, and the ritualized love language of the day. For these are the matters at the heart of Arienti's tale.

First the anticlerical strain. The removal of the papacy to the Southern French city of Avignon in the early fourteenth century, and the infamous Great Schism, with its late spectacle of three contending popes during the years 1409 to 1415, had opened the way to increasing misconduct on the part of the clergy, especially in Italy. And the periodic return of plagues and epidemics in the later fourteenth and early fifteenth centuries, while producing occasional frenzies of piety, had also disrupted episcopal administration and the cure of souls. There was a marked growth in clerical delinquency, turning more and more of the laity, in the cities most of all, against the bands of so-called copulating, gluttonous, mendacious, thieving priests and friars. Their misdeeds fill contemporary reports and stories. Consequently, Friar Puzzo [Friar "Stink" in the Tuscan tongue], as victim or reprobate, fits into a strong current of anticlerical polemic. Whether purely imagined or partly real, he is the type of the carnal, pushy, pleasure-loving, hypocritical, fifteenth-century cleric, and the head of his convent to boot. But he is no coarse lout, or not merely this; he speaks the language of gentlemen. Unknown to most modern readers, though at once obvious to his contemporary audience, Arienti has packed the tale with the ritualized love language of the age, an idiom which belonged firstly to the usage of educated, ambitious, or courtly men; and the friar handles this idiom with ease.

Entering Monte San Savino as a girl "come out of Paradise" is the sixteen-year-old priest, Ser Francesco di Ludomero, that is, Mr. Frank Pure-Games-and-Sport (in keeping with the Latinate pun on his patronymic, Ludomero). He is accorded "a place of honor among the other women," and is so "miraculous" a beauty, that "the eyes of all men and women" turn his way, "gazing upon and contemplating his angelic visage, modest bearing (*onesti portamenti*), and noble manners." The gazing eyes seem insatiable and men fall immediately in love with "her." These are the very words and properties applied or ascribed to the beloved lady of amatory verse, ranging from Guido Cavalcanti's generation in the late thirteenth century to Pietro Bembo in the early sixteenth century, although there were, inevitably, shifts in themes and accents. What is more, Friar Puzzo appears to slide quite naturally into the idiom. Ignorant or silly he may be, as when he calls Cupid the son of Pluto, god of the underworld, when all literate men knew that he was the offspring of Venus and Vulcan. Nonetheless, he invokes poetry's language of the burning lover: "I am all on fire with love for her," culminating with the exclamations, "Help me; alas, I'm dying, I'm burning, I'm consumed." The irony is that having summoned the son of the god of the underworld, he may be acting out his true future condition in the fires of hell. In any case, the parodic masterpiece in the amatory idiom is the letter to his beloved. The opening sentence catches the fifteenth century's elevated (male) way of praising the loved one:

I feel obliged to heaven, beautiful young lady, whom I love more dearly than anything else in the world, only because it has made me worthy of seeing your beauties, which are more heavenly than human, and which delight me as much as anything I ever saw in this world or believe exists in heaven.

Although this is a sacrilegious affirmation, in issuing from the mouth of the prior of an Augustinian convent, it strikes us as ridiculous because of the unfolding prank and the man's office. At a Renaissance court, in the study or setting of a great urban mansion (*palazzo*), or better, in the love poetry of the Bentivoglio circle of Bologna, such amatory expression—if a little less impious—was not only typical and common but also necessary, if it was to fulfill the expectations of love, genre, and milieu. Hence the flicker of mockery and derision in the letter's exordium is a satiric assault on the friar, not on its own ritual language. In the 1470s, for example, Matteo Maria Boiardo refers to his loved one, in his verse, as that "heavenly beauty about which I reason," and elsewhere, "O heavenly whiteness [the lady], not understood by human eyes and human deliberation," and again in another poem, "nor even by thinking can one reach her beauty, because Heaven hides it from human intelligence."

Friar Puzzo's letter goes on to utilize other locutions that are also lifted from the stock of the same amatory lexicon: thus his "lofty" love, her face as a second sun which obscures the real one, the happy blessedness (*beatitudine*) of her face, her "noble virtues," the "consolation of my amorous soul," the "magnanimity of your generous look," "a lover unworthy of your lofty value," "don't disdain my infinite love," "you whence all my health and happiness proceed," and "God . . . make you take pity on me." This elevated and courtly language is carried over even into the friar's exchange with the young go-between: "Most greatly do I commend my suit to your prudence."

In the fifteenth-century setting, these are the words of a gentleman in the mouth of a near lout, but obviously an educated lout who has done some reading and knows his way around. After all, he is the prior of his convent, a post which ordinarily required certain social and administrative skills and a good, late-medieval, Latinate education. For all his rascality, the prior is a man of parts and is well-acquainted, we may remember, with one of the well-born Aretines.

But what shall we say of the young men from Arezzo and their ravishing friend, the priest? As would-be fifteenth-century readers

and listeners, we are clearly meant to sympathize and even identify with them. For they are rather like us, in the Bentivoglio circle
or at the court of Ferrara: nobly born, endowed with landed or other income, proud, carefree, fond of throwing their/our weight
around, and thirsting for amusement. And if, along the way,
they/we can expose and chastise a vile scoundrel, so much the
better. In some respects, they are also thoroughly indulgent: they
cultivate the friendship and encourage the transvestite antics of a
young priest as beautiful as heaven itself, a maiden in everything
but his private parts.

The literary and social ambiguities of the story converge here,
in the priest, since this character both makes the story and is the
occasion for the bringing forth of a revealing set of fifteenth-century attitudes. The appropriate questions bring these forth. Had Ser
Francesco taken final holy vows and was he tonsured? At age sixteen, could he really be old enough to be charged with the care of
souls? Not normally in canon law, but dispensations were procur-
able by means of money and the right contacts, just as they were
for boys of illegitimate birth, who otherwise were debarred from
entry into the priesthood. So, did Ser Francesco have influential
patrons in high ecclesiastical place? Why was he able to travel
and dally about with a company of worldly-minded pleasure seek-
ers? And on the occasion of a country fête to honor the Queen of
Heaven, what about the action of dressing him up as a dazzling
maiden and taking him out to where he would seem the most
queenly and heavenly creature ever seen?

I am not suggesting that the author's fifteenth-century audience
consciously raised these questions. Something, however, in their
implied attitudes does. For in their sympathy with the Aretines,
and by their pleasure in the anecdote, they themselves connived

with the laxity of the Italian Renaissance Church. Men from their social class tended to occupy the positions of command within it, as demonstrated, for instance, by the sale and purchase of cardinalships and curial dignities. Thus, Friar Puzzo and the bewitching Ser Francesco, the one as well as the other, belong not only to the moral and social world of the company of Aretines but also—it is one and the same world—to that of our 1470s upper-class readers. Friar and priest, therefore, may be realistic figments ("factions") of Arienti's imagination, but their makings—i.e., their constituent parts and settings—were already in the mental world of Arienti's readers. This audience and their ilk had made the likes of Puzzo and the priest possible in real life.

Late in the tale, just as Ser Francesco concludes his scolding of the friar, there is a hint of the sometime keen rivalry between the secular and regular clergy (priests vs. monks and friars): "How is it," asks Ser Francesco, "that the heavens do not move to punish your sacrilege so as to make you an image of suffering and an example of pain to the other evil and villainous friars?" What *did* contemporaries make of this indictment, coming from one who had taken the rather scabrous charade far enough to be pushed onto a bed, to have his genitals felt, and suddenly to fear that he might be sodomized? Both at the beginning and end of the tale, we are told that Ser Francesco—"virtuous" at the start and still "an excellent priest" many years later—was a good man. It is strongly implied that he is heterosexual and that he even perhaps truly kept his clerical vows of celibacy. Against these claims, however, there is the tale's luminous imagery: Ser Francesco's stunning beauty as a young woman and his egregious feminine bearing. In effect, Friar Puzzo's lechery is constructed and conjured up by this means. There is thus a striking ambivalence at the focus of the tale. And this unstable feature reflects fifteenth-century upper-class (male) attitudes toward homosexuality. In the ambiguity at the heart of this well-turned tale, we touch an aspect of literary expression that was already present in everyday attitudes, and hence in the social and mental structures of the age. Despite the prominence and glamour of the Italian humanist movement, with its overriding emphasis on the study of classical history and literature, there was certainly no popular sympathy around for the common Roman view, in the time of Martial, that all men were bisexual.

The legal codes of all Italian cities carried harsh statutory penalties against male homosexuality, ranging from heavy fines, exile, prison sentences, and the pillory, to bloody whipping, branding, mutilation, and death by fire. There were moments of extreme severity, such as at Venice and Genoa in the fifteenth century; and fearing the biblical examples of Sodom and Gomorrah, governments occasionally encouraged fierce verbal campaigns against the unspeakable sin of sodomy. Now and then, therefore, convicted sodomites were put to death, but this was more likely to be the fate of those condemned for violent homosexual rape; and older men were apt to be more harshly punished than "passive" (female-like) boys and young catamites. Yet in practice, for all their savage laws against "unnatural" sexual activity, most urban governments verged on toleration: they tended to impose fines, to deal out relatively light prison sentences, and to serve warnings; or they simply failed to prosecute. Moreover, to have influential contacts in high office might also save a man, but such means were not altogether reliable.

How can we explain the obvious ambivalence, dithering, or conflict in upper-class attitudes towards male homosexuality? The answer is, in part, that contemporaries had the sense, however obscure, that sodomy was in some fashion connected with the demands of demography, honor, and family social structure, all of which delayed marriage for males and rigorously removed all middle- and upper-class women from sex outside of marriage. In these circumstances, young men of "good family" turned to female servants, female household slaves, prostitutes, and other men. Consequently, in the course of the fourteenth century, many cities relaxed or eliminated their toughest laws against prostitution; and in the fifteenth century, as a matter of candid policy, Lucca, for one, permitted prostitutes to move freely throughout the city, in order to help wean men away from homosexual practice and to prepare them for marriage. There could be no franker acknowledgement, however circuitous, of the links between social structures and male sexuality.

Early Renaissance Italy seems not to have recognized homosexuality in women. This official blindness issued, I suspect, from views which accompanied the dominant social and property relations. Given the subordinate, "passive," "flighty," and "inferior" nature of women, as enunciated in governing doctrine, their sexuality was taken seriously—i.e., seen as potentially menacing—only when it came into contact with men.

Though the foregoing observations may seem a digression, they help us to understand the ambiguous figure of our beautiful, sixteen-year old priest, and really therefore to understand the tale itself. The author's narrative posture fully indulges Ser Francesco, who is a point of dalliance and who provides a pleasant *frisson* even for his Aretine companions. Insofar as he truly has something of the girl or young lady about him, he would appear to be a passive, submissive, and less harmful being. His foil is Friar Puzzo, for whom the whole allotment of abuse and censure in the tale is reserved. Two men in holy orders: one a near boy, a priest, a virtuous beauty; the other an older man, a friar, an unseemly lecher, a likely sodomite. But these two flourish in the mind of an invisible third party: upper-class society (Arienti's intended reading and listening audience) looks on with delight, playing imaginatively with roles and *personae* rooted in everyday strains and stresses. In their dramatic opposition, the friar serves to cleanse the adolescent priest, to lead us away from the scent of his bisexuality. But more importantly for this analysis, the two represent the genial bifurcation of a conflicted historical attitude: all the admiration and indulgence for the one is paid for by the odious other, Friar "Stinker." If we read the tale outside its historical setting, we may appreciate its invention, verve, and ironic contrasts; but we shall miss the living ingredient, the force and timeliness, in the oppositions between angelic priest and sordid friar. These oppositions were lodged in uncertain, divided, and even guilty attitudes toward male homosexuals. Biblical and statutory sanction, as well as the veiled threat to the "loftiness" of the conjugal family, called for the harshest reprisals against homosexuals. And yet, was it not true that death by fire was too brutal a penalty? That in view of the restrictions on the sexuality of "honorable" women, prostitution naturally surfaced? Therefore, that other "excrescences" might also surface? And so, was some degree of lenience not in order? It was easy to scourge older men in holy orders (though the friar, let us remember, was normally heterosexual). But what to do about good-looking young men and boys who turned to homosexual practice? Kill them? No, not normally. Terrorize them? Yes, well, maybe, or from time to time.

In the fifteenth-century setting, and more specifically, among the assembled company listening to *Le Porretane*, the exposure and dismissal of Friar Puzzo is tantamount to a ritual of symbolic cleansing. The "ethnic" invasion by a company of upper-class (urban) outsiders is seen to have been fully justified: they purge an attractive rural community of its hidden corrupter. This is literature as class celebration, though in a slyly devious mode.

FOUR

1.

BIANCO ALFANI

by Piero Veneziano

*The likely author of this story, Piero Veneziano (a nick-
name), was the Florentine wool merchant (lanaiuolo),
Piero di Filippo del Nero, born about 1380 and domiciled
in the Scala district of Florence's Santo Spirito quarter, on
the far side of the Arno river. He seems to have held public
office on occasion, for he served a term as Prato's chief
magistrate (podestà) in 1433. According to a contemporary, Piero Veneziano had the attractive manners of a
"lover" and was a lighthearted and genial man, wonder-
fully inventive when it came to concocting stories.*

ॐ

During the past plague, which came upon us in the year of Christ
1430, I had remained in Florence to see to some business of mine.
And one day in the month of July, when it is really awfully hot, I
was in the loggia of the Buondelmonti in the company of Piero
Veneziano and Giovannozzo Pitti, and we were talking about
recent events and especially the plague, when several fine fellows
joined us, among whom was Lioncino di Messer Guccio de' Nobili.
Lioncino interrupted our conversation, and with a broadly smiling

95

face said: "Come, let the dead bury the dead and the doctors stay with the sick, and let us, the healthy, try to enjoy ourselves and be happy, if we want our health to last. If you'll let me, I wager that I can make you pass the rest of this day in amusement and good cheer." We all replied that he should do as he pleased, that we would follow and obey him; so he set off toward the Ponte Vecchio with Giovannozzo Pitti and Piero Veneziano on either side of him. And having crossed the bridge conversing pleasantly about various things, he led us to the Pitti garden, where Giovannozzo immediately ordered a table to be set beneath a little jasmine-covered trellis, in the middle of which rose a little fountain. The table was laden with all the fruits in season and two cooling-vessels full of excellent white and red wine. And when we had been there a while and had all taken refreshment, Piero Veneziano called us all to attention with a pleasant preamble and began to tell the tale of Mistress Lisetta, which, since I had heard him tell it before, I have already recounted to you. But it was so much more delightful when he told it, in that he imitated all the actions and gestures of the woman and the peasant, laughing and crying at the appropriate times, so that we seemed to see and hear each of them. After he had told the tale and we had laughed about it for a good while, Lioncino turned laughingly to him and said: "Piero, I mean for our dispute, which has gone on for so long, to be settled and for you to see that I am a better storyteller than you. These worthy young men who have heard your tale will be patient enough to listen to me tell another. And if they judge it to be more amusing than yours, from then on you shall call me your master; and if it should be the opposite—which it won't—I shall call you mine." When Piero had agreed to this, Lioncino stroked his beard, took a drink, and began:

* * *

I believe that several of you know Bianco Alfani, or have often heard him mentioned. Although at first glance he looks young, I believe he is more than forty years old. And although he thinks he is shrewd and crafty, his shrewdness is more in keeping with the age he looks than with the age he truly is, as you shall understand before we leave here. From his youth to this day, Bianco has almost continuously been warden of the Stinche [the city's chief jail], where, making the poor prisoners pay him bribes, he piled up a fortune. But since he's always been sociable and a fellow who loves the sight of a woman's face—especially a young one—he's held on to little of his earnings, and you shall hear how that came about.

Last year Bianco used to come often to the New Market, and in the evening after supper he was always surrounded by a circle of young men, drawn to him like ducks to a decoy to hear him boast and tell stories, which gave them great delight. It happened that on one of those evenings Messer Antonio, jester to the lords,[1] and Ser Niccolò Tinucci and I were at our usual bench, and Bianco was nearby, surrounded, as was his wont, by a group of young men. Overhearing their conversation, we began to delight in his simplicity and in what the youths were saying to him. And after we had listened to them for a while, Ser Niccolò said to us: "I want to make you laugh. A year ago there was an executor[2] from Norcia

1. Messer ["my lord"] Antonio was actually Florence's poet-herald, a functionary who served the Lord Priors, the city's highest executive body (nine men). Although he was certainly no longer a comic figure, the poet-herald was often referred to as a "jester" (*buffone*).
2. Executor of the Ordinances of Justice, one of Florence's four principal judges, all of whom were recruited from abroad and served six-month terms.

by the name of Giovanni di Santi, with whom this simpleton (who had been to Norcia once on some business or other) was on very friendly terms. Now, since I am a close friend of Giovanni's and frequently had occasion to visit him on behalf of some friends of mine, I often found Bianco there; and Giovanni got the greatest pleasure in the world out of making Bianco rant and rave, as you have seen him do this evening. On one occasion, Giovanni had given him some trifling errand to run—for he made use of Bianco in such little matters—and he said: 'Get on with it, Bianco my friend, and come back quickly with the reply; and do not doubt that I will repay you in due course for all your trouble, and it won't be with mere trinkets or trifles.' 'Of course you shall repay me,' Bianco replied, 'don't I know what you folks from Norcia are like?' 'I don't care what you know,' said Giovanni, 'because I've decided, once I return home, never to rest until I make you captain of Norcia.'[3] 'Listen here,' said Bianco, 'that would really be something, and I would wield that staff [of office] as well as you do this one.' 'Very well,' said Giovanni, 'we shall soon put you to the test.' 'The sooner the better,' said Bianco, and went off to carry out the errand for Giovanni, happy as could be. When he had gone, Giovanni began to laugh, and turning to me he said: 'What think you, Mr. Attorney? This fellow surely believes that he shall become our captain, and I don't think they'd even want him as chief of our guardsmen. But do you know what? I shall amuse myself by keeping his hopes up, and he shall do my bidding all the more diligently.'

"What will you say when I tell you that Bianco got this crazy idea into his head to such a degree that afterwards I never came upon him there when he wasn't going on about it, and he was

3. A third-rate provincial judgeship, normally held for a six-month period.

mocked and ridiculed about it by all of Giovanni's servitors, including even the guards, and he never realized it. In fact, when the time finally came for Giovanni to leave Florence and I accompanied him as far as Bagno a Ripoli, Bianco came to see him off and warmly reminded him of his promise. And our friend Giovanni said to him: 'Be of good heart, for I shall keep my promise to you,' and Bianco expected it as sure as death—or so I gathered from what he said to me as we returned to Florence together."

Having heard what Ser Niccolò said, I began to laugh, and said: "We could have a great deal of fun with this man, if what you have told us is true. If we send him a letter that seems to come from this Giovanni di Santi, in which he all but confirms Bianco's appointment, he'll go crazy over it and we'll hear a thousand stories from him here every evening." "Without a doubt," said Ser Niccolò. And Messer Antonio said: "Come then, I'll compose the letter, for I can fake the speech of Norcia better than any of you, and your task, Ser Niccolò, shall be to send it, for I shall give it to you tomorrow." And so he did, for the next morning he came along with a letter written in such a way that no one would have known that it was written by someone not from Norcia. The letter said that a relative of Giovanni's had been chosen elector of the captain, and that he truly hoped to have Bianco elected, but that he shouldn't speak about it yet. Ser Niccolò had the letter properly copied by a notary friend of his and sent it to Bianco via one of his servants, who passed himself off as a courier. The servant was all covered with dust from the country, so that it truly seemed he had come a long way, when he went to the Via dell'Orto behind the church of San Piero Maggiore, where Bianco lived. There he asked where Bianco's house was; it was pointed out to him; and finding Bianco in the doorway, he bowed to him and gave him the letter. And after Bianco had read it, he took the courier joyfully by the hand and insisted on giving him supper. And when Bianco inquired about Giovanni, the servant replied as he had been instructed to do by Ser Niccolò. After supper, the courier said that he wished to depart early the next morning and that Bianco could send an answer if he pleased; and once he got it, he took it straight to Ser Niccolò. When Ser Niccolò met us, he read out Bianco's reply, and we realized that this man was living in the firm hope of being elected captain—all the more so when, on that very day, we went over to the jail and found him replying to whatever any of the prisoners or guards said to him by remarking, "I'll be out of here and away from all you knaves for one time anyway, as not a month will pass before you'll see whether I'm a nobody or a somebody." And he said a thousand other nonsensical things, all of which confirmed our belief that we could take the joke even further. So we wrote another letter, again in Giovanni's name, and sent it to Bianco a few days later by the same courier, informing him that he had been elected and that in a few days Giovanni would send him the official notice, but that he should keep the matter a close secret until the confirmation arrived. We immediately received such a reply to our letter that we decided to carry the hoax all the way. So a few days later Ser Niccolò made up a formal notice of election with a big seal scrounged from Ciave [a Florentine seal maker] and wrote another letter in Giovanni's name, and we sent these on by the same courier, instructing Bianco to be at Pergola, three miles from Norcia, on July 24, and saying that he had only to furnish his own banners, arms, and some linen, and that Giovanni would provide the other things, but that above all he should make sure to have a qualified knight.[4] And when he found Bianco, the courier pretended to be very happy, and doffing his cap as he gave him the notice, he said: "Much good may it bring you, my lord." Once Bianco had read the letter and seen the election notice, his happiness knew no bounds. He took the courier home and gave him forty silver pieces, promising to give him even more when he arrived in Norcia. And after he had given the courier his reply, it seemed a thousand years to him before he could present himself at the marketplace, to which he repaired immediately after supper. There he approached a group of men standing very near to us, and interrupting every conversation, he said: "Do you think Bianco is well known, or that he's a nobody?" The company turned to him, saying: "How now, Bianco? What do you mean?" With the notice in his hand, he answered: "Well, if this doesn't lie, I'll see if I can wield a little staff [of office] like the rest of you do." And soon he told them that he had been elected captain of Norcia; then he began to boast, and they to taunt him, so that it turned into quite an amusing scene. After he had been there a while, we saw him coming up to where we were, and turning to Ser Niccolò, he said: "Our Giovanni is really a man of parts, for he has fully, and without too much delay, obtained what he promised me in your presence." And holding up the election notice, he said: "This is that affair." "What affair?" said Ser Niccolò. "What!" said Bianco, "It's my appointment as captain of Norcia." "By your faith?" "By my faith, and if you don't believe me, read it." Having read it, Ser Niccolò said: "So it is. He's telling the truth. Now, Bianco, you must do something. You must honor him who does honor to you." And everyone encouraged him to go

4. To enhance the dignity of their offices, outside judicial magistrates, such as Bianco thought he was going to be, were often expected to arrive with a knight in their train, i.e., a mounted gentleman who had been dubbed a knight.

to Norcia in the most dignified way; and after much talk we parted. Bianco went home, but we went off to howl with laughter, for it had been very hard not to burst out laughing in his face.

The next morning, with the notice still in hand lest he not be believed, Bianco went all around Florence, as he should not have done, flaunting his new appointment. And this went on for many days, for though he had the formal notice, he was more disbelieved than believed. But then, when people saw that he had his banners made and had bought horses, many began to believe his story, however greatly they marveled. Now it happened that after he had spent a good deal of money, and needing to spend still more, he found that he had run short. But then he recalled that Ser Martino, who at the time was chief attorney for legislation [*notaio delle Riformagioni*], had asked Bianco several times to sell him the piece of land he owned behind the church of San Marco, because he had a chapel in that church and wished to endow it, but Bianco had never been willing to sell it. Now, he thought, it would provide for his needs. So he quickly went to see Ser Martino, and said to him: "You have wanted to buy my piece of land near San Marco, and up to now I have not wished to give it up, because it's been in our family for a long time. But now I need to sell it." And then Bianco told him the whole story, adding: "If you want it, make me an offer; for though I do so unwillingly, I would rather sell my land and honor those who honor me, than do otherwise. Then afterwards, on my return from Norcia, with the money remaining to me, I shall buy some shares in the Monte,[5] which will be worth more than the piece of land." Having heard him out, Ser Martino wished him well and said: "Bianco, you are

5. Bianco is talking about making an investment in Florence's funded public debt.

certainly showing that you descend from the Alfani lineage and that your spirit is like unto that of your ancestors; and you are very right to do things honorably and proceed to Norcia in the proper style. And in order that you may lack nothing, I am content to do as you wish; so you set the price yourself." Since Ser Martino was a judicious and honorable man, they easily came to terms on a fair price. And having the deed of sale drafted that very day at the bank of Esaù Martellini, Ser Martino had the money paid to Bianco, who then outfitted himself with all the things he still needed. And as the time for his departure approached, he hired a judge, a knight, and a notary, as called for by the election notice, and likewise servants and pages. And a few days before his departure, he want all over Florence, followed by an attendant, taking leave of all his friends and acquaintances and promising everyone that he would acquit himself with honor so that this magistracy should not be his last.

When the day of his departure finally came, Bianco sent his guards ahead on foot, while he followed with the rest of his mounted company, including eight horses in all; and they took the road to Arezzo. On arriving there, he visited the captain and the *podestà*[6] and did the same in Castiglion Fiorentino, Cortona, and Perugia, also visiting any Florentines living in those towns. And when these compatriots of his saw Bianco with such a grand retinue and he told them where he was going, knowing him as they did, they were amazed; yet out of respect for their native Florence, they treated him with much honor. After leaving Perugia, he rode all the way to Pergola, arriving there on the 24th, as he had been instructed to do in the letter; and there the innkeeper welcomed him warmly, as innkeepers customarily do. When Bianco had dis-

6. Arezzo's chief magistrates, two offices filled by Florentines.

mounted and had tended to all his gear, the innkeeper, seeing such a presentable figure, said: "Gentle sir, if I may ask, where are you going as magistrate?" "What do you mean, where am I going?" replied Bianco. "I am the captain of Norcia." Stunned, the innkeeper thought a moment and said: "Are you joking? The captain, a worthy man from Rome, took office not fifteen days ago." "Go on, my good man," said Bianco, "you must mean the *podestà*, for I am the captain; and if you have any doubts, read this," and drawing the election notice out of his breast, he put it in the innkeeper's hand. The innkeeper, who could read well enough, understood the sense of the letter and almost decided that he had made a mistake. Then, shrugging his shoulders, he said: "Obviously I'm out of my mind this evening," and deftly changing the subject, he ordered supper to be served. Turning to his retinue, Bianco said: "This man has a fine hold on the art of memory. He can't tell the *podestà* from the captain." And when they were well into their supper, the innkeeper turned matters over to a nephew of his and a servant, mounted his mare, and rode straight into Norcia, where he ran into a crony of his, and said: "Listen, man, the strangest thing in the world happened to me tonight," and told him the whole story. His friend began to laugh, and said: "I don't know which of us is the pregnant fool[7] here, but what a dolt you seem to me! Don't you know that the captain came in on the eighth of this month, and that the *podestà* took office less than three months ago? Either this fellow is pulling your leg, or he's crazy." "How the devil can that be," said the innkeeper, "when he showed me his formal notice of appointment?" And as they were talking thus, they arrived at the town square, where in speaking of

7. The intertextual reference here is to the gullible Calandrino in Boccaccio, *Decameron*, IX, 3.

the case to other people who were gathered there, some of them laughed about it and others were astounded. But being encouraged by a number of them to make it known to the town priors, the innkeeper went to them accompanied by several townspeople. And when the priors heard the story, having no idea what to make of it, they decided to send their chief clerk to Bianco, with a view to clearing up the mystery. The clerk set off with the innkeeper, discussing the matter with him on the way, and finally they arrived at the inn at quite a late hour. The innkeeper had two torches lit and sent word to Bianco that the chief clerk of the town priors of Norcia had come to visit him. Since Bianco did not know that the innkeeper had gone into town, he took it for certain that the clerk was there to visit him as the new captain.

When the two had met, each respectfully doffing his hat to the other and shaking hands, Bianco turned to the innkeeper and said, laughing: "Well, innkeeper? Now you can see how well you remembered when the captain took office." To this the innkeeper replied: "You speak the truth; but soon you shall have greater doubts than I had." Hearing all this, the clerk felt more like laughing than anything else; but he wisely held his laughter in check and turning to Bianco, began to speak: "Sir, my lords have heard of your arrival, and about your saying that you are to be captain of Norcia, which amazes them no end, since the captain took office on the eighth of this month. And they have sent me here to you to find out what this means and what your reason is for speaking this way." When Bianco heard these words, he was so distressed that he looked more dead than alive, and barely managing to open his lips, he said: "Do you have more than one captain?" "No, by God," replied the clerk. Bianco pondered a while, and feeling that he had been duped and that only someone from Norcia could have done this, all his anguish turned to fury, and going all red in the face, he drew the notice of appointment from his breast and said with venom in his voice: "Surely, if this does not lie, I shall be captain of Norcia. And if I have been wronged, I am from such a city that I shall know how to strike back." And becoming ever more fierce, he said: "Perhaps you people think you're dealing with mountain folk, but you shall find the citizens of Florence to be of a mettle different from that of such people. We have humiliated the Duke of Milan and others of similar ilk,[8] bigger fish by far than you people from Norcia. Don't think you've made me come here for an office given to another man, without me making good my rights. Oh, if I hadn't come in time, what the devil would they have done?" And besides this he said a thousand other foolish things, too long to retail here. He finally said to the clerk, who wanted to see the formal notice of appointment: "Go now, go. Tomorrow I shall come to your lords and show it then, and we shall see what they say." Hearing Bianco talk this way, the clerk took him for some kind of a lunatic, and without wasting too many words, took his leave. He returned to the town, accompanied by the innkeeper, and told the priors what had happened. Marveling at what they heard and not knowing what to think, the priors said: "Let us wait until morning and see what he has to say." Bianco conferred with his aides, and after carefully considering both the appointment notice and what they had heard, the only conclusion they were able to reach was that the town of Norcia, constrained by the pope or some other lord, had granted the office to another man after they had already sent the notice of appointment to Bianco. At long last, since the hour was very late, they all went to bed.

8. A reference to Florence's wars with Milan, the papacy, and other Italian powers.

But Bianco didn't sleep a wink all night; indeed, in thinking about what had happened, it seemed a thousand years to him before day would come and he could learn whether or not he was captain. So no sooner had dawn broken than he arose, mounted his horse, and he and his whole company rode directly into town. And since the story had already spread throughout Norcia, everyone ran through the streets to see this new captain, who rode with his head down, not knowing where to turn his eyes from the shame of it all, and looking as if he had lost his wife in a fire. When he reached the Palace of the Priors, he dismounted, and entering he sent word to them that he had come. At once assembling in their public chamber, the priors summoned him and sat him down beside them. And after sitting thus for a few moments, Bianco stood up, and having been instructed by his judge on their way into the town about what he should say, he began like this: "My lords, about three months ago Giovanni di Santo, who was our executor in the past year, wrote to me to say that he intended to have me elected as your captain, and then after some days he wrote that he had had me elected, and finally he sent me the formal notice of appointment. Here it is. Wishing to please your lordships and to reap honor, as my ancestors always have, I decided to come and serve you; and I equipped myself and made all the preparations required by the office, in keeping with the letter sent to me, and I have come here with a company of servitors, as you see, and at great expense, for I have spent more than 200 gold florins. And last evening, first from the innkeeper and then from your chief clerk, I heard that it's already been fifteen days since you gave the office to another man, which astounds and grieves me, just as the case warrants. For this does not seem to me to be keeping faith, as is fitting for a town such as yours, nor does it show the courtesy required by the love that has always existed between the people of Florence and yourselves. And I wouldn't want you to think that you've tricked some little craftsman, because the Alfani house (not to disparage other families) is one of the greatest and oldest in our city, and by bringing such shame and injury to me, you would not bring praise upon yourselves. Yet if you can see to it that my honor is maintained and that I do not lose what I have spent, I would be willing to accept what has happened thus far. Kindly have a care for both your honor and mine." And after he had said this, he put the appointment notice in the hands of the head prior, saying: "This is what makes me speak as I do." Seeing that Bianco was now silent, the prior said to him: "Kind sir, I hope you don't mind waiting outside for a few moments. We shall assemble and give you a reply." Bianco retired to another room across the way from the audience chamber, and waited there with his judge, to whom he said: "How I wish you had heard me, for I promise you I spoke to them in such a way that I cannot believe that in some fashion they will not look to their own honor and mine. For I perceived all too well that they feel they have done wrong; and out of shame, not one of them dared to look me in the face."

The priors met behind closed doors and had the appointment letter read out, and seeing that it had not been written by their clerk, that it conformed in no way with their mode of selecting a captain, and also because of the larger salary, the bigger retinue, the judge (an official not required by their captaincy), and the fact that the document did not bear their seal, they knew immediately that Bianco had been duped. And after laughing among themselves for a while, they summoned him again, invited him to sit, and one of them, speaking for all the priors, began in this manner:

"Gentle sir, having heard what you had to say and now having seen this appointment letter of yours, these lords are moved to wonder and compassion. They are amazed, for they cannot imagine how a trick on such a scale could have been played on you, nor that in all this time you never realized it; for you were never elected to this office, nor was this document drafted here, nor does it bear our seal, nor is it in keeping with the form of letters of appointment for this office. Judging by your speech and demeanor, they take you to be a man of gentle birth, and they have compassion for you, both because of the offense done to your honor and the great injustice that we see you suffering. They would like to be able to satisfy you in both parts, as well out of consideration for yourself as out of respect for the city from which you come, for which city and its citizens we bear a singular affection. But all the offices allotted [to outsiders] are presently filled, nor is any of them about to be vacant, so they see no way to help you in anything other than greatly to lament all this along with you. And finally, they urge you for the sake of your honor to return home as soon as you can, for the longer you stay here, the greater your shame shall be." And at this point he ceased speaking.

Hearing this reply, which was completely contrary to what he was expecting, Bianco was most aggrieved and could say nothing for some moments. But then, with tears in his eyes, he said: "My lords, the only one who could have done this to me is that traitor Giovanni di Santo. This is how he repays me for the services I rendered him in Florence. I have here the letters in his hand. Pray, may it please you at least to send for him and have him compensate me for my losses, and then let him go his way as he pleases, for I shall know how to avenge the injuries to my honor, if God grants life to me and my brothers." The priors replied by saying:

"If it be true that it was he, we shall see to it that you are compensated for your losses, and then we shall so punish him for his error that you won't have to seek much revenge." And in fact they sent for Giovanni, who came quickly, for he too had come to the town square along with the others to see who this new captain might be. And when he entered the priors' chamber and saw Bianco, he was astonished. Then one of the priors, speaking for the others in a very formal voice, told Giovanni why he had been sent for, and demanded to know what reason or impudence had moved him to disgrace and ruin this honorable man and to bring their lordships into the matter as well. Hearing this, Giovanni was even more amazed, and said: "My lords, it is true that when I was executor at Florence, Bianco here was of such help to me that I promised, to the best of my ability, to help obtain this office for him, so that I do consider myself obligated to him; and such are his qualities that if the lot to elect him had gone to someone whom I believed could have served me, I would gladly have intervened for him. But I never heard anything further about all this, and if you find that I ever did, then have my head cut off." Hearing this, Bianco drew the letters out of his breast and said: "My lords, see with what a face this man denies this. Make him read these letters, and see if they are from his hand." The priors made him read the letters, and he declared that he had not written them, owing to which, after the priors and Bianco had had their fair say, they dismissed Giovanni. And wishing to show Bianco in some way that they were sorry about what had happened to him, they ruled that the innkeeper be paid by the town and take nothing from Bianco. You can all imagine Bianco's spirits as he set out for the inn, accompanied by Giovanni and with everyone in the town pointing him out to each other in astonishment. Giovanni commiserated with him greatly, adding that in view of what had happened he could no longer see how he could ever obtain what he had promised him. When they arrived at the inn, Bianco decided to depart without delay, for it was still early; and having taken leave of Giovanni, he started back again for Perugia.

Since Bianco rode all alone up in front, the judge (who was from around Perugia) and the knight and the notary began to talk among themselves and to say: "This man has foiled us on our way to good positions. If he has been tricked, should we suffer for it?" And having decided among themselves what they should do, but saying nothing to Bianco, when they arrived in Perugia, they had his horses, baggage, and all his effects confiscated. Seeing this, Bianco pleaded greatly with them, but to no avail. And finally seeing that it was all no good and that it would be better for him to come to terms with them, he sold the three horses that belonged to him,[9] his trappings and the clothing off his back, obtaining half or less of what the lot had cost him. For since he was forced to sell, he saw himself squeezed by every buyer; and in the end, of all his provisions there remained only the banner with his coat of arms, which he removed from its rod and wrapped in a dirty old piece of cloth. With this on his shoulder, he set out on foot for Arezzo, and then from Arezzo he went on to Ortignano in the Casentino, where he had some relatives. And since he was ashamed to return to Florence, he lingered on there for weeks and weeks, grieving over his misfortune and not knowing or being able to imagine who had done the deed. But spurred on by the desire to find the man if possible, he decided to return to Florence. And when he arrived home and his brothers saw him on foot and in such a sorry state,

9. The other five horses were evidently the property of members of his hired retinue.

they were dumbfounded and of course asked him what had happened. After telling them everything, he then said: "My brothers, you must help me to avenge myself." And being of the same cloth as he, they all swore death to whoever had worked such an outrage. Bianco spent several days in and around the house before he dared venture forth into the city. Yet having to go out, he went about in a daze and with his eyes cast down. And when his friends and acquaintances spoke to him and asked if he had discharged his office so soon, turning red with shame, he would answer that something had prevented his going to Norcia, but that he had been with relatives of his in the Casentino; and pretending to be very busy, he would quickly break off the conversation. But the real story began to be told by people arriving from Norcia and Perugia, so that in a short time the whole city was full of it, and everyone taunted him so much that it was pitiful to see, as each of you knows. But the worst thing for Bianco was that a number of artisans, waiting and expecting to be paid out of his captain's stipend, now began to press him, demanding to be paid. And as he had sold his parcel of land to Ser Martino, not knowing what else to do, he also sold him his two small houses on the Via San Gallo, which Ser Martino really bought more to please Bianco and out of pity for him than for any other reason. Moreover, on hearing the story from him, Ser Martino urged Bianco not to talk about it, nor to probe any further, for the more he talked the more shame he brought on himself; and Ser Martino assured him that the deed could only have originated from among the inmates of the Stinche prison. This, at any rate, was the general opinion; so when Bianco received the money from Ser Martino, he followed his advice, probed no further, and paid off his creditors. And since he no longer had any hope of ever setting forth as rector,[10] he took the banner with his coat of arms into the church of San Marco and fixed it over the tomb of his father, who had died a few years before, and returned to his post at the Stinche.

If he had been severe with prisoners before, now, believing that they had gravely offended him, but not knowing exactly which of them it had been, he was much worse, and in order not to miss the guilty party he was as nasty as could be with all of them. For this reason, the prisoners gathered together several times, and not knowing what to do to improve their lot, Lodovico da Marradi, a wily man, as you know, finally said: "Look, there's no way we can get this man to let up on us. He insists that we're the ones who sent him off to Norcia, and we can't budge him from this belief, whatever we say. And every day, mulling over what happened to him, he makes life hell for us. Our misfortune is to have been brought to this miserable place to be tormented by him, and there's nothing we can do about it. Well then, let's do one thing at least, so that amid all this affliction we may taste the sweetness of revenge, which in my opinion surpasses all other delights in the world. Let's report him to the tax authorities,[11] informing them that he went to Norcia to serve as captain and failed to pay the tax [on his captain's stipend]. To amuse themselves, the officials there will then summon and harass him, causing him great anxiety; and besides, while he is there, we shall have got him off our backs. And even if he thinks we were the instigators, he can do no worse than he's doing now. Anyway, he who fights a good war will have a good peace." They all agreed to this, whereupon Lodovico penned

10. i.e., as captain of Norcia.
11. Actually, to the *Gabella del vino*, the office charged with collecting the taxes (*gabelle*) on the salaries of Florentines who went as rectors to other towns.

an anonymous denunciation and a friend of theirs got it into the special public coffer [*tamburo*] of the tax office. When it came to their attention, the officials there split their sides laughing, then sent for Bianco. And when he arrived, one of them, speaking for all, said: "Bianco, you have been denounced for having gone to Norcia as captain and not having paid the tax. So now you must pay double the sum, for you've incurred a fine." When Bianco heard this, he began to weep loudly, saying: "My lords, have pity on me," and he told them what had happened. Pretending not to believe him, the officials kept up the farce for quite a while and finally concluded that he should appear before them again. Lodovico's plan succeeded all too well, for every time these officials had some persisting disagreement among themselves, one of them would say: "Since we can't agree on these other matters, let's send for Bianco and see if we can agree about him." And they would send for him and keep him a while, and having amused themselves, they would then leave him in suspense. This went on for a good many changes of officials, for whenever the newly-elected ones met for the first time, they would send for Bianco, and then do so again every so often, as they saw fit. This was no little thing for him, nor a matter of minor anxiety, not to mention the fact that it cost him many florins, for he would bring small objects such as brushes, spindles, or mirrors for one or another of the tax officials, depending upon what he thought might please them. Meanwhile the prisoners, through a messenger from the tax office, arranged to hear the news, day by day, of what was going on there, and they never tired of thanking Lodovico for the plan he had devised, which so delighted and consoled them that they were able to bear everything else patiently. I shall leave out how we heard of everything that happened from the attorney who accompanied Bianco to the tax office, and pass over all the fun we had on many occasions and the many tricks played on him by the prisoners, so that by dint of contending with them, he ended up poor, beggarly, bizarre, and gouty.

* * *

When Lioncino had finished his story, he turned laughingly to Piero Veneziano and said: "Well now, what do you want to do, Piero? Do you give in, or do you want to go on being stubborn, as you usually do? Don't you think my story is better than yours?[12] Go on, judge for yourself, so as not to embarrass these young men." "No, no," said Piero, "we need something more here, for however fine and amusing your story, mine far surpasses it. I imitated the very speech of my characters, whereas you did not. Besides, my story has all the ingredients that make for that certain end which always produces laughter, and which generally most delights the ears of listeners, whereas yours does not. All the same, I have no wish to avoid the judgment of these able and discerning young men." Turning to us, Lioncino said: "I'm not surprised that Piero won't concede, for that would go against his nature; but considering your good judgment, I'm not afraid that you shall wrong me. And to keep from tiring you any further, I shall not repeat the many delightful elements in my story; but I do believe that knowing Bianco as you do, and having surely heard that what I have recounted actually happened, my account ought to give you more pleasure than anything in Piero's story. So please judge according to your conscience."

12. The reference here is to the risqué tale of Lisetta, also by Piero Veneziano.

115

We held differing opinions, some of us claiming that Piero's story was better, others preferring Lioncino's. And since we were unable to reach a decision, we promised Giovannozzo that this would not be our last meeting, and agreed that the next time they should tell two more stories and then we would render our judgment. But the plague continued to spread, and with it came Lioncino's death, which distressed everyone; and since we all fled from Florence, some here and some there, the contest was never decided; so I defer both to your judgment and to that of those who shall read the two tales.

2.

The Wages of Social Sin: *Bianco Alfani*

It is Florence in the year 1430, and we are outside Giovannozzo Pitti's house, somewhere on the grounds of the present-day Pitti Palace and gardens. In the trellised shade of a hot July sun, a small company of men sit around a table, eating fresh fruit, drinking cool wines, and chatting. In a moment, Lioncino de' Nobili will begin to regale the group with the story of an insidious prank. Here are the major ingredients of a living and changing oral tradition: an urban setting and men sitting around—in a private garden, as it happens —eating, drinking, gossiping, and telling stories. One other decisive ingredient was necessarily invisible: some vivacity or dynamism in the directly impinging historical and social world, working to renew the vitality of the oral culture.

In view of the dialogic spin and remarkable changes of voice in *Bianco Alfani*, this story calls for its teller to be something of an actor, a resource which evinces the energy of the oral patrimony. Lioncino himself emphasizes the importance of the dramatic element, for after hearing Piero Veneziano's tale of Mistress Lisetta, in the telling of which Piero "imitated all the actions and gestures of the woman and the peasant, laughing and crying at the appropriate times, so that we seemed to see and hear each of them," he challenges Piero's verve and rushes in to tell his own story of the deluded Bianco Alfani. There follow in the story the changing voices of the braggart and fool, foreign voices (from Norcia), the voice of injured pride, a lacing of diplomatic language (in Bianco's first encounter with the lord priors of Norcia), and the voices of rage, humiliation, pity, revenge, and petty wheedling: all making for an actor's paradise of opportunities. And although, according to Piero, Lioncino did not seize the opportunity to act out his telling of *Bianco Alfani*, we can imagine what a *raconteur* like Piero would have done with it, in looking to make the story's points more effectively, the more to captivate and delight his audience. With a brilliant recitation of Bianco's prating, in the context of the daily hands-on and eye-to-eye encounters of that serried urban community (Florence), Piero would surely have seemed the man's worst enemy, second only to the two men who cooked up the plot against him, namely Lioncino himself and the attorney, Ser Niccolò Tinucci.

I stress the theatrical aspects of *Bianco Alfani*, the immediate rapport with an audience, in order to bring out the liveliness and force of the oral culture of the period. Florentine humanists of the fifteenth century loved the literary form of the dialogue not only because it had been favored by the ancients and especially by Cicero, but also because of its convivial features: it gave formal expression to the sociability of their everyday urban experience and to their claim that humanity best realizes itself in and through civic life. Ever since the thirteenth century, Florentines with an interest in ideas, literature, and public life had met in informal gatherings; and afterwards, from the late fourteenth century, they collected at the *Studium* (the University), in the neighboring countryside (e.g., at the *Paradiso degli Alberti*), the convent of Santa Maria degli Angeli, in private houses and in public places, such as by the Tetto de' Pisani, on the fringes of the government square (Piazza della Signoria). Bologna had similar meeting places, and sixteenth-century Venice was to have numbers of aristocratic households that were also gossipy enclaves with talk about art, literature, politics, current ideas, and of course personalities.

Bianco Alfani, then, is the product of a vibrant oral culture. They flourished best in Florence who best used the spoken word. Storytellers, public reciters or performers of verse (*canterini, cantimbanca*), town criers, gossips, circulating rimes and songs and abusive verse, telltale travelers and merchants, and even preachers: all these were the mass media of the day, the equivalent of our newspapers, magazines, TV, and radio shows. Without them life in Renaissance cities would have been less rich and lively, and also far less verbal. A Florence without its cascades and crossfires of words, so often put together artistically, could not possibly have been Florence. Here, roughly halfway between the main government square and the cathedral, the two key points of the city, was the small Piazza di San Martino, a square reserved for public verse recitations and performances. Florence's ruling body, the Lord Priors, employed a full-time poet herald.

In this intensely loquacious culture, once Bianco Alfani had been duped, what was he to do? How was he going to hold his head up and look people in the face when walking through the streets of Florence? The disgraced Grasso in *The Fat Woodcarver* could not, and he abandoned the city altogether. No wonder, therefore, that Bianco delayed his return to Florence for many weeks. Revealingly, too, he returned with nothing but an emblem of his vaunted historical roots: the banner of his family coat of arms, flagging his ill-fated mission. For of honor and reputation nothing remained to him but an ancient and illustrious surname, Alfani, once an outstanding Florentine lineage. Moreover, since the prank had all but slain his previous social identity, it was entirely appropriate for him, in ritual and emotional terms, to lodge the family banner over the tomb of his dead father, which now became, by symbolic extension, the tomb of his former (proud) identity. In real life, he was to die before the end of 1430.

There is far more to Bianco than meets the literary eye. He is the product of a story-teller's imagination only in part. The rest of him, the larger part, is a real historical figure—the carrier *ipso facto* of fragments of the history of Florence. For the story is constructed out of historical building blocks: every individual, office, practice, place, and ambition there named was real. The men lived; the offices and magistracies existed; the described practices were observed; the loggia of the Buondelmonti, the Via del Orto, Giovannozzo Pitti's garden, the Stinche, Bagno a Ripoli, Norcia, the church of San Marco, and so on—all were there. Characteristically, too, external (foreign) rectors employed their own officials and guardsmen, had their own banners made up, bought or hired their own horses, and served short-term tours of duty in office. It was also a fact that certain Florentines yearned to go abroad as foreign rectors (e.g. *podestà*, captain, appellate judge), both because of the need for added income and in the avid quest for honor and reputation. In fact, it would be reasonable to ask the question, where exactly is the fiction in *Bianco Alfani*? If Bianco was not tricked in exactly the manner narrated, something much like that trick actually took place; or at the very least, given his deluded view of himself, the trick was entirely feasible as a practical joke.

Since *Bianco Alfani* is a "story," a complete narrative with a plot and characters, there is obvious reason for historians to suspect the story-teller and the truth of the whole central anecdote. Moreover, the rich framework of supporting verisimilitude could be seen as a device for enlisting the credibility of readers. Accordingly, to obtain a better fix on our story, let us briefly consider its apparent inventions and unrealities, with a view to converging upon its extraordinary realism; for with all its fictions—and they are not easy to pick out—*Bianco Alfani* is a window through which we peer into Florentine society.

Much of the story is about appearance and reality, and there is something perhaps "literary" in this interplay. Thus the convivial pleasure-seeking of the two story-tellers and their listeners is a foil, like the salutary Pitti garden, for the death and disease all about them; and Boccaccio's *Decameron* is the most obvious source—though not the only one—for this narrative ploy. Furthermore, Bianco is old but appears young; he bears a distinguished family name on the outside, but the inner man is hopelessly unworthy of the honor; supposed friends are enemies; forgeries appear real; and the real—Bianco's vanity and silliness—is decked out with name and position.

Some of the story's pivotal conversations and descriptive details appear more fictional than any of the preceding ironies. After all, the narrator, Lioncino, was not present at the times and places of Bianco's duping and humiliation. None of the pranksters was witness to the dealings between Bianco and Ser Martino, the attorney who bought his piece of land behind the church of San Marco. Nor, of course, was any member of Lioncino's circle present at the exchanges between Bianco and the Norcian innkeeper, or at his harrowing confrontations with Norcia's chief clerk, with the lord priors of Norcia, or with Giovanni di Santi. Yet all the particulars of these scenes and conversations are reported to us with as much aplomb as if the story-teller had been present. Are they, therefore, invention or reality? Put thus, in a stark either-or fashion, the question might even be raised of much newspaper reporting in our own day. But in the case of *Bianco Alfani*, as we shall see, judging by evidence both from inside and outside the text, it is clear that the incident at the heart of the story had generated a profusion of talk. Word-of-mouth stories about it were rife, so that our storyteller was providing scenes and conversations that were the common property in gossip of hundreds or even thousands of Florentines in the 1420s. Not surprisingly, therefore, the story raises substantive questions about narrative viewpoints and about time versus contemporaneity. These matters lead us back to the nature of the story's historicity.

The scholarly consensus attributes *Bianco Alfani* to a certain Piero di Filippo del Nero, "detto" (known as) Piero Veneziano, one of the two storytellers present in the account itself. But the first-person narrator of the opening and closing pages is another "I," not Piero's. Moreover, as in immediate personal exchange, this "I" addresses another unknown person in the familiar "thou" and "thy" (*ti narrai, tuo giudizio*). Two possible interpretations of this may be offered here. The pronouns are either narrative lapses or they refer to real men whose names we are unlikely ever to establish conclusively. If the latter—the option favored by scholars— then we may be touching on a patron-client relationship, a perfectly realistic possibility in the world of fifteenth-century Florence. This is to suggest that a client or protégé is presenting a friend or patron with a story written by someone else, though that someone is Piero Veneziano. To add to the confusion here, there is evidence that in 1433 Piero sent the story to his friend, the Florentine nobleman, Galeotto da Ricasoli.

These perplexities return us to the matter of viewpoint (pronouns) as a narrative resource. For in its pronouns, the story of

Bianco is remarkably in line with the oral traditions and historical structures of the age. That is to say, in a tight and neighborly (but also suspicious) urban society, such as Quattrocento Florence was, all sorts of tales, poems, songs, and sayings were collective. Circulating freely within an animated oral culture, they belonged as much to the city as a whole as to the individual *raconteur* or writer; and I's (egos) then were much more fluid, more community-bent, than they are in our own day in industrial or post-industrial Western society. Thus, *Bianco Alfani* begins and ends with singular pronouns (I, me, thou) that have the feel of something personal, while yet not truly being so. The narrative passes from one teller to another: first the mysterious I-me, next Lioncino, then Ser Niccolò Tinucci, again Lioncino, then on to the I's of the different interlocutors in this dialogue-like story, and occasionally to the implied "we" in the imperatives of small groups of men, such as Bianco's listeners. The story is retailed not by one story-teller (Lioncino) but rather by a community of them speaking through him.

In effect, then, the shifting points of view in *Bianco Alfani* add up to a collective narrator and a civic or communal viewpoint. A rather fierce and clever oral culture presents us with Bianco, who is himself (as yarn-spinner) possessed and pervaded by it. In presenting himself, he at the same time presents the workings of critical aspects of that culture, such as its ideals and its ways of transmitting moral or social meanings. The process is circular: everytime he speaks, albeit immoderately, Bianco is both telling on himself and on Florentine community expectations, envies, ambitions, and fears.

Such is the immediacy of the communal, narrative viewpoint in *Bianco Alfani* that unless we bear the question of time in mind, we shall not notice that its handling of chronology is fudged. The opening sentences place the storytelling in July of 1430. On many evenings during the past year (1429–1430), Bianco had much frequented the New Market, treating his young cronies to tall stories. It was on one of those evenings, having overheard the chatter of the prison warden, that the attorney, Niccolò Tinucci, spoke of the gentleman from Norcia, Giovanni di Santi, who was on familiar terms with Bianco. Giovanni had exercised the office of executor of the ordinances of justice, one of Florence's premier judgeships, the year before, hence sometime in 1428–29. A term in this magistracy lasted for six months, and all contemporaries would have known this. It was therefore during that year, 1428–1429, that Bianco came to believe that Giovanni would seek to procure Norcia's captaincy for him. Consequently, the plot against the prison warden had been hatched and carried out sometime in 1428–29: actually, according to Vittorio Rossi, in the interval between April and July, 1429. Yet the story is being told in July, 1430, when Bianco still looks young and can still collect young men about him, happy to listen to his prating.

How could this be? In 1430, Bianco was still plunged in public disgrace and hounded by shame. The story suggests that he would not have had the face to appear so soon and so brashly in public places, certainly not in the New Market which, evenings, was an even more popular haunt for garrulous men than the main government square. Furthermore, owing to the tricks played on him and to his dealings with the Stinche prison inmates, by the end of the story—and at this point we are still in July 1430—Bianco had already "ended up wretched, beggarly, bizarre (irascible), and gouty" (*rimase povero e mendico, bizzarro e gottoso*). It is only thereafter that Lioncino is struck down by the summer's rampant disease and that the two stories, including the one about Mistress Lisetta, are passed on in written form for the "judgment" of the unidentified "you (thou)" and for others "who shall read the two tales."

The story, then, has two temporal continuums. The events as such, followed by Bianco's ruined and ravaged condition, require a minimum period of several years. But with an eye to tone, conviviality, and immediacy, the author squeezes the lot into a mere fifteen months or so. Near the end of the story, Lioncino observes that his listeners had "surely heard that what I have recounted actually happened." He hereby acknowledges an impinging oral current and blithely undermines his earlier claim concerning Bianco's good spirits the year before (but after the disgrace). In brief, the temporal conflict in the narrative suggests that the *raconteur* had retold a recent story lifted from the omnipresent oral culture. Something much like the reported events—or the spicy beginnings thereof—had actually taken place; but in working them up for written presentation, the author has not bothered to get his temporal logic right because there was no strict requirement about this for good yarns in fifteenth-century oral civilization, with its easy and busy Christian transactions between time and eternity. The point was to tell a good story, even at the expense of violating (superficial) temporal logic. And if the expectations of listeners called for a moral twist of some kind, such as in a man's physical payment for his vanity and cruelty (Bianco's relations with the prison inmates), then let him end, as in this case, "wretched, beggarly, bizarre, and gouty," despite any violation of the temporal continuum.

If the author plays fast and loose with historical time, it is something else again with his treatment of the real world. For as I noted at the start, every part of the story's framework involves real Florentine citizens and fifteenth-century realities. Arriving from neighboring and more distant urban centers, external "rectors" or magistrates (*podestà*, *capitano*, *vicario*, etc.) entered into cities for six-month tours of office, a time-honored practice which went back to the thirteenth century. Ciave, the man who produced the seal for the phony election document, was the goldsmith Andrea di Piero, detto (called) Ciave, who resided in the Scala district of the Santo Spirito quarter of the city. Isau (Esaù) Martellini, the banker who hands the cash over to Bianco for the land parcel bought by Ser Martino, was also domiciled in the same quarter, on the far side of the Arno, and was one of the richer men in Florence, as revealed by his tax returns (*catasto*) of 1427. We know more than merely the full name of the alleged buyer of Bianco's bit of real estate—Martino di Luca di Martino Martini (d. 1433). Since all attorneys and public notaries of the period were styled "ser" (in English a kind of "Sir"), contemporaries rightly referred to him as "ser" Martino. During the years 1414–29, when he was one of the city's chief chancellery clerks or secretaries, he was charged with the correct drafting and registering of all Florentine legislation; but he was also an influential and cagey political figure, much involved with the powerful Medici faction in the very year of his being sacked from office (early 1429). Ser Niccolò Tinucci (ca. 1390–1444), another attorney and one of the prime movers of the plot against Bianco, was also a familiar figure in Florentine political circles, having served for years, up to about 1433, as first secretary to the republic's authoritative wartime commission, the *Decem Baliae*. Giovanni di Santo sprang from the Collatini family of Norcia and did in fact hold for a term the Florentine office of executor of the ordinances of justice. Giovannozzo Pitti, host to

the company and aged about thirty-three, was Giovannozzo di
Francesco di Neri Pitti, who in the 1440s and 1450s would be a
prominent member of the Medici oligarchy. His storytelling guest,
Piero di Filippo del Nero, known as Piero Veneziano, also from
Pitti's side of the river (Santo Spirito), was actually a wool merchant (*lanaiuolo*). But we must cross the river to the other side, to
the Vipera section of the Santa Maria Novella quarter, to find the
house of the sixty-three-year-old Lioncino (real name, Lionardo)
di Messer Guccio de' Nobili, our chief storyteller, who twice held
office in the city's supreme governing council, back in 1401 and
1414. And, finally, on the same side of the river, but to the north-
east, in the Ruote section of the Santa Croce quarter, was the seat
of the Alfani lineage. The full name of our unhappy central character was Bianco di Giovanni di Ser Francesco Alfani. Bianco,
however, was a nickname noted even in his last will and testament, as Rossi established. His baptismal name was Lottieri
("Locterius").

   In this cast of real figures, we come on one curiously referred to
as *messer Antonio buffone de' Signori*, "my lord Antonio, jester to
the Lords [i.e., the lord priors of Florence]," the man who produces the Norcian dialect in the forged letters to Bianco, "because
I can fake the speech of Norcia better than any of you." He was
Antonio di Matteo di Meglio (1384–1448), poet-herald of the
Florentine republic since 1417, an employee of the city's governing body, the lord priors. His office was a composite dignity that
went back to the early fourteenth century, when the job called for
a kind of jester and rhymester, who was also mockingly entitled to
be called "my lord" (*messer*, *mio-sire*). But in the 1420s and
1430s, Antonio's distinctive job was to compose poetry for political, celebratory, and religious occasions, as well as to entertain

and even instruct the lord priors with his verse recitations. In the story, interestingly, we find him in the company of Ser Niccolò Tinucci, who also had some local standing as a poet (and some of his poetry, like Antonio's, comes down to us). Was there, accordingly, some devious attempt here, on the part of the writer, to associate his storytelling with a literary circle in Florence? Not necessarily, for Antonio and Ser Niccolò would inevitably have known each other. Their official functions in the 1410s and 1420s took them, often almost daily, into the palace of the lord priors; and their common interest in poetry would have brought them more naturally together.

Having reviewed the story's factual framework, we may turn next to the anecdote proper. Nearly a hundred years ago, struck by the apparent realism of *Bianco Alfani*, Vittorio Rossi set out to ascertain its truth as chronicle. His true aim, however, all but openly confessed, was to try to prove that the central anecdote was a fiction. He wanted his literature—or at least some part thereof—unadulterated by chronicle realism. The result was a major 1901 article based on sustained archival research, confirming the names of all the characters involved and noting their ages, domiciles, and properties. Having established all this, he then highlighted Domenico Maria Manni's eighteenth-century discovery that the Norcian, Giovanni di Santo, held his Florentine office not in 1428–1429 but rather back in 1421, during the six months from April 18 to October 17. Bianco Alfani, moreover, was not head jailer in 1428–1429; nor was there any trace, in Ser Martino's property inventories for his 1430 tax returns, that Bianco had ever sold him two houses on the via San Gallo or a piece of land behind the church of San Marco. What is more, Lodovico Marradi, actually Lodovico Manfredi, Lord of Marradi, a mercenary jailed for treason to his employer, the Florentine republic, was put into the Stinche not before June 1425, hence nearly four years after Giovanni di Santo had been executor in Florence. Rossi thereupon concluded, in his nineteenth-century empiricism, that *Bianco Alfani* could not possibly be an "historical account"; and although maintaining that the anecdote was a made-up historiette inserted into a structure of chronicle realism, he admitted the plausibility of Manni's old suspicions that the story might hold elements of truth, harking back to 1421–1422.

Yet the archival evidence adduced by Rossi is, as a matter of fact, astonishing in its support of Manni's suspicions and of my claims regarding Florence's energetic oral culture. For Bianco's tax returns of 1427 establish the following: (1) that he had two houses on the Via San Gallo and "a field behind San Marco," which all together brought in a yearly income of 22.00 florins; (2) that he had sold his jail warden's post and was waiting to collect a final 7.00 florins on this transaction; (3) that he still owed 50.00 florins to the Hospital of Santa Maria Nuova for monies previously lent him, plus another 70.00 florins in back taxes; and finally (4) that at the age of fifty-one "I have no trade whatsoever and I no longer do anything." When combined with the main provision of his last will and testament of 1423, Bianco's tax returns also reveal that his debt to the Hospital of Santa Maria Nuova was for a considerable sum of money which had been lent to him back in 1422. The inevitable question comes of itself: since Giovanni di Santo had left his Florentine post in the latter part of 1421— sometime after October 17, owing to his having to submit to a regular inquest ("syndication")—had the 1422 loan to Bianco anything to do with expenses for the inglorious Norcia captaincy? We must suspect so. After all, the detailed information in the story is uncannily accurate for an account that came by word of mouth; so much the same was perhaps also true of some of the other circulating oral versions. Thus, there is the historical reality of all the characters, including the nicknamed Ciave; and there are Bianco's properties and residence in the parish of San Pier Maggiore, the prison wardenship, the fact that Ser Martino's family truly had a chapel in the church of San Marco, and even Bianco's dire material circumstances in 1427–29, as attested by his 1427 tax returns. About forty-six years old in 1422, but apparently much younger looking, Bianco could easily have aged dramatically over a period of six or seven years, if he fell victim to the sort of plot described in the story. Consequently, we may well ask, had he sold his prison post because life in the Stinche had become intolerable for him? Being without a trade, doing nothing, and plagued by debt, he would truly appear to have "ended wretched, beggarly, irascible (*bizzarro*), and gouty," as if already on the way to his death in the epidemic of 1430.

By the 1440s, "to be a Bianco Alfani" in Florence was already a turn of phrase for saying that a man was a ridiculous fool. This expression was the product as well of an oral "text" as of a few manuscripts, and chiefly, I suspect, the former—an account that went by word of mouth. But the venom and tenacity of the story suggest that there was some strong, particular business behind the destructive practical joke, something more than just the desire for a good entertainment. The written account itself provides the clues, and most of these point to an act of revenge.

Having sold the office of prison warden, Bianco had doubtless bought it (or his family had), so that he had quite possibly occupied it "ever since his youth." As boss of the main Florentine prison, Bianco superintended a system whose inmates and detainees were often debtors, bankrupts, and citizens who had defaulted in their payment of income and property taxes. Such men could be pounced upon in the streets of Florence—a common enough occurrence—and carted off to prison. Moreover, they were more likely to remain long-term prisoners than were common criminals, who normally faced flogging, mutilation, execution, exile, and/or heavy fines. Inevitably, therefore, many Florentines, such as ex-prisoners and relatives or friends of inmates, harbored strong resentments against debtors' prison. Accordingly, how could Bianco, or any long-term prison warden in Florence, not become heir over the years to an accumulation of animosity, particularly if, as alleged in the story, he had regularly squeezed bribe monies out of prisoners? Their food and comforts depended on the support of relatives and friends, on charity, or occasionally on loans from money lenders. It may even be that Bianco "amassed a fortune" by his "cruel" dealings, if we understand this to mean something in the range of, say, 150 to 300 florins. The administrators of Florence's famous *catasto* levy of 1427 operated on the principle that 200 florins of rental capital brought in a yearly income of seven percent (14.00 florins), which was roughly one-third to one-quarter the annual wages of a skilled textile worker. But even if Bianco amassed much less than was rumored, the resentment and stories against him were bound to multiply.

When combined with vanity, self-delusion, cruelty, and prating—all of which the story ascribes to Bianco—the distinguished old name of Alfani served as an additional incitement to rumor and fabrication. And among knowledgeable Florentines, the well-placed, the articulate, or the literary, if there was some thirst for vengeance, what more damaging way to inflict it than in the recording or continual retelling of the prank? In a city where life for the well-known or well-connected was life in a public arena, as we also learn from two other stories, *Ricciarda* and *The Fat Woodcarver*, how could a disgrace like Bianco's not be a searing mode of social castigation?

In the fleeting indication that Bianco spent some of his ill-got gains on young women, the story suggests that he paid court to whores: only thus in Florence could a man spend money on "a woman's face," unless, of course, she was his wife. Prior to the prank, therefore, as he grew older, with his name, fortune, solid position, and presumed heterosexuality—for any rumor of a homosexual penchant would have provoked mockery—it is likely that Bianco cut an increasingly eccentric figure both in his idle boasting and in his failure to marry. Recent study has shown that in his class and station, the overwhelming majority of Florentine men had married by the age of forty, and so his lay celibacy must have added to any airs of extravagance or bizarrerie on his part, rendering him all the more inviting a target for derision.

Lodovico, Lord of Marradi, announces his scheme to betray Bianco to the *gabelle* officials with the claim that "the sweetness of revenge . . . surpasses all other delights in the world." This view verged on the proverbial in quattrocento Italy, but it is not the story's first broaching of the subject. When the shamed and ruined Bianco finally returns to Florence in search of his tormentors and vengeance, he says to his brothers, "you must help me to avenge myself." And "being of the same cloth as he, they all swore death to whoever had worked such an outrage [against him]." Here, tellingly, the story suddenly strikes out beyond Bianco himself to sneer at the lineage by asserting, in effect, that in that branch, at any rate, all the Alfani males were jerks and loud mouths. Admittedly, in Renaissance Italy, the kinship group tended to bear the reputation of its best or worst members, depending upon the influence or impotence of the lineage. But here there is no doubt of it: the storyteller goes out of his way to snipe at the entire clan, and this again is why we pick up the scent of a desire for revenge. In late medieval and Renaissance vendetta—in this instance against Bianco—the revengers might target all the adult males of the closer kinship group, not merely the individual who had inflicted the original injury.

By 1430—in some eight years or less—the Bianco Alfani affair had been absorbed into the oral culture, when the attempt is suddenly made to freeze it, so to speak, into a fixed narrative: our written story. Originally moved, it seems to me, by the obscure wish to settle a score with Bianco, several men dupe him, whereupon a current of ill will against him is at once released, adding speed to oral accounts of the trick, as these course their way through Florence. Piero Veneziano's narrative codifies the circulating story and either adds, or merely passes on, in its revenger's anatomy, the slanting insult against Bianco's brothers. Were the plotters of 1429—Lioncino de' Nobili, Ser Niccolò Tinucci, and *messer* Antonio—the original tricksters back in 1421? No one can say. In an alert, quick, practical, and malicious society, such as Florence was, Bianco's vanity, babble, and jailer's job had doubtless caused him to be surrounded by secret detractors and enemies. But whoever the original plotters were, they had to be men from the city's political and governing circles, because they alone possessed the experience and audacity to counterfeit the formulae which convinced Bianco of his elevation to one of Norcia's major dignities.

To understand the scope of the story's realism, it is important to grasp that the successful tricking of Bianco hinged entirely on the forgeries—letters, Norcian dialect, fake Norcian seal, the official language of the appointment letter—and that these were the work of experts: the poet-herald, *messer* Antonio, whose job required that he have a keen ear and strong mimetic gifts; Ciave, the goldsmith and skilled seal-maker; and *ser* Niccolò Tinucci, poet, war-office functionary, and public-law attorney, hence a man thoroughly schooled in the drafting of public instruments. It should be emphasized, too, that *office was honor* in all Italian Renaissance cites, and the higher the office, the greater the honor. This was a rule of urban existence, which also held true for appointments to magistracies abroad. If, then, Bianco was ambitious, vain, and a trifle credulous, why would he have been moved to mistrust the letters put before him? On the contrary, ardently desiring to believe what they said, he was far more likely to further the schemes of his hidden enemies.

Whatever our views regarding Bianco Alfani as chief jailer, we may feel, nevertheless, that the joke played on him was too cruel to rank as anything humorous. But humor, like so much else in our lives, is subject to the tides of history. Branded as vain, venal, cruel, and a braggadocio, Bianco is seen to get his comeuppance. His penalty is financial ruin, infamy, and bitter shame. Whether or not he merited such punishment is a non-historical question and an unanswerable one. Contemporaries laughed delightedly . because they saw him getting what they believed he deserved. This was certainly the view of the prisoners under his harsh regime.

I have claimed that the deceiving of Bianco was motivated, in the first instance, by an obscure desire for revenge, in all likelihood entertained by a scatter of Florentines. Here was a motive which modern readers are able to understand. But there was also another emotional ingredient at work in the Bianco affair, one more difficult to reconstitute in the modern consciousness: I refer to the Florentine need or itch to teach a lesson to a citizen who was a pertinacious and indiscrete prater. In our time, boarding schools, street gangs, and exclusive clubs know all about the varieties of punishments and stratagems for use against members who step out of line. One of Boccaccio's young storytellers observes that "in our native city [Florence] . . . fraud and cunning prosper more than love or loyalty" (*Decameron*, III, 3). Perhaps this was one reason why Florentine advice to boys and young men, as recorded in family memoirs, proverbs, letters, and books of conduct, urged and stressed the importance of secrecy in personal and family affairs, particularly concerning finances, property, and political ambitions. In a city where private life was already more than half a public affair, caution and discretion in speech had to be a rule of life and conduct. In brashly and routinely breaking this rule, Bianco turned himself into a ready victim for the most dangerous of all Florentines: those who were themselves the consummate practitioners of secrecy and clandestine dealing—namely, men from the city's governing circles. Such men were the reported agents of his undoing: Lioncino de' Nobili, Ser Niccolò Tinucci, and even the herald, *messer* Antonio. That these were the sort of men, or their sons, whom Bianco was in the habit of addressing is made clearly evident on the evening when, waving the bogus appointment letter, he rushes into the New Market, accosts a group of men, and says: "if this [letter] doesn't lie, I'll see whether or not I can wield a little staff [of office] like the rest of you do." Thus, they were the sort of men accustomed to serving in offices abroad. Days later, in his negotiations with Ser Martino Martini, one of the city's leading chancellery attorneys, Bianco again reveals his naïveté by announcing that he would use his Norcia earnings to buy shares in Florence's communal debt (the *Monte*) and thereby improve on the act of selling his San Marco land parcel to Ser Martino. Most informed Florentine citizens—Ser Martino, for one—knew that active investment in the *Monte* was a subtle and tricky business, better left to the experts and big-money men.

No sober or sensible man of the political class would have carried on in Bianco's manner, constantly baring his soul to all of watchful, pragmatic, and secretive Florence. Though he seems never to have held a notable office in the city, Bianco's last name gave him some title there, and his ambitions, in his eyes at least, put him into the office-holding class. His chronic and mad indiscretions, therefore, had to be seen as a challenge to one of the rules by which civil and reasonable men lived. If such men held their tongue, watched others, lived by the rules, and suffered some constraints, why should Bianco not be made to pay dearly for his flagrant infractions, his brazen social sins? What is more, he must be made to pay whereby he sinned: in public and in a public mode, that is, in a ridiculous and shaming spectacle for the delight of the whole community whose rules he had flouted. As head jailer and heir to an old name, he was worth castigating and certainly well-enough placed to amuse the entire city; but as a little man too—little because at bottom he had no real political contacts—he could be duped with impunity. In the later thirteenth century, the males of the main Alfani line were rich and eminent Guelf bankers; in the fourteenth century, they had eight terms of service in the city's chief governing council (the *Signoria*), two of these as gonfaloniers of justice, the supreme dignity. Since then, however, they had fallen on bad times; they failed to marry well or, like Bianco, did not marry at all; and they no longer had any political standing. By contrast, arguably, no one would have dared to trick (in the Norcia captaincy manner) a man from one of the eminent political lineages, such as the Capponi, Rucellai, Strozzi, or Castellani; for then the response would have been a serious blood-feud with possible fatalities.

The more we study *Bianco Alfani*, the more we see the lineaments of a conformist society, where the individual was expected to live in accordance with its social-structural ideals, as expressed by the desires and expectations of those around him. Men could certainly get away with eccentricities—the poet Burchiello did, so too did the sculptor Donatello and the humanist Niccolò Niccoli—but they could safely do so only if they possessed countervailing, positive qualities that gave something back to the surrounding society. Otherwise they submitted themselves to the dangers of being ritually cut away from the civic community.

FIVE

1.

GIACOPPO

by Lorenzo de' Medici

*Statesman, poet, art collector, and musician, Lorenzo the
Magnificent de' Medici (1449–1492) was the Florentine
republic's political boss, with quasi-princely powers, from
about the early 1470s. Although André Rochon,in his* La
Jeunesse de Laurent de Médicis (1449–1478), *does not
discuss* Giacoppo, *the consensus in scholarship attributes
the tale to Lorenzo's youth; and the late 1460s work best as
the most likely time of his authorship.*

&

It must be common knowledge that there has always been an
abundance of gullible, foolish men in the city of Siena. I don't
know whether the air there naturally produces such men, or if it is
a natural thing that this tree, having sprung from bad seed, should
bear fruit similar to its seed. Indeed, since they say a good son
resembles his father, perhaps the sons, not wishing to bring shame
upon their fathers, endeavor to behave in such a way as not to seem
to be bastards.

So it was that not many years since, there was a citizen of Siena
called Giacoppo Belanti, a man of about forty years of age and of

considerable wealth but few brains. And it was his good fortune—though some might say bad luck—to have a very pretty wife, for in Siena prettiness seems to be as natural in women as a touch of stupidity and vanity is in the men. And this wife of his was about twenty-five years of age; and, as happens to pretty women, she was courted by a handsome young man. This gentle lady was named Cassandra; the young man, called Francesco, was Florentine by birth and had been at the University in Siena for a long time, and had always been in love with Cassandra. Whence it had logically to follow that she loved him no less than he loved her, for Francesco was a very comely young man, and she of an age to know bad from good, and to know as much as a woman can know. For truly, that is the best age to make love to women; because when they are younger, shame and lack of spirit usually hold them back; and when they are past this age, either because they have lost the nerve needed for such ventures, or because their natural passion has cooled, they are a bit too frigid for a lover's purposes.

Since Francesco had been pursuing Cassandra for so long, without succeeding in snaring her, he could think of nothing else day or night except how to obtain what he had so long desired. And what inflamed him most was knowing that the means alone were lacking, since the two parties were willing and eager. For Cassandra was very fond of him, although this love of hers was somewhat curbed by fear for her honor, and no less by Giacoppo's jealousy. For Giacoppo behaved toward her as most husbands who have a pretty wife are wont to do. And since Cassandra was so very pretty, so much the less willing was she to bear the jealousy, seeing herself married to an old and ill-favored man who showed little prowess on the battlefield of love. And her chief motive for seeking a new partner was knowing her husband to be a half-wit.

These reasons would have been sufficient to kindle a flame less ready than hers. Moreover, it is very natural, when one has the possibility to choose between the good and the bad, to prefer the good; indeed, it would have been crazy of her, and an action worthy of shackles, if she had done the opposite. For truly women's misfortune seems to me to be a great one, and men to have a great advantage: since no matter how insignificant and pathetic a man may be, when he takes a wife, he always wishes to choose one who pleases him, or not take her at all; whereas a woman, without knowing what or why, is subject to the wishes of others and must take what is given to her in order not to have worse. And many women have to resign themselves to things that cause them to die a thousand deaths a day. So it is no wonder that transgressions are discovered every day, which should be judged with more sympathy than is usually done, and we should be lenient with them for the said reasons.

To return to our story, the only thing Cassandra and Francesco lacked was the power to attain happiness—to their great shame, since the only obstacle in their way was a blockhead, although it was more by watchfulness than intelligence that Giacoppo barred their way to bliss. So Francesco, having thought of the thing over and over again, and trusting in Giacoppo's simplicity, devised the scheme about which I am going to tell you. First of all, he made a show of having renounced his love for Cassandra. And having kept this up until Giacoppo was almost reassured about him, one day he pretended to receive letters from certain relatives of his in Florence, regarding his taking a wife. And his friends and acquaintances soon spread the news, for he was well known and loved in Siena, and so it became common knowledge. And among others it reached the ears of Giacoppo, who was beside himself with happiness about it, for he thought that he was now totally sure of his wife. For he believed that Francesco would have to leave Siena, or take his mind off the things that had formerly occupied it, as some men do when they take a wife. Then, once Giacoppo's suspicions had been lulled, Francesco began to say that he had no desire to leave Siena, for having studied and worked so hard until now, he did not want to abandon his education just when he was about to take his doctorate. Therefore he intended to bring his bride to Siena and keep her there until he had finished, in his own good time, what he had come there to do. And acting upon these words, he rented a house for himself and his wife to live in (since the one he had before was not suitable), not too near to Giacoppo's, but in a place where Giacoppo often passed. Nor was it long before Francesco said that he intended to go to Florence for the wedding and bring his bride back to Siena; which he duly did.

When he arrived in Florence, Francesco went to see a prostitute. She was one of those who practice the profession more decorously but no less assiduously than the public ones; her name was Meina[1] and she lived in a place called Borgo Stella. Now Meina had a very pretty face and a very nice appearance; and Francesco agreed to pay her a specified amount if she would go with him for a certain period of time. And so he brought Meina, who was very happy with the arrangement, in honorable company to Siena, saying that she was his wife. And since everyone believed this, she was treated with courtesy by the gentlewomen of Siena, and was often invited by them.

Meina, who was crafty and shrewd, knew very well how to conceal her innumerable shames beneath her pretty ladylike garb,

1. A diminutive form of the name "Bartolomea."

and gave the appearance of being a very decent woman who was revolted by improper things. And having been instructed by Francesco as to what she should do, she would sometimes stand at the window, which, as we've said, overlooked a street by which Giacoppo often passed, because it was handy for several of his errands. And as she was often on the balcony, he had the bad luck to look up at her on one occasion, whereupon she threw him an encouraging glance and he returned it with pleasure, and felt a hankering for spring figs even though he was well beyond the age for this. Now Giacoppo began to say to himself: "This is rich!— that Francesco, young and handsome as he is, should have ogled my wife for so long without ever getting so much as an encouraging look from her, and I, old as I am, in such a short space of time have found favor with this woman. It looks as though Francesco is going to end up like Mainardo's dog, which tried to bite and was the first to be bitten."[2] And moved as much by vanity as by love, Giacoppo began to pass that way more often; and finding that the terrain was better and better every day, he often boasted to a circle of young men, saying: "The fact is that old men too can get women to fall in love. You young men spend your lives in trying to woo, yet you never accomplish anything; while I, as old as you see me, have recently had a stroke of luck for which each of you would pay a tidy sum." But with all this talk he couldn't find a way to confess his love to her. So one day, since he was not making a move, Bartolomea (for that was what she was calling herself, to appear respectable and so that her true identity should not be known) had to send a maidservant to him with a letter, in which she said that she was dying for him and that for God's sake he must help her, for she feared that he had cast a spell on her.

2. A proverbial expression.

Beside himself with joy, Giacoppo sent back a reply as foolish as himself. And not much time passed before Bartolomea, after first pretending to have had great difficulty in bringing it about, gave him an appointment for one evening, saying that Francesco had gone with a Sienese friend of his to some country estate. When evening came—and it seemed to Giacoppo a thousand years before it did—she gave him the arranged signal, and Giacoppo soon found himself in the house. Then Bartolomea, doing all the things that people usually do when they are on fire with love, led him into a bedchamber and hid him under the bed, saying that he must stay there until she sent a certain maidservant to sleep, because she wanted the affair to be a secret. And he did so, remaining there for about two and a half hours. Later, when Bartolomea returned to him, she made a pretense of being very sorry about his discomfort, but said he must be patient. And when they were together, pretending to act in the heat of passion, she scratched his face, tore his eyes open, and bit him so hard she left marks. And he, believing that this was how lovers acted, not only accepted it all quietly, but also felt as if he could touch heaven with his finger. Then, having achieved that end for which lovers so yearn and suffer, the old man, struggling and straining, finally got to where he wanted to go. And she, pretending to be amazed that a man of his age should make such a good showing, made the poor fellow almost kill himself doing that which seemed impossible. And finally, returning home more dead than alive, all battered and bruised, though it seemed to him as if he had come from heaven, he had another battle to wage with his wife; for in order to justify himself, he had to do in one evening what would normally have been not only difficult but impossible for him in a whole year.

Instructed by Francesco, Bartolomea, not wanting the prey to slip through her fingers, continued to be attentive to Giacoppo. And though he came to her often, he did little more than to return home covered with scratches and bites. And this he did many, many times, and this state of affairs lasted many months, producing as many amusing words as it did deeds. For, being moved by vanity, Giacoppo did nothing but boast to young and old alike of his good fortune, not knowing that he was weaving the very net in which he himself would be snared. Things had gone on in this way for quite some time, when Lent arrived; and Bartolomea begged Giacoppo to give her a little holiday, at least until those holy days passed, for it was time to attend to one's soul, although it seemed hard to her to have to do without him. These words moved Giacoppo to go to confession and acknowledge his sins.

Now his long-time confessor was a Franciscan friar called Frate Antonio della Marca, with whom Francesco, knowing him to be Giacoppo's confessor, had already reached an agreement. For although he was a friar, Antonio believed that one of the seven works of mercy was to succor the afflicted, and he wanted to make the proverb come true which says there is no trap or treason that does not involve a Franciscan. Thus he consented to Francesco's entreaties without much difficulty. So when Giacoppo was at his feet confessing, the friar began to question him as usual. And when he got to the sin of lust, Giacoppo began to tell him about his affair with the woman he believed to be Francesco's wife. Hereupon the friar stopped and said: "Alas, Giacoppo, how did the temptations of the devil gain such power over you, that you have been led to this unforgivable sin, for which it is neither in my authority, nor in that of the pope, nor even in that of Saint Peter if he rose from the dead, to grant you absolution?" And Giacoppo said: "But I've heard you say that there is no sin so great that it cannot be absolved." To this Frate Antonio replied: "That is true, but it is necessary to do something I know you would never do." And Giacoppo said: "There's nothing I wouldn't do to save my soul; I'd even sell myself and my wife to do so." And Frate Antonio said: "If you are of this mind, I shall tell you. But I'm sure that you will promise to do it and then won't keep your promise." Giacoppo said: "I'm surprised at you; I love my soul more than anything in this world." Frate Antonio said: "Very well, then, I shall tell you. Haven't you heard it said that sins against a man's honor and taking things unjustly can only be pardoned by giving those things back? So it is in this case: having deprived that young woman and her husband of their honor, your sin cannot be forgiven unless you return their honor to them. And you cannot return it to them unless you bring her husband, or if she has no husband, the closest male relative she has, to lie with your wife, if you have one, or if not, with your closest female relative, as many times as you have lain with his wife. We read how when David committed the sin of adultery, he gave his wife to the man who had given his own wife to him; and thus was he forgiven. So you see what you have to do." Hearing the priest's words, Giacoppo realized he had done wrong, and said to himself: "Now I see that *I* shall be Mainardo's dog." Then turning to the friar, he said: "Spiritual father, although it seems to me very difficult, nevertheless I must love my soul more than the things of this world. And I shouldn't be ashamed at all, since David, who was a king, also did this, and I am a citizen of Siena. So come what may, I wish to save my soul before doing anything else." Hearing Giacoppo's pious words, the friar said no more, but embraced him and kissed him on the forehead; and, after holding him a little while, said: "My spiritual son, I see that the grace of God has enlightened you; and I see you taking a path that shall lead us to our goal. May you be a thousand times blessed. I see now that this matter shall turn out well, praised be our Savior. But since this sin is so great, I must advise you that even with all this it cannot be absolved without a particular penance. And therefore I have decided that you must go to Rome to atone for this and your other sins. And in this way one attains the glory of eternal life, and this life joyfully passes. So go, blessed son, and do what you have promised me." And he gave him his blessing.

Giacoppo rose from his place at the priest's feet and returned home, absorbed in thought. In the end, after debating with himself, his conscience won out and he decided to go call on Francesco to restore his honor to him. And this faced him with another difficulty; for he did not know how to tell Francesco without putting himself in great danger. But believing he had found a way to save himself, overcome by his conscience, and thinking that since these were holy days he might be safer now than at another time, one day he went to call on Francesco with these words: "Francesco, I've always loved you as if you were my son, which you are young enough to be. Now sin has led me to do something for which I greatly repent; and I beg you to forgive me, as God has done. And before I tell you any more, promise me that you will not harm me, but by the passion of Our Lord swear that you will forgive any injustice that I have done you." Francesco said: "I have always revered you like a father; and even if you had killed my own father, first out of love of God in this holy time of Lent, and then out of love for you, I promise on my faith to forgive you for any injury you may have done me." Giacoppo threw himself at Francesco's feet, saying: "I'll not tell it to you save on my knees." After finally convincing him to get up, Francesco began to listen to what he knew much better than Giacoppo. And when Giacoppo had spoken with many tears, Francesco pretended to be very disturbed, saying: "You had great foresight when you made me swear not to harm you; for if it weren't for that, I would have done something that neither you nor that whore of my wife, nor even I myself, once the deed were done, would have liked. But I love my soul better than you have loved me; so in short, I forgive you for everything from this moment. Now get out of my sight." Giacoppo, thinking he had accomplished a great deal, said: "You must hear a little more from me, and help me to get God to forgive this sin." And he added that Francesco must go lie with his wife. To this Francesco replied: "That I did not promise you; I do not wish to be wicked and a traitor as you have been. It's more than enough that I have forgiven you for such a great injury. So do not speak to me of this, for I do not wish to hear anything about it, and again I tell you to get out of my sight if you know what's good for you."

Fearing worse, Giacoppo left Francesco and returned to the friar. And when he told him how things had gone, and came to the part where Francesco refused to hear anything about going to bed with Giacoppo's wife, the friar said: "Oh, you haven't accomplished anything; for that is the way that you must restore his honor. Otherwise, it's as if you had done nothing." Giacoppo, not knowing how to go back to Francesco, said to the friar: "Perhaps it would be better if you sent for him, and I shall be present, and you make him understand that it isn't a sin. Perhaps for you he will agree to what he would not agree to for me." The friar said: "That is a good plan; but I do not know him. I shall send a young friar of mine with you and you shall point Francesco out to him from a distance, so that it won't look as though I am sending for him about this." Giacoppo agreed and left with the young friar, to whom he pointed out Francesco, and the young friar then gave Frate Antonio's message to Francesco. Going immediately to the church, Francesco found the friar in a little room outside his cell; and pretending to have a noisy argument, they laughed about their jest for some time. Then the friar called Giacoppo, and said to Francesco: "You must by all means console poor Giacoppo here, not for love of him, because he doesn't deserve it, but for love of the Lord Jesus, who will also show mercy to you and will not count as a sin what you do for love of His name; and I shall remain in your debt along with Giacoppo for this." At these words, Giacoppo threw himself at Francesco's feet, begging him to go lie with his wife. Francesco, pretending to weep with compassion, said: "Come now, I agree to do it. And I wish to make a gift to God of this injury and this favor that I shall grant you, and for His love I shall do what you ask of me, although to my conscience it seems very hard."

Giacoppo, delighted with this reply, now began to worry about something else: how to persuade his wife to agree. Nevertheless, heartened by the knowledge that he could dispose of his own wife as he wished, he went home. And he believed that he had found a clever way of making a cuckold of himself. As soon as he entered the house, he began to weep piteously so that his wife would ask him why he was crying. And the ruse succeeded just as he planned, for she very insistently began to ask him the reason for so many tears. To which Giacoppo responded: "I have good reason to weep, for I am damned and cannot save my soul." Cassandra, who had been primed, began to weep harder than he, and said: "Alas! How is this so? What have you done? Is there no remedy at all?" Her husband said: "Yes, but it is very hard, very hard indeed." To which Cassandra replied: "Why don't you tell me what it is? And if anything can be done, we shall do it." Giacoppo said: "I shall tell you: it's up to you whether I am saved or damned." And he began to tell her. And when he came to the part about what she must do, she acted very offended. And, to make a long story short, he was obliged to go down on his knees and beg her to grant him this favor. And after he got her to agree, so that he could be absolved as soon as possible, he went to Francesco and said: "Tonight's the night; you shall come to supper with me, and then in the name of God you'll begin to help me to expiate this great sin." Happier than ever, Francesco made a face as if this were bad news for him, and pretended that his going was a special favor. But for all that it seemed a thousand years to him before evening came. And when it did, he went to Giacoppo's home. There, after a lavish supper, he left Giacoppo in the dining room and went as he had so long desired with his Cassandra into the bedchamber and then to bed. And everyone can imagine that things there went differently from the way they had with Giacoppo and Bartolomea. Later, in order to atone for all of Giacoppo's sins, it was necessary for Francesco to return many times. And since Giacoppo then went to Rome for his penance, as he had been ordered to do by Frate Antonio, there were few nights when Francesco was not with Cassandra. And thus at last they consummated the love they had felt for so long. And may it please God to give ours the same happy ending.

So the jealous Giacoppo, on his bare knees, had to beg Francesco to do what Francesco desired more than anything else in the world, in order to be absolved of a sin for which he had suffered the penance before committing it—thanks to Frate Antonio, who did as some clerics are wont to do. For just as friars and monks are often the cause of infinite good, so they are also at times the source of many great evils, and all on account of the inordinate faith that men undeservedly put in them.

2.

A Patriotic Prank: *Giacoppo*

Passing a tart off as his new spouse, a handsome young Florentine in Siena seduces the wife of an older Sienese gentleman by having the tart seduce the husband, who, believing her to be the wife of the youth, is then so overcome by the fear of eternal damnation, that in atonement and to save his soul, he begs the Florentine to have intercourse with his wife.

So far as this elegantly-turned anecdote seems to us a humorous frolic, it is still achieving, we may suppose, its prime fifteenth-century aim. But let us try to retrieve its dark and rather savage undercurrent, as this will give us a more focused view of the mental world of early Medicean Florence and more specifically, perhaps, of its worldly (male) elite. I propose to broach seven of the many themes brought into the tale, with an eye to drawing out elements which, though somewhat concealed from us or likely to be misconstrued, were plainly evident to, and rightly angled for, a Renaissance audience. The seven themes are local patriotism (*campanilismo*), religious credulity, the reputation of the Franciscan order of friars, aging and average age at marriage, the incidence of female adultery, prostitution, and the use of amatory language for satiric ends. I shall also touch on Lorenzo de' Medici's immediate ambience.

In its fifteenth-century context, the tale must be said to begin with a kick at Siena: "As many people must know, there has always been an abundance of gullible and foolish men in the city of Siena." And the kicks continue right through the tale. Unquestionably the leading state in fertile and industrious Tuscany, Florence was often regarded as a menace by its two neighboring republics, Lucca and Siena. Had not the Florentines bloodily conquered once-proud Pisa as recently as 1406? The tale, therefore, could have been set in Lucca, but for the fact that this little state had no university, hence Francesco's residence there would have required some other pretext. Yet despite the fact that Florence was the foremost regional power, Florentines had long looked upon Siena and Lucca as enemies, because they perceived them as vulnerable points in any Milanese or other foreign penetration into Tuscany. As a result, keen animosity and jealousy flourished among the three republics. Moreover, all the cities of central and upper Italy were heirs to ancient and vital traditions of local patriotism. In the appropriate metaphorical term, *campanilismo*, urban folk were emotionally attached, ardently so, to the sound and sight of the church bells of their parishes, neighborhoods, and cities. But owing to the fierce and chronic regional wars of the thirteenth and fourteenth centuries, love of one's native place also spawned distrust and hatred—occasionally turning into downright xenophobia—of neighboring foreigners. Consequently, the disdain for Siena in Lorenzo de' Medici's tale is no minor ingredient; it is a shaping motive when seen in relation to Florentine reading and listening audiences. To put the matter succinctly, the metaphors of our tale are such that through the actions of Francesco, Giacoppo, and Cassandra, Florence both cuckolds Siena and "screws" it. Insofar as Siena *is*, by synecdoche, its foolish men, it is (in an Elizabethan term) "hornified"; but insofar as it is, also by metaphorical extension, their pretty wives, it is—in the most appropriate term—"fucked." The second paragraph of the tale all but asserts this; for in Siena, we find, being good-looking "seems to be as natural in women as a touch of stupidity and vanity is in the men." That is to say, pretty Sienese wives are ready prey for clever foreigners. And all Siena gets in return, in Lorenzo de' Medici's exchange, is a sly Florentine whore. What is more, by introducing her, Meina, into the society of upper-class Sienese women, the author commits the ultimate moral outrage. He deliberately soils the honor of Siena in its most precious and tender part: its pool of gentle mothers, wives, daughters, and sisters. Is it any wonder that with these attitudes, Florence in the sixteenth century, under the first Medici duke, would at last take Siena by force of arms?

The opening lines of the tale brandish malice against that tiny republic: not only are the men of Siena fatuous and gullible, they are also a bad and bastard race, and they are so by nature, as implied by the metaphors of the seed, tree, and fruit, sheltering under skies of unhealthy air. But the true hallmark of Sienese men is their folly and credulity; hence in the figures of the handsome Francesco and wicked Meina, Florentines—with a peninsular reputation for wit and cold cunning—are to be their foils. Then there are names. For the malice is heightened by the fact that though Giacoppo seems to be a fictional character, his last name is not a fiction: Belanti was the name of a well-placed Sienese family, a name which, like Cassandra (bad news for Giacoppo), probably holds a note of vengeful scorn. For many a fifteenth-century tale, there was something in a name. Thus, while Giacoppo is given a real family name, the Florentine is given only a first name, Francesco; and this is because, etymologically, the "frank" and

"free" Francesco is meant to be a Florentine, rather than a particular individual. In Florence, moreover, his hired prostitute is
known by the diminutive and over-familiar nickname, "Meina"
(Bartolo*meina*), but in Siena, to gull the Sienese, she ascends to
the dignified "Bartolomea."

Now when Bartolomea set her trap for Giacoppo, she was doing
what all middle- and upper-class urban women were sternly
warned not to do: she was making eye contact from her balcony
window with a strange man on the street below. One current of
advice held that women should stay away from windows altogether. Stories of the period—with a good deal of exaggeration, I suspect—often feature such transgressive behavior. Yet it is not
Giacoppo's simplicity and vanity that get Francesco into bed with
Cassandra; it is his religious credulity. And this brings up a difficult theme for historical study. For first we should have to define
"credulous," and having done so, we would find it impossible—
given the ambiguities of any such definition—to do a study of the
sort fit to tell us something, in quantitative terms, about the social
range of "credulity" in fifteenth-century Italy.

Suffice it to say, accordingly, that Renaissance prose and poetry teems with the evidence of people—humanists, poets, lawyers,
merchants—who have a notion of "credulity" in that they draw a
line, however uneven or undeclared, across the extent of religious
belief: on the one hand is, by implication, a solid, sensible, and
necessary belief; on the other is credulity, something excessive, a
type of belief fit for peasants, simpletons, the uneducated, perhaps
women especially, or even just the common run of people. In the
fiction of Boccaccio and Gentile Sermini, wives may achieve adulterous aims by exploiting the credulity of their husbands, who
agree to perform modes of prayer, penance, or abnegation that free

wives for adulterous action. Similarly, shrewd friars, priests, miracle performers, and possessors of "true" religious relics trick people out of money or valuables by manipulating their simple religious faith. And again, in letters, verse, and fifteenth-century treatises, lawyers and humanists lash out at clerics who are villains but who successfully pass themselves off as saintly men: here too there is a supposition regarding the gullibility of the laity in matters of belief.

Giacoppo obviously belongs to this class of believers, only he is worse, more credulous, because he is also a "blockhead" (*scimunito*). Inevitably, therefore, the impact of Lent, his confession, his guilt, and the outrageous theology of his cagey confessor betray him into believing a load of codswallop: namely, that having seduced Francesco's "wife," he can only receive absolution for his sin and save his soul by allowing Francesco to lie with his own wife. It is to be tit for tat—and why not?—for "I love my soul more than anything in the world" and "There's nothing I wouldn't do to save my soul."

On the face of it, being vain and a boaster, rich and wellborn, and perfectly capable of showing off to young men, Giacoppo appears to have at least an ordinary intelligence; but though we know him to be a bit of a nitwit, let us bear in mind, too, that he has fallen into the hands of two crafty Florentines and a persuasive Franciscan friar, his own confessor, who is in effect playing the pimp. Moreover, his wife's burning love for Francesco—lust actually, as we shall see—is also a key factor in the cuckoldry. We may say, accordingly, that in the role of the Franciscan as procurer, in this man's lascivious use of the sacrament of penance, hence in his sacrilege, and in a rather jeering view of marriage, the tale offers us action that is no mere frolic. Not surprisingly, then, it does not seem to have done the rounds much in manuscript, and was not finally printed until 1865.

Within two generations of its founding in the thirteenth century, the Franciscan order of preaching friars had split into two very hostile groups, one of which held more strictly to the Franciscan vows of poverty and chastity. By the fifteenth century, the truly strict ones, the Fraticelli, had been hounded out of existence as heretics, while the two remaining wings, conventuals and observants, generally took a lax approach to their rules. As for their mendicancy, their commitment to begging, for all practical purposes, this had been cast aside. Their contentious spirit, however, persisted; and they were dogged by an unsavory fame for vice, hypocrisy, ignorance, and pleasure-loving. Our friar, Antonio della Marca, is deftly inserted into the framework of this malodorous notoriety. And remarkably, while he is not depicted as doing his deed—the tricking and betrayal of Giacoppo—for money, any fifteenth-century reader would have taken such a transaction for granted. Yet by not mentioning money, the author appears, cleverly, to blunt the edges of his fleering indictment of the Franciscan order, which is made to seem very nearly synonymous with lubricity and treachery. For "Antonio believed that one of the seven works of mercy was to succor the afflicted," that is, to help Francesco and Cassandra satisfy the lust which afflicted them; and he wished to prove the truth of the proverb "which says that there is no trap or treason that does not involve a Franciscan."

For all the fun and cunning of the basic anecdote, these matters were not pure comedy in the fifteenth century, and particularly not so in the light of the tale's flaunting of sustained blasphemy, for which in real life people occasionally suffered grievous physical penalties. Yet again and again in the tale, the name and love of

God are invoked for the purpose of getting Francesco into an adulterous bed with Cassandra. Thus, tormented by his supposed sin of adultery against Francesco, Giacoppo pleads with him: "You must . . . help me to get God to forgive this sin [by lying with my wife]." Friar Antonio declares: "You must by all means console poor Giacoppo here [and lie with his wife], not for love of him . . . but for love of the Lord Jesus, who will also show mercy to you and will not count as a sin what you do for love of His name." Francesco finally agrees: "I wish to make a gift to God of this . . . favor that I shall grant you [Giacoppo], and for His love I shall do what you ask of me [have intercourse with Cassandra]."

What are we to make of this sacrilege *par excellence*, this candid pilfering of God's mercy and loftiness for lecherous ends? Write it off as humor? The soiling and burning of the American flag might be a joke, if done privately today in the United States of America; but if brazenly done in public, it would certainly lead to an arrest or even, in some quarters, a lynching. We may argue, therefore, that *Giacoppo* was intended as private entertainment for the restricted circle around Lorenzo de' Medici. Evidently, too, in the early years, that circle cultivated and tolerated a certain degree of irreverence for their society's religious practices. The dubious fame of the clergy generally—not just of the Franciscans—had contributed to this mischievous turn. Clerics were often regarded as living in flagrant violation of their vows; and the more austere of them—e.g., San Bernardino of Siena—were even suspicious of any regular, official contact between women and confessors. They did not trust their own religious confreres. All the Italian city-states reported scandalous cases of convents which routinely violated their own rules governing claustration, and the religious houses of some nuns seemed little better than clandestine brothels.

Understandably, therefore, in the second half of the 1460s, just as the brilliant young Lorenzo began to dole out significant favor, write verse, and collect protégés, a circle gathered round him which gave voice to blasphemous views, while also expressing broader, popular sentiments, such as anticlericalism and scorn for Siena. The members of the circle counted the sparkling Luigi Pulci (a major poet), the learned and sprightly Braccio Martelli, the seductive Dionigi Pucci, the rich and talented Bernardo Rucellai, the politic Pietro Alamanni, and later on the beautiful Sigismondo della Stufa—all, of course, Florentines and part of the Medici claque. Lorenzo's private tutor—he was still around—had been the eloquent and clever priest (later bishop of Arezzo), Gentile Becchi, who could himself be remarkably irreverent about religious matters. Yet within a few years of the likely dates of *Giacoppo* (1468–70), Lorenzo became Florence's undisputed (behind-the-scenes) political chieftain, and in the 1470s the alleged "freethinker" Luigi Pulci, was banished from his side. As *de facto* head of state, Lorenzo had to keep up religious appearances. But he had always been sensitive to convention, self-interest, and *force majeure*. In the very last sentence of the tale, in the artful and compromising balance between good and bad priests, he is already charting a moderate course.

The sacrilegious features of Lorenzo de' Medici's tale are occasioned by Giacoppo's credulity and in a sense are all about this, but they do not touch the main source of his original troubles with Cassandra: the age difference between the two. Here at once we shall see how historical—how much subject to change—the notion of age is.

Giacoppo was about forty years old and his wife about twenty-five. This difference was consistent with demographic figures cast for Florence, where average age at marriage in 1427 was, in round figures, about eighteen for women and thirty for men, for a difference of twelve years. But very often the age gap was more like fifteen or twenty years, so that the Giacoppo-Cassandra ratio was perfectly in line with historical findings. In addition, this aspect of the tale draws upon the traditional theme of the *malmaritata*, stretching back to the mid or early fourteenth century: the theme in song and ballad of the lamenting girl, unhappily married, or about to be married, to an old man. In an urban society where marriage was, as we saw in *Ricciarda*, arranged with a view to the solidities of property and status, the *malmaritata* would long endure as a plangent voice, though a voice fostered by historical realities.

In our day, a man of forty or more would scarcely be thought too old to have "spring figs" or "figs out of season" (sex outside of marriage); but in the fifteenth century, sex *in* marriage for such a man might already be viewed as a problem, and perhaps rightly so in many cases, owing to maladies, nutrition, and social expectations. Recent study has shown that in Italian Renaissance views, old age was assumed to commence at some point between forty and forty-five, and our tale certainly gives support to this finding. Giacoppo, we are told, is old enough to be Francesco's father, and Francesco can allege that he has always revered Giacoppo as a father. But there may also be a dash of generational rivalry and exaggeration in the tale, if the young author, Lorenzo, then about twenty years old (perhaps a little younger than Francesco) and living under a gerontocracy, looked upon men in their forties with a measure of illwill or uncharitableness.

Giacoppo is so aroused by Bartolomea, that for all his age and lack of salt in the brain (*sciocco*, foolish, lacking in salt), he is able to perform wonders—not, however, with impunity, for his face is made to bear the stigmata of his passion in the scars and bruises of Barolomea's bites and scratches. In a society which often punished whores, bawds, and thieves by branding or otherwise marking them, and where the ubiquitous imagery of saints depicted these with the marks and signs of their martyrdom or sanctity, the bruises of our old man of forty are meant to be seen both as punishment for his idiocy and as a jeering parody. Toward the end of the tale, he is again put through ludicrous ritual action—kneeling, praying, and pleading, which, though normally intended for God and the saints, is in this case directed at Francesco and Cassandra, as he prays them, in effect, to cuckold him. The satire is unrelenting.

As the tale opens, in the passage pertaining to age and sex in marriage, Lorenzo de' Medici's cold eye is also cast upon matters that are never discussed in historical writing. For one thing, there is the ruthless assessment by a fifteenth-century Florentine rake, looking upon the type of the twenty-five-year-old wife (of another) as perfect quarry. The perfection lies in the fact that she is then still young enough to retain ardor and strong impulse, but old enough "to know as much as a woman can know [thanks to her bedroom experiences]" and to have put shame and timidity behind her. Directing his tale at a circle of knowing males, and in the wish to appear tolerant and wise, Lorenzo suggests that given the marriages imposed upon them, middle- and upper-class women are often involved in adultery: "it is no wonder that [such] transgressions are discovered every day." This must be seen as an exaggeration. There may have been more of this than we have hitherto suspected, but the question has yet to be studied. What can be confidently asserted is that the obstacles and bars erected against the adultery of propertied women—such as fear, conditioning, the omnipresence of telltale servants and neighbors, and above all the loss of dowry and expulsion from the household—were so formidable, in a way which we can barely imagine today, that we must take Lorenzo's suggestion with a grain of salt. In striving to tell a good story, he is egging his male audience on, while also giving voice, perhaps, to perennial male fears. In the very same paragraph, however, apropos of the subject of arranged marriage, Lorenzo makes an observation which is startling in its justice and accuracy: "women's misfortune seems to me to be a great one, and men to have a great advantage: since no matter how insignificant and pathetic a man may be, when he takes a wife, he always wishes to choose one who pleases him, or not take her at all; whereas a woman, without knowing what or why, is subject to the wishes of others and must take what is given to her in order not to have worse." This glancing *aperçu* includes some exaggeration, for men were also fully subject to the pressures of arranged marriage, and many women must have found contentment in their marriages. In the patriarchal urban societies of Renaissance Italy, owing to the power of the father and elders, owing to their control over jobs and vocational futures through their disposition of property, assets, and private education, marriages were arranged for *both* sexes. But in this business, men often had a voice which could not be claimed by their sisters, who, having been reared to be more obedient, timorous, shy, and passive, were much more likely to accept unquestioningly the decisions and urgings of their elders. There were no poems or songs of the *malmaritato*: i.e., of the lamenting, unhappily married young man. If nothing else, he could find his pleasures outside the household, as is clear from indications in four of the six stories in this collection. Among the pleasures outside of marriage for married men, or at least for some married men, including young bachelors, was the brothel. The subject itself is introduced by the figure of Meina (Bartolomea).

Most city-states had legal and licensed houses of prostitution by the late fourteenth century. The Florentine statutory code of 1325 reveals that the activity of prostitutes had been formerly illegal in Florence and even then was restricted by law to areas completely outside the city, though off the main roads and at some distance from certain churches. In the course of the fourteenth century, houses were licensed inside the city, always within appointed areas. Like most of the peninsula's major cities, Florence taxed such houses and derived a small income from them. One argument forcefully used to justify the licensing of prostitutes held that it was more natural and less sinful for men to frequent brothels than to have congress with homosexuals. Prostitution could be seen as a way of preparing young men for "natural" (conjugal) sex.

But there was something special about Meina. "She was one of those [prostitutes] who practice the profession more decorously but no less assiduously than the public ones" (*di queste che fanno l'arte piú onestamente ma non meno che le publiche*). Here is one of the earliest of all references to women of the sort who would be more numerous and much more fashionable in the sixteenth century: courtesans or *cortigiane*, "classy" tarts for rich men of the upper classes. In the key adverb that tells all, Meina operated *onestamente*: in context, this is to say that she operated privately, therefore discreetly or decorously. Public women were in brothels, under the control of bawds or pimps; they were expected to keep to designated streets and, when in public, had to wear the distinguishing items of their trade—a yellow sash, or gloves, or high-heeled shoes, and occasionally bells. Not, however, Meina; she suffered no such indignities; she was her own mistress. And if we are to judge by the established picture of courtesans in early six-teenth-century Rome and Venice, we might assume that she hailed originally from a good family, had the speech and manners of women from the middle or upper classes, and was visited at home only by well-to-do men and patricians, from whom she was likely to have picked up certain airs. The tale, therefore, may real-istically claim that Meina was successfully introduced as Bartolomea into the society of Sienese gentlewomen. Necessity had sharpened her wits and mimetic ways.

Since it is clear that Cassandra connived with Francesco from start to finish, when we consider that they achieved their amatory aims with the help of a tart, a villainous Franciscan, and a half-wit of a husband, it is difficult to think of their "love" (again in the fif-teenth-century context) as anything elevated. At best, they have cheated conventional, upper-class society and slaked their physi-cal desires; at worst, they have verged on damning their souls, though the tale turns its back on this possibility by enlisting our sympathies for them and our laughter against poor Giacoppo. Nevertheless, what Francesco says in irony about Bartolomea, "that whore of a wife of mine," Giacoppo could afterward have said of Cassandra, although without the irony, owing to her com-plicity with all of Francesco's stratagems.

I single out these matters to make a point about love. There are moments in the tale when the refined language of fifteenth-centu-ry love is used to characterize the passions of Francesco, Cassandra, and Bartolomea's relations with Giacoppo. Thus, Francesco "had already been in love with Cassandra"; she "was courted by a handsome young man"; or Bartolomea carried on as if being "on fire with a great love" and claimed "that she was dying for him [Giacoppo] and that for God's sake he must help her." Bartolomea's antics are a hoax. Even, however, in the case of Francesco and Cassandra, it is soon made clear that keen physical desire is the theme. In the amatory discourse of the day, love, it is true, could only take place outside of (arranged) marriage; but it must remain "noble" or elevated, ergo largely unphysical, or its whole face and character changed. In drawing on the serious language of love, even if sparingly, Lorenzo de' Medici is stealing value and refinement from another discourse in order to dignify Francesco and Cassandra, but in so doing, he is also playfully mocking the cheated discourse. On the other hand, Bartolomea's bandying about of the terms of love simply makes Cassandra's husband look more patently ridiculous.

The howling derision directed at Giacoppo is an episode in the history of Florentine attitudes towards Siena; but it is also, more pointedly, a social lesson about the oblique and terrible dangers that attend religious credulity. Whatever the views of the large multitude of believers, for an elite of young men from the worldly-wise ruling class, such a weakness could be turned into a gateway for dirty tricks. This exposed the sanctity of the household—hence male honor and identity too—to the treachery of others, and "all on account of the inordinate faith that men undeservedly put in [priests and friars]."

Looking around for additional subtlety in Lorenzo de' Medici and his circle, might we say that from a Florentine viewpoint Siena was, like Arcadia, a distancing locale where disreputable behavior was less real, and so less offensive and threatening? If so, then Lorenzo's assault on marriage becomes less transgressive or shocking, and the friar's behavior more fanciful. It was all happening elsewhere (not here), in a country of nitwits, hardly a real place at all. It was not the real Siena, but rather the "Siena" of joke and polemic, a place of the imagination where married women are pretty, men silly, and friars corrupt.

Aside from the fact that some friars *were* corrupt, such a reading takes subtlety too far. We are not in England, at the notoriously anxious court of King Henry VIII, nor in a totalitarian state, where the expressive imagination may be pressed into labyrinthine ways. Lorenzo, in any case, did not go public with his tale. He meant it for the men of his immediate circle. The devious mode in Florence, at that point still a few years from being much talked about, would be Ficinian Neoplatonism; and this way of seeing the world would not be articulated by means of whores, silly husbands, lusty wives, and squalid Franciscans.

SIX

1.

THE FAT WOODCARVER

by Antonio Manetti

The Florentine architect and writer Antonio di Tuccio Manetti (1423–1497) knew Brunelleschi, the prime mover in this story, as well as many of his acquaintances. His biography, Vita di Filippo Brunelleschi, *is the major historical source on this architectural genius. He wrote the* Story of the Fat Woodcarver *(*Novella del Grasso Legnaiuolo*) in the 1480s; and although there are other, shorter versions of the story, even in verse, gleaned from a lively oral tradition, Manetti's construction is the most complete and best account.*

&

In the past, and especially in more recent times, the city of Florence has had many men of a beguiling and amusing sort. Thus, in the year 1409, in keeping with their custom, a spirited group of respectable citizens met one Sunday evening for supper at the house of Tomaso Pecori, a most respected, entertaining, and clever man who delighted in their company. These men were from the governing class and from among the masters of the more intellectual and imaginative of the crafts, such as painters, goldsmiths, sculptors, woodcarvers, and the like. When they had finished their happy meal, since it was wintertime, they sat by the fire; and while conversing both generally and more separately about a variety of pleasant topics, mostly connected with their own crafts and professions, one of them asked: "What are we to make of the fact that Manetto the woodcarver didn't come this evening?" For this was the name of one of them, familiarly known as Grasso ("the Fatman"). It then came out that one of them had told him about the supper but had not, for some reason, been able to get him to come. Now this woodcarver had his workshop in the Piazza di San Giovanni and was considered at that time to be one of the finest masters of his craft in Florence. Among other things, he was famous for his skill in making panel-painting pediments, altarpieces, and similar things, which not every woodcarver of the day could do. And he was a very likable person, as most fat people are, about twenty-eight years of age, large of build, and stout, which was why everyone usually called him Grasso. And to tell the truth, he was a touch simple, but it would have taken a shrewd man to notice this, for he was by no means a fool. And as he was in the habit of joining this company but had not come that evening, they wondered why and could think of no reason for his absence, unless it was due to some mad whim, for he was prone to these. So, feeling a bit snubbed—since they were almost all of a higher rank and station than he—they began to amuse themselves by thinking up ways to avenge this snub, and the man who had spoken first said: "We could play a prank on him to teach him a lesson." To which one of the others replied: "What could we do, apart from tricking him into paying for a dinner that he himself would not attend?"

One of the men present was Filippo di Ser Brunellesco, whose marvelous intellect and genius are still widely remembered. Now Filippo, who at that time was about thirty-two years old, was very familiar with Grasso and had taken his measure and sometimes discreetly amused himself at Grasso's expense. After some thought, and with the self-confident grin that came so naturally to him, Filippo said: "I would like to play an amusing joke on him of the sort which, in revenge for his not coming this evening, would bring us great pleasure and entertainment. If you play along with me, I'd love to do it. And I've just thought of the way: we'll make him believe that he has become someone else and that he's no longer Grasso the woodcarver."

Although the company knew Filippo to be very clever at whatever he put his hand to (for truly he is blind who does not see the sun), still, despite their having some idea of how simple Grasso was, what Filippo was proposing seemed impossible to everyone. But Filippo, who was very good at such things, gave them so many clever, subtle reasons and arguments that he succeeded in convincing them that it could be done. And having agreed as to how they would keep the thing a secret, they gleefully decided that the vendetta should be carried out and that Grasso should be made to believe that he had become someone called Matteo, who was known to some of them and to Grasso as well, but who was not part of the intimate group of friends who used to dine together. And laughing wildly, several of them, going off to one side, decided to carry out the plan as soon as possible.

The jovial tale was soon launched. Indeed, it started the next evening in this fashion. Since he was on very friendly terms with Grasso and knew everything about him as well as he knew himself, for the woodcarver good-naturedly confided everything to him (otherwise he could not have proceeded with his designs), Filippo went to Grasso's workshop, where he had been a thousand times before, just at the hour when such artisans usually close their doors and work inside by lamplight. And after the two had been talking for a while, a boy arrived, as planned, all out of breath and asked: "Is Filippo di Ser Brunellesco here?" Whereupon Filippo, stepping forward, said: "Here I am. What do you want?" The boy replied: "If you are he, you must go home immediately." Said Filippo: "God help me! What has happened?" The boy replied: "I have been sent running to you and the reason is that two hours ago a grave accident befell your mother, who is near death. So come quickly." Filippo made a show of being very surprised, and again commending himself to God, took leave of Grasso. But Grasso said to his friend: "I will come with you, in case something needs to be done. Everyone should pitch in at a time like this. I'll close the shop and come away with you." After thanking him, Filippo said: "I don't want you to come for now; this matter surely cannot be of much importance. But if I need anything, I'll send word to you. If you wish to help me, stay here in your shop, and do not leave for any reason, in case I should need you. Then, if I don't send word to you, go about your business." Having thus kept Grasso in his shop, Filippo left, and after pretending to be going home, doubled back the other way and proceeded to Grasso's house, which was near the cathedral of Santa Maria del Fiore. And having opened the door with a knife, being the kind of fellow who knew how to do such things, he entered the house and bolted the door from the inside so that no one could get in.

Just at that time, Grasso's mother had gone to Polverosa, in the country, to do laundry, cure meat, and attend to other such tasks, and Grasso was expecting her back any day. That, as Filippo knew, was why he had left the door on the latch. Grasso stayed in his shop for a while and then closed it, and to keep his promise to Filippo yet more fully, he walked up and down outside the shop, and after having done so many times, he said: "Things must not be going badly for Filippo. He won't be needing me." And with these words he set off for his house, and when he arrived at the door, which was at the top of two flights of stairs, he went to open it as he usually did; and having tried several times without success, he realized that the door was bolted from within. So, knocking loudly, he said: "Who's there? Open up," imagining that his mother had returned and bolted the door from the inside either from some kind of precaution or by an oversight. Imitating Grasso's voice, so that he sounded exactly like him, Filippo called out: "Who's down there?" Although thinking that voice very unlike his mother's, Grasso said: "It's Grasso." Filippo now pretended that the man calling from outside the house was the Matteo they wanted Grasso to think he had become, and so he said: "Go on, Matteo, go with God; I have a world of things to do. Filippo di Ser Brunellesco was in my shop a while ago, and they came to tell him that some hours ago his mother was in danger of death. So it's a bad evening for me." And turning around, he pretended to say to Grasso's mother: "Get my supper ready; you've come home two days late, and on top of that you've come at night," and he added several reproachful words. Hearing someone in his house scold his mother with what seemed to him not only his own voice but all his own actions and mannerisms, Grasso said to himself: "What does this mean? That fellow up there seems to be me, to hear him say that Filippo was in his shop, and how they came to tell him his mother was ill. And besides, he's shouting at Monna Giovanna, and his voice sounds just like mine. Am I losing my mind?" And as he went down the stairs and stepped back to call through the window, there arrived—as planned—the sculptor Donatello (whose fame is known to everyone), who had been at the dinner and was one of Grasso's friends. When he approached Grasso standing there in the twilight, he said: "Good evening, Matteo, are you looking for Grasso? He went into his house a little while ago." And Donatello didn't stop, but went on about his business. If Grasso was amazed before, he was more amazed than ever now to hear Donatello call him Matteo. Startled and stunned, with yes and no contending in his head, Grasso set off toward the Piazza di San Giovanni, saying to himself: "I'll stay here until someone who knows me passes by and says who I am," and going on, "Woe is me! Am I like Calandrino,[1] turned into someone else so quickly without realizing it?" With Grasso half out of his wits, there suddenly arrived, again as planned, six guardsmen from the Mercanzia [Merchants' Court] and a bailiff, and with them was a young man pretending to be a creditor of the same Matteo whom Grasso was almost beginning to believe he had become. And this man, coming up to Grasso, turned to the bailiff and the guardsmen and said: "Take away Matteo here. He is my debtor. You see, I've tailed you until I caught you." The guardsmen and the bailiff seized Grasso and started to lead him away. Turning to the man who was having him arrested, Grasso said: "What have I to do with you, that you are having me arrested? Tell them to let me go; you've mistaken me for someone else; I'm not who you think I am, and you're committing a great injury by shaming me like this when I have nothing to do with you: I am Grasso the woodcarver, not Matteo, and I don't know what Matteo you're talking about."

1. The proverbial Boccaccio character (*Decameron* VIII, 3 and IX, 3).

Then he made as if to strike them, for he was a big, strong fellow. But they quickly seized him by the arms and the creditor came forward, peered carefully at his face, and said: "What! You've nothing to do with me? Don't I know who Matteo my debtor is, and who the Fat Woodcarver is? I had your name entered in the debtors' book, and what's more, I got a judgment a year or more ago. What! You have nothing to do with me? And he says he isn't Matteo, the scoundrel! Take him away. This time you'll pay before you get out of it. We'll see whether you're Matteo or not." And thus quarrelling together, they led him off to the Mercanzia [court and jail]. And because it was about a half-hour before suppertime and quite dark, they met no one there, nor on the way, who knew the Fat Woodcarver.

When they arrived at the Mercanzia, the chief clerk pretended to write Matteo's name in the register and then put him in jail, for he knew all about the plot from Tomaso Pecori, with whom he was on intimate terms. The other prisoners, who had heard the commotion on Grasso's arrival, and hearing him called Matteo several times, received him as if that were his name and asked him nothing else, none of them, as it happened, knowing him except by sight. And hearing and seeing himself called Matteo by everyone, like a man possessed, he was almost certain that he had become someone else. And when asked why he had been arrested, he replied in complete confusion: "I owe a good deal of money, that's why. But I shall get out of here early tomorrow morning." And the prisoners said: "As you see, we're about to have supper. Eat with us and then tomorrow you'll get yourself out. But we'd better warn you that one always ends up being here longer than one might think. May God grant that this doesn't happen to you." Grasso accepted their invitation and ate a little; and when they had eaten, one of them lent him the corner of his miserable little pallet, saying: "Matteo, stay here as best you can for tonight and if you get out tomorrow, fine, and if not, you can send home for some bedding of your own." Grasso thanked him, and settled down to sleep as best he could.

When the youth who had played the creditor had done what he thought was necessary at the Mercanzia, Filippo di Ser Brunellesco met with him and got all the details of how Grasso was arrested and taken to jail. Meanwhile, Grasso, lying on the edge of the mat and mulling things over, kept saying to himself: "What am I to do if I've become Matteo? For from all the things I've seen, it seems certain to me by now, and everyone agrees. But which Matteo? If I send word home to my mother, and Grasso is at home (for I heard him there), they'll make a laughingstock of me." And so he endured until the next morning, thinking these thoughts, believing he was Matteo one moment and Grasso the next; and he scarcely slept, if at all, but kept tossing and turning and agonizing over it all. And when he got up with all the others, he went to the window of the jail, imagining that someone who knew him was sure to happen by, to release him from his doubts of the night before. And then Giovanni di Messer Francesco Rucellai entered the Mercanzia. He was one of the dinner company and privy to the jolly plot, and he was very well known to Grasso, who at this time was carving the top of a frame for a Madonna for him. In fact, just the day before, Giovanni had been in his workshop for quite a while, pestering him about it, and Grasso had promised to give it to him in four days. Now when Giovanni reached the Mercanzia, he put his head inside the window to the jail, which at that time was on the ground floor, where Grasso was standing. And when the woodcarver saw Giovanni, he began looking at him and grinning; and Giovanni, as if wondering who he was, looked at Grasso as if he had never seen him before, for either he didn't know Matteo, or was acting as if he didn't, and said: "Why are you laughing, partner?" Grasso said: "No reason." And seeing that Giovanni didn't recognize him, he asked: "Sir, do you happen to know a fellow called Grasso, who has his workshop in the Piazza di San Giovanni, and is a woodcarver?" "Are you talking to me?" asked Giovanni, adding: "What! I know him very well. In fact, he's my man,[2] and I'm going to see him shortly about a little job he's doing for me. Is he the one who had you arrested?" Grasso said: "No, by holy Mary!" Then he went on: "Forgive me, but I would like to ask you in confidence to kindly do me a favor. Since you are going to see him anyway, please tell him this: 'A friend of yours is in jail at the Mercanzia, and he would like you to come have a word with him'." Said Giovanni, staring him fixedly in the face and struggling to hold back his laughter: "Who are you? Who should I say is sending for him?" (this was so that he would confess to being Matteo and could be teased about it sometime later). Grasso said: "Never mind, it's enough to say what I've told you." Then Giovanni said: "I shall do so gladly, if that's all you want," and left; and when he ran into Filippo, he told him laughingly of everything that had happened. Grasso remained at the prison window, saying to himself: "Now I can be sure that I'm no longer the Fat Woodcarver. Oh! Giovanni Rucellai never took his eyes off me, yet he didn't recognize me—he who's always in my shop, and *he* isn't out of his mind! It's certain that I'm no longer Grasso and have become Matteo. Damn my luck and my misfortune! For if this gets out, I shall be humiliated and taken for a madman and the children will taunt me and I'll run a thousand risks on account of it. And also, what have I

2. The Italian text reads: *egli è tutto mio.* This is a patron-client expression of the period, meaning something like: "I am his patron; he is my servitor, and he would do just about anything for me."

to do with another man's debts, or the scrapes he's gotten into—I, who have always avoided this and a thousand other dangerous mistakes? And I can't confide in anyone, or ask for advice, and God knows I need it! I'm really in trouble. But let's see if Grasso comes, and if he does, maybe I'll understand what all this means. Could he possibly have become *me*?" And caught up in such thoughts, he waited a long time for him to come; and when he did not come, Grasso drew back to let another prisoner take his place at the window, while he proceeded to wring his hands and roll his eyes up and down from floor to ceiling.

On that day a judge—whose name it is well not to reveal—was also being held in the jail for debt. He was a man of considerable merit, known no less for his literary than for his legal fame. Now this man, although he did not know Grasso and had heard nothing about him, seeing him so downcast and distraught, and believing that he was upset because of his debt (and since he had already resolved his own case and was about to be released), tried to comfort him out of charity, as one sometimes does, saying: "Come, Matteo, you couldn't be more miserable if you were about to die, or were in danger of some great disgrace. According to what you say, it's only a small debt you owe. One mustn't give in to misfortunes like this. Why don't you send for some friend or relative of yours? Don't you have anyone? Come, try to pay up or reach some kind of agreement, so you can get out of jail, and don't be so downcast." Seeing himself comforted so compassionately and with such kind words, Grasso did not say to the judge, as another man might have done, "Why don't you mind your own business?" Wisely, instead, knowing him to be a respected man, he decided to speak to him with every reverence, though he too was in jail, and to tell him his whole story. Accordingly, he drew the judge off to a corner of the jail and said to him: "My lord, although you do not know me, I am well aware of who you are and I know that you are a man of distinction. This is why—and your kindness moves me to do so—I have decided to tell you what is troubling me so much, for I do not wish you or anyone else to believe that I am in such distress for a small debt, even though I am a poor artisan. In truth, something else is weighing on me, and it may be something that has never happened to anyone in the world." The judge was quite amazed to hear him say this, and listened with great attention.

Grasso began at the beginning, relating everything that had happened to him up to that moment, struggling to hold back his tears, and urgently imploring the judge to do two things: first, in all honor never to talk to anyone else about this, and second, to offer him advice and help, adding: "For I know that you have long read about many things, including stories of ancient and modern men, and men who have recounted many events. Did you ever come across anything like this?" Having heard him out, the worthy judge quickly considered the matter and concluded that one of two things had happened: either the man had been driven out of his mind by an overwhelming melancholy, brought on by his present trouble (if he was a man of little spirit) or by another matter, or else someone was playing a trick on him, as was indeed the case. And in order to understand better which it was, the judge replied that he had often read of one man becoming another and that it was not an unheard-of thing. In fact, there were worse cases, as when men became brute animals, such as Apuleius, who became an ass, and Acteon, who became a deer. "And one reads of many others, which at the moment don't come to my mind," said he, now seeking to amuse himself a bit. To which Grasso said: "Oh, I never would have believed this!" And he took it for gospel truth. Then he added: "Now tell me, if I who was Grasso have become Matteo, what must have happened to *him*?" To which the judge replied: "He must have become Grasso; this is a case of changing places, for that's how it usually happens, to judge by what one reads and the examples I've seen up to now. It cannot be otherwise. I would really like to see this fellow. This is truly something to laugh about!" "If it's not happening to *you*!" said Grasso. "That's true," said the judge, "these are great misfortunes. May God protect every man from them. We're all at risk. I used to have a worker to whom the same thing happened." Grasso sighed deeply, not knowing what else to say, since that's how things were. To entangle him even more, the judge added: "We read the same about the companions of Ulysses, and others who were transformed by Circe. It is true, from what I hear and have read, if I remember well, that some people have come back to themselves, but it happens rarely if the transformation lasts even a little while." Grasso was stunned to hear this.

He was still in this state at around three o'clock and hadn't yet eaten, when two of Matteo's brothers came to the Mercanzia and asked the bursar if a brother of theirs named Matteo was a prisoner there and how much he was in for, because they wanted to get him out. The bursar said yes, and pretending to look for his name in the book, after turning some pages, said: "He's in for such-and-such an amount, at the petition of so-and-so." "It's too much," said one of them. Then they said: "We'd like to talk to him a little, and then we'll give the payment order for him." And they passed on to the jail, where they said to a man at the grating: "Tell Matteo that two of his brothers are here, and have him come to us," and looking in, they immediately recognized the judge, who happened to be talking with Grasso. After receiving the message, Grasso

asked the judge what happened afterward to his worker; and when
he was told that the man never became himself again, Grasso, now
twice as worried, came to the grating and greeted them, and the
older of the brothers began to say: "This is just like you, Matteo,"
never taking his eyes from Grasso's face. "You know how often
we've warned you about your misconduct and how many times
we've gotten you out of this jail and others, and it does no good to
tell you anything, for you go from bad to worse. God knows better
than anybody how hard it is for us to get you released, for you've
already eaten up a fortune. And what good has ever come of anything you spent? Really, you've just frittered and thrown it away.
Not to mention the fact that everyone cheats you at gambling.
Hasn't half your money been stolen? And we suffer for it, and the
shame is all ours, because you don't mind at all. In fact, it seems
that you do everything to shame your friends, and think you can
justify it by saying, 'You've mistaken me for someone else.' Are
you a child? You've long since left childhood behind. But you can
be sure of this. If it weren't for our honor and the urgings of our
mother, who worries us more than you do (for she is old and frail),
this time we'd leave you to your own devices, so often have you
done this to us. And we're telling you once and for all that if you
ever get into trouble again, come what may, you'll stay in jail a lot
longer than you'd like. Let that be enough for you for now." After
pausing for a while, without saying anything, the brother continued: "And so as not to be seen doing this all the time, we'll come
for you tonight around the hour of the Angelus, when there'll be
fewer people around, so that everyone doesn't learn of our misfortunes and we won't be so shamed on your account." Grasso turned
to them with appeasing words, fully believing by now that he was
Matteo, since they were paying for him and had both continually

looked him in the face, and it wasn't dark. He told them that indeed he would never again cause them trouble and that he would mend his ways, and that if he should ever again misbehave, they should harden their hearts against him and his mother and any excuses he might use. Now fully resolved to be Matteo, he begged them for the love of God to come for him at the appointed hour. They said that they would do so, and departed, and Grasso turned back and said to the judge, drawing him close: "We're into an even prettier fix now, for Matteo's two brothers came here to me—the Matteo with whom I've been exchanged (how can I say this?)"—he looked the judge in the face—"and they both spoke to me face to face, and in the light, as you could see, just as if I were Matteo, and after scolding me for a long time, they told me that they would come for me at the hour of the Angelus and get me out of jail." Then he added: "Up to now I would never have believed it; but now I see clearly what you are saying," and then he asked: "So that worker of yours never came back to himself again?" "Never, poor man," said the judge. Grasso heaved a deep sigh and then said: "So, they get me out of here, but then were shall I go? Return to where? I can't go back home—but which is my home? That's the beauty of it. Just consider," and he looked at the judge, "if I go home, and Grasso is there (as he surely will be, for I heard him with my own ears), what shall I say so that I won't be taken for a madman or a fool? Oh, you know very well that if I go into the house as if it were mine, and Grasso is there, he'll say: 'Has this fellow gone mad?' And if he isn't there and returns later and finds me, what will happen? Who should stay, and who should go?" And he added, "You can be sure that if I hadn't been home when my mother returned from the country, she would have had me searched for and found me even if I had been up in the stars. But

since she sees him there before her, she doesn't know what happened to me." The judge fought hard to keep from laughing—he
was enjoying himself no end—and said: "Don't go home. Go with
these two who say they are your brothers, and see where they take
you and what they do to you. What have you got to lose? Anyway,
they're paying for you." "That's true," said Grasso, and the judge
went on: "You'll get out of jail, and since they have no doubt that
you are their brother, who knows, maybe you'll be better off.
Perhaps they are richer than you."

While they were speaking of these things, night began to fall
and the judge couldn't wait to get away from Grasso, so that he
could finally laugh, for he could no longer keep a straight face. The
two fellows who were pretending to be Grasso's brothers had been
there at the Mercanzia, waiting for the appointed hour and laughing the whole time. They saw the judge's case settled and watched
him emerge from the jail, looking as dignified as if he had just
come from talking to a magistrate about a client in a lawsuit (as
jurists sometimes do), and saw him go off. After the bursar had
returned to his place, they came forward and pretended to make a
payment to the creditor and the bursar, who then got up again from
his seat with the keys to the jail, and going over to where the prisoners were, said: "Which of you is Matteo?" Grasso stepped forward and said: "Here I am, sir," no longer doubting that he had
become Matteo. The bursar looked at him and said: "Your brothers
here have paid your debt for you, all of it, so you are free to go,"
and opening the door of the jail, he said, "This way."

When Grasso came out it was already quite dark, and he was
delighted to be out of jail without having disbursed a penny. And
because he had gone all day without eating, the moment he was
out the door he thought of going home. But then, remembering

how he had heard Grasso's voice there the evening before, he changed his mind and decided to follow the judge's advice, and so he went with the two men, who lived near the church of Santa Felicita, at the beginning of the Costa San Giorgio. On the way, they scolded him gently—not harshly, as they had at the jail— telling him how distressed their mother was and reminding him of the promises he had made to change his ways on other occasions. And when they asked him why he had said that he was the Fat Woodcarver—whether it was because he really thought he was, or so that the guards would believe that they had mistaken him for Matteo and would let him go—Grasso did not know what to answer. He grew pensive and began to regret having gone with them, for he hated to admit that he was Matteo. But on the other hand, he said to himself: "If I again say that I am Grasso, perhaps they won't want me, and I will have lost both their home and my own." So he promised them that he would mend his ways, and did- n't answer the part about why he had said he was Grasso, but stalled for time. Thus they arrived home, where they took him into a room on the ground floor and said, "Stay here until it's time for supper," as if they didn't want their mother to see him in order not to grieve her. A fire was lit and a little table set in the room, and one of them stayed with him by the fire, while the other went to the priest at Santa Felicita, who was their parish rector and a good person, and said: "I am coming to you in confidence, as one neighbor should go to another, and also because you are our spiri- tual father. In order that you may better understand things, so as to do what is best, I should say first that we are three brothers who live close by, as you may perhaps know." "Yes," said the priest, who knew them slightly. The brother went on: "One of us, named Matteo, was arrested for debt yesterday and detained at the

Mercanzia. And because this isn't the first time we've had to bail him out, he is so distressed about it that he seems to have gone half out of his wits, and seems obsessed by this thing, although in every other way he is the same Matteo as usual, or almost. What's different is that he has gotten it into his head that he's become somebody other than Matteo. You never heard such a fantastic thing! He says he's become some fat woodcarver—though a man known to him—who has his workshop behind the baptistery of San Giovanni and his house beside the cathedral of Santa Maria del Fiore. We've tried in a number of ways to get this idea out of his head, but nothing has worked. So we got him out of jail and brought him home and have him in a room, so that people won't hear about these crazy antics of his. For you know that once someone begins to show such signs, even if later he becomes the most sober person in the world, he'll be teased and mocked ever after. Also, if our mother became aware of it before he recovered, it might cause her some ill effects. Who can tell? Women are faint-hearted, and she is frail and old. So, to conclude, we beg you for pity'sake to come to our house and try to get this fantasy out of his head, for we know you to be a good person who would scruple to reveal such a disgraceful thing. This is why we have turned to you rather than to anyone else. And we shall always be obliged to you and may it gain you merit in the eyes of God. Not to mention the fact that you are charged with his salvation, for he is one of your flock, and you have to render an account of him. For if, with his brains overturned, he were in a state of mortal sin and died without recovering his wits, he would perhaps be damned." The priest agreed that it was indeed his duty, adding that he was not only eager to help but also would spare no pains to do so. For, duty aside, he was an obliging man by nature. Then, after a pause, he said, "And maybe the pains will not be wasted. Take me to him," adding, "unless he's dangerous." "No, by holy Mary," said the brother. "Ah, I see. You fear he might be in a mad frenzy." "As you well know," said the priest, "people in that state have no regard for their own father, let alone a priest, for what they see appears to them to be something other than what it is." "Reverend sir, I see your point," said the brother, "and you are right to ask. But, as I told you, he's more deluded than raving mad, and to see him, neither you nor anyone else would be aware of his condition. And in truth, if he were raving, we would give up all hope and would not be going to all this trouble, for rarely or never do such people recover. One might say that he has lost his way just a little, rather than lost it entirely, and we don't want our mother to know anything about it. It's because we have hope that we are taking this action." "If that's how it is, then I want to see him," replied the priest, "and make every effort to cure him. For really, in a case of this sort, it is everyone's duty to help. I realize the danger to your mother, as you say, and it is best to spare her this trouble, if possible." The brother thereupon brought him home and into the room where Grasso was.

When the woodcarver, who was sitting there lost in thought, saw the priest's cassock, he stood up. The priest said, "Good evening, Matteo," and Grasso replied, "Good evening and happy new year." "It is, now you say so," said the priest, for Grasso already seemed well to him. Then he took him by the hand, and said: "Matteo, I have come to stay with you a little while." And he sat down by the fire and drew him onto a small chair beside him. And seeing that he was giving no sign of insisting that he was the woodcarver, as he had been told, the priest began to have some hope of a good outcome, making signs to the brother who had brought him there, indicating that so far things looked very good. And he gestured to the brother to stay out of the room, and this he did. Then the priest began to speak as follows: "You must know, Matteo, that I am your parish priest and your spiritual father; and that it is our duty to comfort all our parishioners as much as we can in spirit and in body. I hear things that trouble me greatly: it seems that recently you've been in jail on account of your debts. I want you to understand that these are not unusual things for you or anyone else, nor should they seem so; for this world brings such misfortunes, and lesser and greater ones, every day, and one must always bear them with fortitude. I say this because I hear that you have cast yourself into such a state that you've been on the point of going mad. Men of worth do not behave this way, but confront adversity, insofar as they can, with the shield of patience and fore-sight; and that's good sense. What folly is this, among others I hear you have been committing, that you say you are no longer Matteo, but keep insisting that you are somebody called Grasso, who is a woodcarver? This obstinacy of yours is bringing shame on yourself and turning you into an object of ridicule. Truly, Matteo, you are to blame when on account of a small adversity you have grieved yourself to the point of losing your senses. For six florins! Oh, is that such a great thing? Especially now that they have been paid! My dear Matteo," said the priest, squeezing his hand, "I don't want you to do this any more; and for my sake (and for your own honor and that of your people here, who seem to me to be such good folk) I want you to promise me that from now on you will rid yourself of this fantasy and attend to your own affairs, like any upstanding, sensible man. And commend yourself to God, for any man who places hope in Him does not do so in vain. The result will be that you will do yourself good and bring honor to yourself and to your brothers here, and to everyone who loves you, and also to me. Come! Is this fat woodcarver such a great master or so rich that you would rather be him than you? What advantage do you see in doing this? Let's even suppose that he is a worthy man and richer than you (though from what your brothers tell me, he is rather some degrees lower). Saying that you are he will not get you his honors, nor his wealth, if he has any. Do as I tell you, for I am advising you for your own good. Alas! Among other things, if you brought such a disgrace upon yourself, you would run the risk of having the children taunt you in the streets, and you would be in trouble and shame all the rest of your life. That's all you would have gained by this. And I promise to report well of you to your brothers so that they may love you as a good brother and always be eager to help you. Come now, Matteo, act like a man, not an animal, and leave off this foolishness and forget all this nonsense about the fat woodcarver. Do as I say, for I'm giving you good advice." And he gave him a gentle, steady look.

Hearing how lovingly the priest said all this to him and the seemly words he used, and having no doubt at that moment that he was Matteo, Grasso replied that he was willing to do whatever he could of what the priest had told him to do. And because he realized that everything the priest said was for his own good, he promised from that time on to make every effort and never again try to convince people that he was Grasso, as he had done until then—that is, unless he became Grasso again. But if it were possible, he wanted a favor from the woodcarver: he wanted to have a chat with him, and for a good reason; for by speaking with him, he believed he could easily put an end to his error. But if he did not meet the woodcarver and speak with him, he was afraid he wouldn't be able to make any promise that he could keep. At this the priest grimaced and said: "My dear Matteo, all of this is contrary to your own best interests, and I see that you have not yet rid yourself of your delusion. What do you mean, 'unless I become Grasso again'? I don't understand. Why do you need to talk with him? What have you to do with him? For the more you talk about him, and the more people you talk to, the more you will broadcast this affair, and the worse it will get and the more it will be held against you." And the priest said so much about this that Grasso gave in, though he did so unwillingly.

When the priest left, he told the brothers of his conversation with Grasso and of what Grasso had finally and reluctantly agreed to do. But, from something Grasso had said—though he had not quite understood it—the priest suspected that he might not keep his promise to him. However, he had done what he could. One of the brothers placed a silver coin in his hand to make the thing more credible, and they thanked him for what he had done, and begged him to pray to God to return Matteo sane to them. The priest opened his hand and grasped the coin, and having taken leave of them, returned to the church.

While the priest had been with Grasso, Filippo di Ser Brunellesco had arrived on the sly, and, drawing aside one of the brothers amid gales of laughter, got him to relate everything: about freeing Grasso from jail, and what they had told him on the way home and later on. And in recounting all of this to Filippo, the brother told him about the judge whom they had seen talking with Grasso in jail, and how they had seen him being released. Filippo carefully noted and committed everything to memory along with what the creditor who had Grasso arrested had told him. And having brought with him a beverage in a little phial, he said to the brother:

"While you are dining, see that you give him this to drink either in wine or however you think best, as long as he isn't aware of it. This opiate will make him sleep so soundly that even if he were beaten, he wouldn't feel it for several hours." After arranging this with them, he left.

The brothers returned to the room and sat down to supper with Grasso, for it was already past nine-thirty. And while they were supping they gave him the beverage, which was neither evil-tasting nor bitter, so he was not aware of it. When they had finished supper, they remained a while by the fire and went on talking about his misdemeanors, begging him to keep his promise and refrain from such behavior, and especially for their sake and that of their mother to leave off the folly of believing he had become someone else. This was very wrong of him and he shouldn't wonder if they begged him to stop, for it hurt them almost as much as it did him. That very day, they told him, it had happened that while they were walking through the New Market to procure the money for his release, one of them heard someone behind them say: "Do you see that fellow who's lost his memory and forgotten who he is, and thinks he's become someone else?"—although another man said: "That's not the fellow, it's his brother." And while they were talking about this, the opiate began to work, so that Grasso couldn't keep his eyes open. They said to him: "It seems you're falling asleep on your feet, Matteo. You mustn't have gotten much sleep last night." And they were right. Grasso replied: "I promise you, I've never been so sleepy in my whole life." They said to him: "Go right to bed." With difficulty he managed to undress and get into bed; then he fell asleep so soundly that, as Filippo had said, even had he been beaten, he would not have felt it; and he was snoring like a pig.

Since the woodcarver was big and fat, Filippo came back at the agreed time with six friends. All six had been at the supper in Tomaso Pecori's house and were robust, high-spirited fellows who wanted to take part in the prank, having heard how it had begun from Filippo, who had described it all with the greatest glee. On entering the room where Grasso was, and hearing that he was sound asleep, they picked him up, put him in a hamper along with all his clothes, and carried him to his own house, where, as luck would have it, his mother had not yet returned from the country. They knew all this because they were keeping an eye on everything. And they put him into bed, and placed his clothes where he usually put them. But they put his feet where he usually put his head. And after having done this, they took the key to his workshop, which was hanging from his belt, went there, entered, and moved all of his tools around from one place to another. And they did the same with his planes, turning the blades upside down, and the same with the handles of his hammers, and they arranged his saws with the teeth on the inside. And they did this to all the tools that lent themselves to such reversing, and turned the whole workshop topsy turvy, so that it looked as if devils had been there. And after putting everything in a fine mess, they locked the shop up again and took the key back to Grasso's house and hung it where he usually did; then they left the house and closed the door again and went to sleep in their own homes.

Drugged by the potion, Grasso slept all night without ever waking up. But next morning, awakening to the sound of the Angelus from Santa Maria del Fiore, when the effects of the potion had worn off and it was already daylight, he recognized the sound of the bell and, opening his eyes, saw some chinks of light in the room and realized that he was in his own house, and his heart was suddenly filled with great joy, for it seemed he had become Grasso again and was master of all his possessions, which he had thought might be lost to him. And now he almost wept, he was so beside himself with joy. Yet he was disturbed and amazed to find his head where he usually put his feet in the bed. And remembering the things that had happened, and where he had gone to sleep the night before, and where he was then, he suddenly fell into a reverie of uncertainty about whether he had been dreaming then or was dreaming now. And he vacillated between the one and the other, and looking around the room, cried: "This is the room I had when I was Grasso, all right, but when did I get here?" And he kept touching first one arm, then the other, and then touching his chest, to make sure he really was Grasso. Then he said to himself: "If this is so, why was I arrested as Matteo? For I still remember that I was in jail and that everyone took me for Matteo, and that I was bailed out by those two brothers; and that I went to a house near Santa Felicita and the priest talked to me a lot and I ate supper and went to bed there, for I had gotten so very sleepy." So again he was in the greatest confusion as to whether he had been dreaming then or was dreaming now. And he began to feel anxious again, but not so much as not to feel a persisting glimmer of joy when he remembered what the judge had said to him in jail, for he believed that it was more likely than not that he had turned back into Grasso. And although he remembered everything that had happened, from his arrest up to the time and place where he had gone to bed the night before, it didn't bother him, since he had become Grasso again and it seemed that things had turned out all right. But then his thoughts would turn back to the things that had happened and he would again say to himself: "Who knows if I dreamt it, or if I'm dreaming now?" and after several heartfelt sighs, he said: "God help me." After getting out of bed as he always had and getting dressed, he picked up the key to his workshop and went there, and when he opened the door he saw the whole place, as well as every one of his tools, turned topsy-turvy. On seeing this, still baffled as to how he had reached his bedroom, he was immediately assailed by new thoughts that blotted out the old ones. And while he was pondering the state of his affairs, and unsure as to whether he was awake or dreaming, but delighted to be Grasso again and in possession of his own belongings, who should appear but Matteo's two brothers. Finding him in such a state and pretending not to know him, one of them said: "Good day, master." Turning around and recognizing them, but without returning their greeting, and with no time to think about what he should reply or to take counsel with himself, Grasso said: "What do you want?" One of them replied: "The truth is that we have a brother called Matteo who was arrested for debt some days ago and took the thing so to heart that he went a little off his head. All to our shame, but that's how it is. And among other things, he says that he's no longer Matteo, which is his name, but rather the master of this workshop, who seems to be called Grasso. And although we have admonished him greatly and have had him warned and berated, we have been completely unable to talk him out of this foolishness or idiocy or whatever we may call it. Yesterday evening we even brought our priest from Santa Felicita (that's our parish and he's a good person), and he promised the priest to give up this fantasy, and dined with the best appetite in the world and fell asleep right in front of us. Then this morning, long before dawn perhaps, without anybody hearing him, and leaving the door open behind him, he left the house. Where he went we do not know; so we came to see if he had turned up here, or if you knew anything about him."

Seeing that these men, who had gotten him out of jail the day before at their own expense, and had taken him into their home and fed him and given him a bed, did not recognize him as their brother, this seemed to Grasso to confirm that he had become himself again, especially as he had just come from his own house; and he got an urge to toy with them, for he was beside himself with joy, and said to them: "I'd look to see if he's at the Foundlings' Home, if he's a child." But then his humor changed. He had been engaged in mending the blade of a plane, which he now grasped firmly in his hand (and it was a very big hand) and looked them in the face. And they, not finding him in the mood they were expecting, suddenly feared that he might hurl it at them, and decided to get away from him and beat a retreat.

Grasso really had no such intention; nevertheless, when the two left, he couldn't figure out what had happened, so he decided to get away from his shop for a while and go to Santa Maria del Fiore to think at his leisure, and to verify whether he was Grasso or Matteo by meeting other men, although, thanks to the fact that he had slept in his own house and that the two brothers no longer recognized him as Matteo, he was almost certain of himself. And again turning over in his head the uncertainty about whether it had been a dream or real, and about who he now was, he would start to reach for his cloak and then forget that he wanted it and turn somewhere else and then back to his cloak, in utter confusion. Yet he finally managed to take up his cloak, and pulling the shutter of his shop down, he made for the church, as he had for his cloak, taking four steps forward and three back. He finally reached the church, saying to himself: "This has been a strange business. Let the judge say what he pleases, I don't know how it came about." Then he said: "There must be something to the fact that everyone, not just one person, mistook me for Matteo." And struggling to free himself of these thoughts and simply to find out whether or not he had truly become Grasso again, he still couldn't get them out of his mind. And he was still afraid that he might turn back into Matteo again, or into somebody else. With his mind in this turmoil, he suddenly decided to find out what had been happening in the meantime to Matteo, in order to check on whether or not what the judge had told him was true. And since he thought no one was there to notice him, he paced back and forth like a wounded lion, as those who happened upon him reported later.

It was a work day and there were few people about and no one was watching, so it seemed to him a good place to vent his feelings. And while he was pacing up and down like this in the church, he came upon Filippo and Donatello, who were chatting there together, as was their habit. But this time they had come deliberately to be on the lookout for Grasso, and had seen him come in. Filippo knew that Grasso had no idea whether what had happened had been a trick or not; nor was there any reason for him to suspect them, for they were sure that they had cleverly covered their tracks. Pretending to be very happy, and going on a bit to make it all plausible, Filippo said: "Things actually turned out quite well with my mother. The attack had almost passed already by the time I got home, so I didn't send for you. She's had it before; old people are like that. I haven't seen you since; what happened to you last night? Did you hear this story about Matteo Mannini? Has he gone mad?" The question was addressed as much to Donatello as to Grasso. Donatello asked: "What happened?" Filippo replied: "Don't you know?" and turning to Grasso, said: "It seems that the night we were together, sometime between eight and nine, he was arrested here near the piazza. And the man who was having him arrested (I don't know who it was, but that has nothing to do with it) was with the bailiffs, and Matteo kept saying to the bailiffs and the guardsmen: 'Who do you want? You've mistaken me for someone else. I have no debts with any-one. I am the Fat Woodcarver. Do you want me?'" Grasso was completely taken in by Filippo and had no suspicion that Filippo knew anything about what had happened to him. Filippo went on like this: "The man who was having him arrested went up to him, for the bailiff had said to him: 'Beware of what you're having us do. We're holding you responsible for this. If this is not the man, you'll lose your expenses, because we mean to be paid. Besides, through no fault of our own, we could also get into trouble for it.' The man having him arrested, who was the collector for a draper's establishment, went up to him and looked at him carefully, and said: 'He's trying to disguise his face, the scoundrel!' Then, after looking him over again, he said: 'He's Matteo, all right, take him away. This time he's going to pay for it!,' and while they were lead-ing him away, Matteo kept saying that he was Grasso the wood-carver, declaring: 'Here's proof that I just locked up my shop,' and he showed them a key" (which were all things he had done, and had happened exactly as the young man had reported to Filippo), adding: "And I hear that it was just as funny at the Mercanzia. Can it be that you haven't heard anything about it? It was the fun-niest thing in the world." Donatello also pretended to know noth-ing about it, and said: "I remember now that they were talking about it yesterday in my workshop; but I was very preoccupied and had a lot to do and paid no attention. But now that I think about it, I did hear the names of Matteo and Grasso and something about being arrested, but I didn't bother to ask about it afterward, because I wasn't thinking about Grasso at the time. But come on, tell us, Filippo, what is this story, since you know all about it? Ah, that's really a laugh, that he was being arrested, and didn't want to be Matteo. How did the story turn out?" Filippo said: "Oh, it's impossible that Grasso doesn't know about it. What happened to you yesterday? Can it be that no one came to your shop to tell you about it? I hear that everybody in Florence was talking about it" (twisting the knife in the wound), "and three or four times yesterday I was on the point of coming to your shop to chat about it, and then for some reason I ended up not coming." Grasso kept looking from Filippo to Donatello, wanting to reply first to the one and then to the other, and he kept biting back his words, turning first one way and then the other, like a man possessed, unable to make out whether they were telling the truth or pulling his leg. After heaving a great sigh, he said: "Filippo, these are certainly strange things!" Filippo knew right away what Grasso meant, and could barely keep from grinning. Then he exclaimed: "You said you hadn't heard anything about it. How can that be?" And they wanted him to sit down with them so that they could listen to him more at their ease. Grasso was sorry he had spoken, and didn't know what to do, and was all tongue-tied, because one moment he thought that they were speaking to him sincerely, and the next moment he thought just the opposite.

Just then along came Matteo, who approached them without their realizing it, for he too had been on the lookout—all on Filippo's prompting. And luck was with them, as he could not have arrived at a more perfect time. Matteo greeted them, and Grasso, totally bewildered, turned to him and was about to say, "Your brothers were at my shop just now, looking for you," but he restrained himself. Then Filippo said: "Where have you come

from, Matteo? We want to know about this, too. We were just talk-
ing about you, and now we're all here." Donatello said to Matteo:
"Were you arrested one of these past nights? Tell the truth, for
Filippo tells me . . ." "Was no one ever arrested before?" asked
Matteo. Then he said to Filippo, who was looking him in the eye:
"I've come from home." "Oh," said Filippo, "people were saying
that you had been arrested." "Well, I was arrested, my debt was
paid, and I got out and now here I am. What the devil is this!
Don't people have anything else to talk about but my affairs? My
mother plagued me about it all morning, from the moment I got
home. And since I returned from the country, those brothers of
mine are sulking and looking at me as if I were growing horns, and
they were just saying to me when they ran into me here: 'What
time did you go out this morning, and did you leave the door
open?' I think they've gone crazy, they and my mother with them. I
don't understand them. And they say something about my being
arrested, and having paid for me—really crazy." Said Filippo:
"Where have you been? It's several days since I've seen you."
Matteo said: "I'll tell you the plain truth, Filippo. It's true that I
had a debt at a draper's shop for six florins of good coinage, and I
put them off for a while because I too was being put off, for I was
supposed to get eight florins from a fellow from Empoli, and I
should have had them several days ago, according to what he had
recently promised me; and I had intended to use that money to
pay off my debt, and would have had some left over. On Saturday,
I promised my creditor I would pay him Tuesday without fail, as
the fellow from Empoli had promised me. And when he secured
the judgment against me (since it's been quite a while really that
I've owed the money to him, because I've been having financial
difficulties), to avoid his doing me an ill turn, I decided to go off to

our place near the Certosa in Galluzzo, and I stayed there two days and that's why you haven't seen me. I returned less than an hour ago. And the oddest thing you ever heard happened to me. I went to the country Tuesday after dinner. And since I had nothing to do and it was a thousand years since I'd been there, and we keep nothing there but a bed (for we send from Florence for wine at vintage time and for everything else in its season), I idled on the way to kill time and drank a couple of drafts of wine at Galluzzo, so as not to bother our worker about supper. And when I got there it was night, and I asked him for a bit of light, and went to bed. What I'm going to tell you now is really funny. I'll say it again—everyone seems to me to have gone crazy, perhaps myself more than anyone. I was getting dressed this morning in the country and had opened a window—to tell you the truth, I don't know whether I'm dreaming now, or if I dreamed what I'm about to tell you. I feel like a different person this morning, Filippo, it's a funny thing, but never mind that. Says my worker, who had given me the lamp: 'What happened to you yesterday?' Says I: 'Didn't you see me last night?' Says he: 'Not I, when?' Says I: 'Scatterbrain! Didn't you light the lamp for me, when I couldn't get it to burn?' Says he: 'Yes, the evening before; but I didn't see you yesterday evening, nor all day yesterday. I thought you had returned to Florence, and I was surprised that you hadn't said anything to me, since I was sure you must have come here for some reason.' So I must have slept all day yesterday. And I asked the worker: 'What day is it today?' And he tells me it's Thursday. Indeed, Filippo, I find that I slept an entire day and two whole nights without ever waking up. It was all one big sleep."

Listening with rapt attention, Filippo and Donatello pretended to be very amazed. Said Filippo: "Whatever you ate the night before must be well digested by now." Matteo said: "I tell you, I'm so hungry I could eat an ox." "Then it wouldn't be a good idea to share a meal with you," said Donatello. But this story about Matteo having slept during the whole time when everything was happening made Grasso marvel, and he said to himself: "There's no help for me, I'm surely going crazy. I never would have believed this three days ago, and yet I'm . . ." Matteo went on with what he was saying: "But I dreamed the craziest things you ever heard." Said Filippo: "Someone's light-headed here. You should eat." Matteo went on: "And I just ran into an errand boy from the draper's where I owe the six florins. He apologized to me and said that he wasn't the one who had me arrested (as he's the one who usually comes to ask me for the money, and is a decent sort), and he said: 'I'm sorry for all the expenses you've had.' And from what I can see, the money's been paid. And when he said that, I understood what my mother and brothers had been talking about when I thought they had gone mad. As I was telling you just now, they paid the money, but how, I don't yet know. I wanted to find out from this boy. And indeed it seems that during the time I thought I was sleeping, however it happened, I was in jail most of the time. You figure it out, Filippo. I for my part don't know how this could have happened. And I couldn't wait to see you to tell you and have a laugh with you about it." Then he turned to Grasso and said: "I've spent most of this time between your house and your workshop. I've got something to tell you that's sure to make you laugh. I find I've paid a debt of several florins, and all this time while I was sleeping, I thought I was a different person, just as surely as I see myself here among you now. But who knows whether I'm dreaming now or was dreaming then?" Says Donatello: "I didn't understand, tell me again: I was thinking about something else.

Oh, you fellows are driving *me* crazy. You just said that you had been in the country." To which Matteo replied: "I know very well I did." Says Filippo: "He must mean that he was there in a dream." Then Matteo said: "Filippo understood me."

Grasso never said a word; he stood there confounded, listening very attentively to see whether Matteo had been *him* during that time. Filippo was as happy as a scratched piglet, and because it looked as though people were beginning to gather around (since now and then one or another of the party couldn't help laughing a little, except for Grasso, who was utterly bewildered), he took Grasso by the hand, and said to all of them: "Let's go a while into the choir stalls, so that people won't gather around; for this is one of the best stories I've heard in all my days. I want to hear this one. Go on, Matteo, tell me this story. And you shall hear another from me later, one that everyone in town has been telling, as you're beginning to make me suspect that the two might be the same story."

They all sat down in a corner of the choir stalls where they could easily see one another. (At that time the choir of the cathedral was between two large pilasters that stand just before the entry to the tribune.) And after being silent for a little while—Filippo was acting as if he were waiting for Matteo to speak, and Matteo seemed to be waiting for Filippo—Filippo began to talk first; and addressing himself more to Matteo, who was playing his part well, than to Grasso, in order not to upset him, he laughingly said: "Listen to what people have been saying all over Florence. I just repeated it to our friends here. Then we shall listen to you, since you want me to speak first. It is being said that you were arrested on Monday evening." "I, arrested?" said Matteo. "Yes," said Filippo, "on account of that debt you were telling us about";

and turning to Donatello, he said: "You see, there was some truth
in it." Said Donatello to Matteo: "It must have been when I found
you knocking on Grasso's door the other evening." Said Matteo:
"When? I don't know that I ever knocked on his door." "What do
you mean you didn't knock on his door?" Said Donatello, "Didn't I
speak to you outside his house?" Matteo acted surprised, and
Filippo continued to address Matteo: "And they say that on the
way you kept saying, first to the bailiffs, then to the fellow who
was having you arrested: 'You've mistaken me for someone else,
it's not me you want, I have no debts with anyone,' and you
defended yourself as much as you could by saying that you were
Grasso here. And you say that you were in the country, and
according to what you say, at that hour you were in bed sleeping.
How can this be?" "Let them say what they want," said Matteo,
"but you really must be joking. I was in the country, as I told you,
so as not to be arrested, because I was truly afraid I might be. As
for what Donatello was saying just now, I would swear on the holy
altar that I never knocked on Grasso's door, then or ever. Now listen to how it really happened, for it's wildly different from that. I
asked an attorney friend of mine who works in the government
palace to get me a safe-conduct against debt and to send it to me
in the country, and I thought I would have it by yesterday. The
attorney wrote me a missive early this morning and sent along a
messenger expressly to tell me that the councillors had not yet
met,[3] for some of them were in the country; and as there was no
other need for them to meet, the Lord Priors didn't want to make
them come back just to issue safe-conducts. And he added that I

3. *Collegi*: the members of the government's chief advisory councils, being the
Twelve Good Men and the Sixteen Gonfaloniers. They advised the Lord Priors on
a regular basis.

could stay out in the country for a few days if I was expecting to be arrested. But I came back to Florence and have been on my guard, and since the debt has been paid, it's all right. Filippo and Donatello, this is certainly the truth. But what I dreamed in the meantime is awfully funny. Filippo, I'm not kidding, I never dreamed anything that seemed so real to me while I was dreaming. I thought I was in this fellow's house" (and he touched Grasso) "and that his mother was my mother. And I was chatting familiarly with her as if she were my own mother, and I was eating and talking about my affairs, and she was answering me. And I remember a thousand things she said to me; and I went to bed in that house and got up and went to his shop, and it seemed to me that I wanted to work as I have seen Grasso do a thousand times when I visit him in his shop. But it seemed to me that there wasn't a single tool in its proper place, so I put them all back where they belonged." Grasso was looking at him like a man gone mad, for he had just had those very tools in his hands. And Matteo went on: "And then when I tried to use the tools, none of them would work for me, and it seemed that I was putting them in places other than where they usually are, with the intention of putting them back in order when I had time, and then I would pick up other tools, but they were all the same. And it seemed to me that I was answering people who came to ask me things as if I were really Grasso, for indeed that's how it seemed to me. And I went to eat and came back to the shop and in the evening I closed up and went home to bed, as I said, and the house looked just as it really does and as I've seen it, for I've been there with Grasso, as he knows."

Grasso had been silent for an hour, for he didn't think there was anything he could say that would help him at all with Filippo, whom he knew to be as sharp as a razor. The story of Matteo's

dream had completely convinced him that he was in an inextrica-
ble tangle. The account of that dream of a day and two nights
seemed to him to correspond perfectly to the duration of his own
troubles. And Filippo and Donatello affected the greatest wonder
in the world over the dream. Then Filippo said: "So it seems that
you weren't the one who was arrested. And yet you say that your
debt was paid while you were in the country; this is a snarl that
not even Aristotle could untangle." Pursing his lips and shaking
his head, and perhaps thinking about Matteo saying that he
thought he had become him, and also about what the judge had
said to him at the Mercanzia, Grasso said: "Filippo, these are
strange things, and from what I hear, things like this have happened before. Matteo has spoken and you two have spoken and I
have something I could say too, but it might make you think I'm
crazy. I'd better keep quiet. Come, Filippo, let's not talk about it
any more." And at that moment he truly believed that what the
judge had told him was a manifest truth, since there was so much
proof of it. And most certainly he believed that he had been
Matteo and Matteo had been he; but since Matteo had been
asleep, his troubles had been fewer, less serious, and less bother-
some than those of the man he, Grasso, had become.

But now he really believed that he had become himself again,
seeing and hearing the story of Matteo, who was no longer Grasso.
And as his mother had not yet returned from Polverosa, he was
keenly impatient to see her, to ask whether she had been in
Florence during that period, and who had been in the house with
her that evening when he knocked on the door, and who had
opened his shop during that time. And he took leave of his
friends, who could in no way make him stay, although they used
only gentle, polite pressure, partly so that he wouldn't take it bad-

ly again, and partly because they wanted to give vent to their
laughter, which they could no longer hold in check. Still, Filippo
said: "We must have supper together one evening," and at this
point Grasso left without replying.

There is no need to ask if Filippo and Donatello and Matteo
now laughed among themselves; for those who saw and heard
them thought they seemed crazier than Grasso—especially
Donatello and Matteo, who all but wept with laughter. Filippo kept
grinning and looking from one to the other. Grasso, as they
learned afterwards, decided to close his shop and go all the way to
Polverosa, where he learned from his mother that she had not
been in Florence and the reason why she had prolonged her stay
in the country. Whereupon, turning this fact over and over in his
mind, and returning to his senses and to Florence, he concluded
that he had been the victim of a practical joke, though he couldn't
figure out how it had been carried out. But that's how it seemed to
him, since his mother had not been in Florence during that time
and no one had been in his house. And he couldn't very well let
on now that he had understood, nor had he the heart to defend
himself for having been duped, should anyone speak to him about
it. And he was particularly affected by Filippo's involvement, for
he didn't see how he could save face with him.

This is why Grasso determined to go away to Hungary, for he
recalled that he had been asked to go, and decided to find the
man who had invited him, a former associate of his who had studied with him under Master Pellegrino delle Tarsie, whose workshop was in the Via delle Terme. This young man had left
Florence several years before and gone to Hungary, where he had
done very well with the help of Filippo Scolari, known as Pippo
Spano, one of our citizens who was then captain general of

Sigismund's army. And this Sigismund, who was the son of King Charles of Bohemia, was himself King of Hungary—a wise, astute king who was later elected emperor in the time of Gregory XII and crowned by Pope Eugene IV. This Spano took under his wing all Florentines who went there and had any intellectual or manual skill, for he was an outstanding lord who loved his countrymen exceedingly, as they must have loved him; and he helped many of them. Now this young man had come to Florence at that time to see if he could recruit any masters of his craft and take them back to Hungary for the many works he had been commissioned to do there, and he had spoken about this with Grasso time and time again, begging him to go and assuring him that they would soon become rich. Grasso ran into him by chance, and going up to him, said: "You have often talked to me about going with you to Hungary, and I've always said no. Now, on account of something that's happened to me and a disagreement I've had with my mother, if you still want me, I've decided to come away with you. But if you agree, I want to leave tomorrow morning, for if I were to stay any longer, my departure would be hindered." The man answered that he was very glad to have him come along, but that he couldn't leave the next morning because he hadn't yet finished his business. But he told Grasso to leave whenever he wanted and to wait for him in Bologna, that he would be there in a few days, and Grasso was satisfied. After they had agreed on things, Grasso returned to his shop, got some of his tools and other small items, as well as some money to take along with him, and having done this, he went to Borgo San Lorenzo and hired a horse which was then to be returned in Bologna. The next morning he mounted the horse and set out for that city as if he were a hunted man, speaking not a word to relatives, nor to anyone else. And he left a letter at home addressed to his mother, inviting her to make up her dowry from the value of everything that remained in his shop, and saying that he had gone to Hungary with the aim of staying there for some years. Before mounting the horse, as he was walking through Florence (for he had to do this, although he showed himself as little as possible during that brief period), he happened to go by several places where he heard people talking about what had happened to him, and everyone was laughing and joking about it. And he overheard someone say that it had all been a practical joke. The first to let the story out had been the fellow who had him arrested, and then the judge who had been with him in jail. Filippo had had a hilarious meeting with the judge, had asked him what Grasso said while he was in jail, and had disclosed the plot to him; and amid gales of laughter, the judge had told him everything. And all over Florence people were saying that the trick had been played on him by Filippo Brunelleschi, which made perfect sense to Grasso, who knew all too well what Filippo was like, and saw that he had been duped and that Filippo was behind it. And all this spurred Grasso on to stick to his decision.

So this is how Grasso left Florence and went with his friend from Bologna to Hungary. The old supper company continued their custom of getting together from time to time; and the next time they met was in the same place, at Tomaso Pecori's house. And with a view to their all laughing together about the prank, they invited the judge who had been detained at the Mercanzia. When he learned who they were, he went along gladly, not only because he knew some of them, but also to find out more about the whole affair, and to tell them his part, for he saw that they were eager to hear it. They also invited the youth who had arrested

Grasso with the bailiff, and Matteo, and the two brothers who had led the dance at the jail and at their house and by the fire. In addition, they wanted to have the bursar from the Mercanzia, but he couldn't come. The judge delighted at hearing everything that had happened, and told them about Grasso's questions and about how he had told him about Apuleius and Circe and Actaeon, and about his own worker in order to make it more plausible to Grasso, adding: "If anything else had occurred to me, I would have told it to him." They laughed their heads off, jumping from one episode to another, as these occurred to each of them. And seeing how the affair had turned out, and how they had been lucky with the priest and the judge and everything else, the judge made this pretty speech to them: that he couldn't remember ever having been at a banquet in his whole life where he had had more or better food; and that most of it had been so good that rarely, if ever, did such food appear on the tables of kings or emperors, not to mention those of lesser princes or private men such as themselves. And he believed that no one could have seen through the trick, so great had been Filippo's forethought and finesse.

When Grasso and his friend arrived in Hungary, they set to work and met with good fortune, for in a few years they became rich, relative to their condition and standing—thanks to Pippo Spano, who made Grasso a master engineer, so that he was called Master Manetto of Florence and had a fine reputation there. And Spano took him into the field with him on maneuvers and paid him well, and every so often, as was fitting for the occasion, gave him fine and lavish presents. For Spano was as generous as if born a king, and he was magnanimous with every man but especially with Florentines—which, in addition to his other virtues, had been one of the things that had attracted

Grasso to Hungary. And when not in the field, Grasso was able to tend to all his own commissions, because he carried out a great deal of work there both with and without his friend. Later, over a span of several years, he returned to Florence for a few months at a time on a number of occasions. And the first time he came back, when asked by Filippo why he had left Florence in such a mad rush and without consulting his friends, Grasso told him this story point by point, laughing all the while, with a thousand amusing details that only he could have known—about both being and not being Grasso, and about wondering whether he had dreamed or was dreaming when he remembered what had happened, so that Filippo had never laughed as heartily as he did then. Grasso looked him in the eye, saying: "You know this better than I, for you were really having me on that morning in the cathedral." Filippo replied: "Never mind. This will make you much more famous than anything you ever did with Pippo Spano or with King Sigismund—people will still be talking about you in a hundred years." Grasso laughed, and so did Filippo, just as much as before. And for all that, Grasso never wanted to be with anyone but Filippo when he had a moment to spare, even though he knew for certain that Filippo had been behind it all. And Filippo would joke when he was with Grasso, saying: "I knew all along that I was going to make you rich. There are many people who wish that they had been Grasso and been tricked like this. You've really gotten rich out of it, and become acquainted with the emperor of the world and with Pippo Spano and with many other great princes and barons." And indeed this return or homecoming of Grasso's, and all the others afterward, since he always kept company with Filippo, gave the latter the occasion and leisure to question him at greater length and many times, and to cross-examine him in minute detail about the things that the judge and the young man [the pretended creditor's agent] had told him. For most of the funny things had happened, so to speak, in Grasso's mind. And this is how it came about that the story of the Fat Woodcarver could be written in minute detail and full information given about it, for Filippo repeated it in all its particulars several times afterward, and the present version was later derived from those who heard it. And everyone who heard him tell it declares that it is impossible to recount every detail as it occurred, without omitting some droll passages from the account and from what really happened. Therefore, after Filippo died, the story was gleaned from people who had heard him tell it several times: for example, from a man called Antonio di Matteo dalle Porte, and Michelozzo, Andreino da San Gimignano (who was Filippo's pupil and heir), Scheggia, Feo Belcari, Luca della Robbia, Antonio di Migliore Guidotti, Domenico Michelino, and many others.[4] Although there was some writing about it in Filippo's time, not a third of what had happened was reported there, and it was fragmented and full of defects. But perhaps it did this much good—that because of it, the story wasn't entirely lost. Thanks be to God. Amen.

---

4. They are *seriatim*: Antonio Gamberelli, the sculptor known as Rossellino (1427–1479); Michelozzo, sculptor and architect (1396–1472); Andrea Cavalcanti da Buggiano, sculptor (1412–1462); Giovanni Guidi, called Scheggia, brother to Masaccio (1407–1480); Feo Belcari, poet and writer (1410–1484); Luca della Robbia, sculptor and potter (1400–1482); Antonio Guidotti, Florentine architect (fl. 1450s); and Domenico di Michelino, painter (1417–1491.)

2.

Who Does He Think He Is? *The Fat Woodcarver*

Reading *The Fat Woodcarver* raises two immediate questions for the modern reader: is this story meant to be funny? and, did it actually happen? Interestingly, both questions are really about history and only contingently about literature. The first is asking about the circumstances that attended laughter and humor in fifteenth-century Florence; the second is a query about psychological feasibilities in the same time and place.

Grasso ("Fatman") looks much like the classic scapegoat: he is picked out of the herd or group, mercilessly derided, and then in effect driven out of the encampment—the corral of Florence's sacred walls—by the whips of shame and humiliation. The only missing element here—but its absence undoes the scapegoat thesis—is the achievement of a feeling of purgation: there is no suggestion at all in the story that the group around him experiences any sense of relief or cleansing. If, following his ordeal, Grasso had committed suicide (and his self-imposed banishment is a mode of symbolic suicide), this act would have stirred up the collective feelings of the group and thus achieved a similar end: the reaffirmation of community coherence in the supper company. As embodied by the group around Grasso, the community closes ranks in the very act of singling him out. In so doing, that is, in its laughter, complicity, and vitalized exchanges, group spirits are rekindled and the individual sense of belonging, the pull of all the old and more recent bonds, is reaffirmed, but all at the expense of one of the members. Cruel? Yes. Life-affirming for the group? In the short run at any rate, yes. Terribly funny? Yes, apparently, in the eyes of contemporary witnesses and of all the pranksters involved. They were to dine out on the story for years.

What has changed since then to exclude us from the intended humor? More accurately, what was there about quattrocento Florence, about its ideals, social structures, and daily rules or expectations, that made the concerted attack on a man's sense of self a thing of comedy? In reply, I shall put forward a series of historical propositions and meditations, rather than, let us say, an enunciative essay. One of the most troubling things about this story, for historians anyway, is that it puts questions before us that have almost never found their way into historical discourse. What is the relation of the "I" or the "me" to the impinging social group? To what extent do we know ourselves in the recognition and confirmation of others? And in any given time and place, how vulnerable may individual identity be to the denials of the (certifying) group? In our time, curiously, it suddenly makes sense for historians to pose such questions, because a leading strain in contemporary philosophy has seriously challenged the notion of the self as a continuous, centralized, organizing quiddity.

Since a member of Grasso's supper company orchestrated the reversal of reality against him, and all the members, reportedly, split their sides with laughter over his temporary loss of identity, the search for the foundations of humor in *The Fat Woodcarver* should center on his relations with the group. So what about the group? Who were they exactly? As so often in Italian Renaissance fiction, the opening page of the story offers us critical information. Practice in the oral tradition of storytelling called for a rapid and clear delivery of essentials, and *The Fat Woodcarver* is in this mode. Any desired suspense would then flow from the plot itself.

Few if any texts from the early history of Florence provide so intriguing and detailed a profile as this one, however laconic, of a mixed group of men who regularly met to chatter and have supper together. But we shall need to bring in supplementary particulars, in order to make up for what contemporary Florentine observers would themselves have brought to the story.

Grasso's friends—and oddly they were this, even after his disgrace—"were a spirited group of respectable citizens," who came "from the governing class (*reggimento*) and from among the masters of the more intellectual and imaginative of the crafts (*maestri d'alcune arti miste e d'ingegno*), such as painters, goldsmiths, sculptors, woodcarvers, and the like." The company thus included a remarkable social scatter, ranging from members of the political oligarchy, such as their host Tomaso Pecori, to a major goldsmith, art theorist, and engineer (Brunelleschi), a vastly gifted sculptor (Donatello), and a highly talented woodworker, Grasso himself. Lay religious confraternities in Florence were also composed of men from the different strata of society; but religious association for ritual purposes was one thing and a chatty company, come together for the business of pleasure, was something else. Moreover, the sort of dining club, with its broad social makeup, which collected at Pecori's house on that wintry Sunday evening of 1409 was rarely to be found outside of Florence in those years, and would have been most improbable either at Venice or one of the princely states, say, Milan or Ferrara. Only Siena, I reckon, and perhaps Bologna, had the social and mental structures for kindred groups and reunions. At that moment, having recently and fiercely defended its liberties against the expansion of

Milanese autocracy under the Visconti, and being much preoccupied with the grand decorating and completion of the city's gigantic cathedral, the republic of Florence was a meeting ground for productive encounters between talented or clever men from diverse backgrounds. Indeed, a minor share of its major political offices, all held for short terms of two to six months, was still reserved for men from the lesser craft guilds, with the result that rich bankers, petty tradesmen, and great landowners regularly served together in public office.

But it would be wrong to imagine that Florence was a democracy, or that reverence and flattery were denied to status, riches, rank, and illustrious ancestry. All these were very much to be reckoned with and played a near-tangible role in daily political and social life. The first page of the story provides seemingly innocent particulars that turn out to be charged with meaning, the thrust of which would have been immediately plain to contemporaries. Of the three men named there, the first is given his full name, "Tomaso Pecori"; the second is called "Manetto the woodcarver," nicknamed "el Grasso" (the Fatman or Fat One); and the third is given his and his father's name, a near patronymic, "Filippo di Ser Brunellesco." To have a family surname in early fifteenth-century Florence was already to be someone. But Tomaso Pecori, a member of the oligarchy, is also accorded a more dignified summing up: "a most respected, entertaining, and clever man" (*uomo molto dabbene e sollazevole e d'intelletto*). Manetto alone is identified by his trade, woodcarver. Then, being at once diminished (however gently or amicably) by the appellative "the Fat One," he is situated in his place of work: "this woodcarver had his shop in the Piazza di San Giovanni." In short, Grasso is known by the work of his hands—"one of the finest masters of his craft in

Florence"—his corpulence, and his workshop (facing the Baptistery). On the other hand, although the author is admittedly looking back as from the 1480s, Filippo di Ser Brunellesco (aged about thirty-two), who started out as a goldsmith and was also a sculptor, is not pinned down by trade or craft. He is elevated: a man of "marvelous intellect and genius." And mention of his father, Ser Brunellesco, calls attention to an attorney (*ser*)—hence to some Latinity and learning—in Filippo's immediate family background. Much employed as an attorney by Florence's War Office (the *Dieci di balìa*), Ser Brunellesco had been an authoritative figure in the recruitment, payment, and provisioning of the foreign mercenaries who captained or served in the republic's professional armies.

The shadowed promise of the foregoing particulars is then swiftly brought to issue. Why had the woodcarver, who was wont to meet with that gossipy company, not joined them on this Sunday evening? Casting round for reasons, they conclude that only some quirkiness, whim, or fancy (*bizzarria*), "for he was prone to these," could account for his absence. And this caused the company to feel that he had "snubbed" them (*tenendosi da lui un poco scornati*), particularly because "they were almost all of a higher rank and station than he" (*perchè generalmente erano quasi tutti di migliore qualità e condizione di lui*). Here suddenly and fleetingly—but is it so fleeting?—an awareness of rank and class sharpens the narrative and turns out to be what lies beneath the nomenclature and descriptive modes singled out above.

Socially, then, the woodcarver was perhaps the most humble member of the group. In this regard he was rather like the young sculptor, Donatello (Donato de' Bardi: ca. 1386–1466), another of Pecori's guests that evening. The son of a small-time employer in the woolen cloth industry, this man was trained as a goldsmith, but seems always to have kept a modest style. Years later, as Vespasiano da Bisticci tells us, on being given a splendid red cloak by Cosimo de' Medici, Donatello refused to wear it, because he regarded it as being above his station.

Grasso was also one of the youngest members of the company, if not quite the youngest. Although the author of the story, Antonio Manetti, gets Brunelleschi's age right, "about thirty-two" in 1409, he may be wrong about the woodcarver, whose age he gives as "about twenty-eight." In 1447, Grasso's Florentine tax returns, filed in his absence (he was in Hungary), list him as being sixty-two years old, for a birth year therefore of something like 1385. We know that in age and other matters, tax returns in Florence were often faulty; but if they are right in this case, then Grasso would have been twenty-four in 1409, about the same age roughly as Donatello. There is no reason to favor Manetti over an official tax record; he wrote long after the 1409 events, drawing heavily from rich and detailed oral accounts; and though these accounts could be remarkably accurate, as we saw in our analysis of *Bianco Alfani*, exact age was not a datum for unquestioning trust. Manetti is right about Brunelleschi's age, but we must bear in mind that he both knew him personally and wrote a *Life of Filippo Brunelleschi*.

If Grasso was the "lowliest" member of our coterie, or nearly so, and one of the youngest, he was not without notable qualities, or he would never have been in that group. Eminent and clever Florentines like Tomaso Pecori did not invite just any man to sit at their hearths. And the notoriously impatient and brilliant Brunelleschi would never have cultivated the friendship of an ordinary artisan, for his closest friend during those years, until they quarreled, seems to have been none other than the young

Donatello. Grasso, moreover, was not only something of a genius in his craft (and this in a city with no shortage of outstanding talents), he was also amiable, apparently meditative, and a trifle quirky—"sensitive" we might say nowadays, even in his streak of simplicity, for "he was by no means a fool."

The members of the company would have known something else about Grasso: that is, that his father, Jacopo, sat in the city's chief governing council, the *Signoria* (a body of nine men) in 1380; and that his grandfather, Manetto, had served a tour of duty in the same body back in 1368. Among men of the governing elite (*reggimento*), such matters were common knowledge. But the Ammannatini family—Grasso's new surname, though it is not given in the story—did not "make it": they failed to establish themselves within the class of active political citizens. Consequently, there would also have been something of the "new man" about this immediate descendant of "upstarts." The taint of newness, or of "base" parentage, hung on in Florence.

We have assembled a profile of the Fat Woodcarver: he was likable (men were attracted to visiting him in his shop), highly talented and sensitive, but also young, big and fat, perhaps a shade whimsical (a dreamer?), and with a touch of the new man. His humble economic circumstances were self-evident; he says as much to the judge; and at the end of the story, he abandons Florence with nothing more than a little cash and some tools—for he proposes to live by the skill of his hands—leaving behind no real property of his own. His mother is to get what is rightfully hers in law, the equivalent of her dowry (*dote*): namely, all the tools and oddments remaining in his workshop, in addition to a house and perhaps some land at Polverosa, although we are not told that these are mentioned in Grasso's letter to Monna Giovanna.

Evidently, her dotal capital had been partly used to help set him up in a woodcarver's establishment.

We also have a sketch of the dinner company: they were comfortable, important, or outstandingly talented men who loved conversation, good spirits, and the exchange of ideas. There was an obvious interest in the "higher" crafts (art); they appreciated wit and intellect; and Brunelleschi's presence, combined with the stimulus of a well-placed host like Tomaso Pecori, meant that the group also encouraged a note of rivalry or competition. In a city already famous for its verbal dexterity, arts, and wit, the Pecori-Brunelleschi circle could not have been anything but remarkable.

The conversations generated by just such a circle—one of the earliest of its type in Europe—would serve over the long term to help revolutionize the traditional medieval view of the artist as artisan: a craftsman who, however skilled or able, worked nevertheless with his hands and so lived from his manual labor. Down to the sixteenth century, princes and rich patrons expected painters to decorate saddles, shields, banners, and paraphrenalia for fêtes, as well as to paint portraits and religious pictures; and sculptors—but not painters—were often full-scale members of a major influential trade guild, the corporation of Silk or Por Santa Maria merchants, but only because this association included the craftsmen skilled in working with gold and gold objects. Like Brunelleschi and Donatello, sculptors were often first apprenticed and trained as goldsmiths. Thus, in traditional occupational terms, Grasso was perforce a man of lower social and economic standing, and a shorter version of the story (*Palatino*, 200) flatly asserts that "compared to the others, he was a man of lowly condition" (*era di bassa condizione a rispetto de gli altri*). Called a *legnaiuolo*, a carpenter or woodworker in more general terms, he was doubtless inscribed, whatever his talents, in the lower or more humble guild of carpenters.

Yet quite apart from the significance of the social breadth of Pecori's guests, among whom there was sincere admiration for the skills of a woodcarver such as Grasso, the very first sentence of the story (in the Italian) is already striving to dignify the skills of the master craftsmen in the group by noting that they were connected with the arts that mixed manual dexterity with intellect and imagination (*maestri d'alcune arti miste e d'ingegno*), "such as painters, goldsmiths, sculptors, and woodcarvers." This Florentine circle, then, marked an early moment in the history of the artist, as he evolved in his identity from craftsman to a more elevated *persona*; but the struggle, so to speak, for the dignity of the artist was to pass over into the sixteenth and seventeenth centuries, when the great and successful artists acceded to the status of "gentlemen," while the common run of artist-craftsmen long held a lesser place and dignity. Precisely, however, because the Pecori-Brunelleschi circle was an early and pivotal group, we may assume that it was subject to subtle social and moral strains. Indeed, I suspect that the coherence of the group derived in part from the redoubtable Brunelleschi, a chameleon-like figure who navigated back and forth between two social worlds: the governing world of Tomaso Pecori and Giovanni di Messer Francesco Rucellai (another member of the circle) and the servitor's world of the gifted artisan, Grasso. Brunelleschi knew how to deal with the *Operari*, the committee of oligarchs, merchants, and great guildsmen who supervised the continuing work of building and decoration for the cathedral of Florence. But being himself a goldsmith, sculptor, budding architect, and draughtsman, he was also thoroughly familiar with the resources, ways, and vocabulary of the medieval and Renaissance workshop. In 1409, perhaps only his famous contemporary, Lorenzo Ghiberti, another goldsmith, sculptor, and art theorist, approached Brunelleschi in his ability to traffic both with artist-craftsmen (like Grasso) and with eminent merchants and politicians. But Brunelleschi's well-known quarrels and impatience reveal that he was also an unquiet presence. Something—ambition, an explosive brilliance, insecurity, or his biochemistry—moved him to rivalry and excellence, to excel. The fact of hailing in part from the world of the workshop—despite his father, Ser Brunellesco—would also have been a spur for him in the presence of men like Tomaso Pecori and Giovanni Rucellai, whom he spent his life impressing. And if he needed models of this sort closer to home, there were the men on his mother's side of the family, the Spini, one of the city's most distinguished lineages.

Well then, enter the young, likable, and talented Grasso—big, fat, surely flattered to belong to such a company, therefore a trifle shy and not altogether sure of himself. Is he already fearful of Brunelleschi, for whom he seems to entertain a degree of hero-worship? But then he fails to turn up at one of their suppers. After the meal, therefore, gathering around the fireplace, noting his absence, and feeling most undeservedly snubbed, they turn on him. They decide to teach him a lesson. And we know what happens next. But *do* we know? Do we understand the authority and impact of the devices unleashed against him, calculated to make him think that he is not who he thinks he is? He is, it appears, a touch simple, but this is not at all obvious, "for he was no fool." On the contrary, he seems to have a strong personality, if we judge both by his extraordinary reputation as a craftsman and by his swift, decisive flight from Florence at the close of the story. In conformity with all the customs and expectations of the day, this

big unmarried man in his mid-twenties, or older, lives with his
mother. Even after marriage he would have moved his wife into
the same household, again because this was Florentine practice,
in keeping with the demands of economic wisdom and family feeling. Yet no sooner does he discover the prank than he flees from
his home, city, and country, without consulting his mother or any
of his relatives. This was not the action of a weak character or personality. He was seized by a sense of shame that overwhelmed all
family feeling. Private sense and sensitivity gave way to public
mortification. To be made the laughingstock of the community, "in
a hundred circles of gossip throughout Florence," made for a
degradation which could not be relieved by private remedies.

The task now is to establish how exactly so strong a character,
so individual a personality, could have been driven to the point
where, for the better part of some thirty-six hours, he verged on
believing that he was no longer *il Grasso*, but rather someone else.
We may even doubt his alleged simplicity—attested, in any case,
only by Brunelleschi; for in a rudely practical world, such as early
Quattrocento Florence was, any oddity or meditative bent was
likely to be perceived as "simplicity." There were no airy philoso-
phers in the Florence of that day; at that moment, even the
humanists were a down-to-earth lot; and Marsilio Ficino was still
nearly two generations away.

The supreme architect of the entire trick, Brunelleschi, begins
it by softening Grasso up with an alarming message regarding his
own mother: she is on the brink of death. In a superstitious and
death-ridden society, with its appalling cycles of plague and other
epidemics of the late fourteenth century, this is a curiously brave
and brazen lie on Brunelleschi's part. Within the hour, being mys-
teriously locked out of his house, Grasso has a good reason for

thinking that *his* mother has returned from their place in the country and is in the house, from whence he also hears a voice sounding
disturbingly like his own. From this moment on, everything moves
like clockwork and he is given little or no time really to think
about things. Already called "Matteo" from inside his house,
Grasso suddenly sees Donatello, who hurries casually by, saying,
"Good evening, Matteo, are you looking for Grasso? He went into
his house a little while ago." The great prankster, Brunelleschi,
here turned playwright, has chosen the perfect time, the twilight
hour, when, because of dinner or supper, the streets are already
deserted and Grasso is unlikely to encounter anyone who recognizes him. The scenario is unfolding with incredible perfection.

And now Brunelleschi strikes with the full force of his instinc-
tive genius. One friend (Brunelleschi in his supposed distress),
the door at home locked from the inside, his mother's unan-
nounced return from the country, and a second friend (Donatello),
have all been used to stir up Grasso's emotions, in effect to
unnerve him. But there is nothing obviously public here: private
matters prevail. The face and force of public authority are still
lacking. Whereupon six guardsmen and an official from the presti-
gious merchants' high court, all doubtless in livery and led on by
an irate creditor's agent, arrive on the scene, identify him as
Matteo, a bad debtor, and arrest him.

That mysterious name "Matteo," with its near pun on *matto*
(crazy), keeps being directed at him. What is Grasso to do, as he
is overpowered by the six guardsmen? In trying to defend himself,
his most pained utterance, addressed to the unknown agent, is a
dignified cry of embarrassment: "you're committing a great injury
by shaming me like this" (*fai una gran villania a farmi questa
vergogna*), a statement shot through with public accents. For *ver-*

gogna—shame and embarrassment—is in the close link between private conscience and public space. *Villania* is injury as insult; it is verbal abuse, incivility, or discourtesy—a pointedly urban word with a pejorative undertow in its view of the countryman or peasant (*villano*), here assumed to be rude and uncivil in his ways. Grasso's sharpest pain, then, is at the point where the "I" or "me" is exposed to the glare of public attention and scrutiny. And that unrelenting pain or shame is to be exacerbated by the intervention of the Florentine commune: his arrest by public officials, the entry of his case into the records of the Mercanzia court, and finally jail and the company of other prisoners who also know him as Matteo.

After spending a sleepless night cut off from the comforting, unofficial world of his own intimates, Grasso's hopes of returning to it are raised when, next morning, a member of his dinner group and close acquaintance, the patrician Giovanni Rucellai, arrives at the court building, looks into the jail, sees Grasso, and, at the moment of eye contact, coldly pretends not to recognize him. Again the script. Stunned, Grasso engages Rucellai in a cagey exchange. But the mode of disclosure, in the course of this brief give-and-take, is all in the use of pronouns that cannot truly be rendered in English. Seeing Grasso grin at him and noting his craftsman's garb, Rucellai speaks but automatically uses the verb form for the familiar pronoun and patronizes him with the epithet "partner" (*compagno*): "Why do you laugh, partner?" Grasso prefaces his business with a deferential expression, *uom dabbene*, something like "Honorable man" or "Good Sir, do you happen to know a fellow [etc.]," and then employs the respectful pronoun of the second person plural, *voi*: the "you" fit for the sort of person who, formally at any rate, is entitled to status respect. But Rucellai remains with the familiar pronoun, *tu*: the *you* or *thou* employed by speakers with their servants, children, workers, tenant farmers, and other social inferiors, or used between equals when these were on familiar terms. The premises of the Mercanzia court held prisoners who were debtors, not jailbirds or common criminals, as Rucellai well knew; so he would not have used the *tu* form with, for instance, Grasso's co-prisoner, the judge (unless, of course, they were close friends); and since he affects to know neither the woodcarver nor the invented "Matteo," his immediate choice of pronouns has to be based on Grasso's artisanal dress and body language. Their pronominal exchange confirms that the two men stand on different sides of a social divide.

The moment Grasso is "arrested" and jailed, he loses the mobility —his ambivalent rise in status—which he enjoys among the members of his dinner circle. He is removed from private to public space, from those who know him to those who do not. The social lineaments of his pronominal exchange with Rucellai, therefore, again come forth, but now in the most significant encounter during his hours of captivity—in his meeting and conversations with the unnamed judge or jurisconsult, also referred to as "the doctor [of law]," though we consistently keep to "judge" in our translation.

Once in jail, even if only for a day or two and for debt, any lower guildsman would soon be made aware of his humble status; but not the judge, who in talking to Grasso automatically uses the familiar pronoun, whereas the woodcarver replies with the respectful *voi*. In fact, his very first word to the judge is a titular expression of respect, *Messere* (*mio-sire*, "My lord"). Grasso claims to know exactly who the man is, but even had he known nothing about him, he would have recognized the judge's status by his dress, specifically by the fur trimming then worn by doctors of law. No casual encounter this, it brought the woodcarver smack up against the world of elite learning: Latin, the law, literature, and the classics—a world which enjoyed then an authority and reputation for which there is no parallel in modern times, unless it be in the aura or kudos which occasionally attaches to Nobel-prize scientists. When, therefore, the unnamed dignitary speaks to him with understanding and sympathy, Grasso, in his despair and confusion, is instantly moved to take him into his confidence; and so he draws the judge aside and tells him all. In the absence of a priest and in the eyes of "a poor artisan," as Grasso calls himself, who could best throw light on his weird transformation of identity if not a learned man? Yet even as he begins his tale, while fighting "back his tears," he begs the judge never to reveal the matter to anyone. So apart from the question of his identity, Grasso's chief worry is his fear of public shame and ridicule; and this returns us to the question of public space in Grasso's life.

How does the woodcarver know about the judge? There is no reason to doubt his claim about this. As we are to learn toward the end of the story, certain members of Grasso's dinner circle were acquainted with him and he must have come up in their conversation, particularly because he seems to have had a name for literary—and perhaps some humanist—learning. In 1409, some of the members of such an alert circle would undoubtedly have heard of men like Coluccio Salutati, Giovanni Gherardi da Prato, Lionardo Bruni, and of all the Florentine jurisconsults of the day. Furthermore, judges and law experts (*doctores*) had their professional beat in and around the streets and squares that Grasso also knew and frequented, because his workshop on the Piazza di San Giovanni was within 250 meters of the principal court venues: the episcopal court in the immediate view of his workshop, the Mercanzia (in a corner of the main government square), in addition to the regular courts situated behind the Mercanzia and the main government palace. Judges and *doctores* could be easily picked out in the streets. Grasso himself, we are told, was quite likely known by sight, but not otherwise, by several of his co-prisoners.

Our subject is the public or communal dimension of social space: specifically, the functioning of such space as a maker and conveyer of meaning. Knowing the judge both by sight and reputation, the woodcarver may filter an image of him through his dinner group, where the man has been talked about. But he also takes the image from his own immediate world of streets and squares: the public world which he, the woodcarver, both fears and loves, trusts and must distrust too. For just as it may recognize and reward him, so it may also turn on him in scoffing laughter and derision ("I will be considered crazy and children will run after me"). In his self-division and harrowing disorientation, he turns for help to the kindly judge, as if to privatize him a bit, to snatch him away from the inimical part of the public world; but his instincts also tell him that he is taking his mental life into his hands, and to be sure he is. The judge's legal and classical learning—as in his references to Apuleius, Actaeon, Ulysses, and Circe—is part of that objective world which Grasso may look upon, but which also, as a part of the judge, looks back at him. Public and private realities will not come apart: they are inextricably linked, in Grasso too. Facing the Baptistery and lying a stone's throw from the cathedral, his own workshop is situated in one of the most public and communal of all Florentine squares, the square of the city's patron saint, St. John the Baptist. Hence the workshop is itself a semi-public place and space, where

228

patrons, prospective customers, friends, collaborating artisans, the curious, and others all come to commission work, to look around, to talk, and to make inquiries. And this traffic, beginning from the time of his boyhood years as an apprentice to a master from near the New Market, has molded Grasso as much as anything. Even his private world—home, conscience, and consciousness—is a shadowy public world. Thence his terror of shame and derision, of public degradation. Owing to the social structures of Renaissance urban life, much the same is also true of men like Brunelleschi, Tomaso Pecori, and Giovanni Rucellai. We may remember that in our first story, *Ricciarda*, the lady's great fear and fury have to do with the threat of dishonor and public shame that hang over herself and her children. In *Bianco Alfani*, Bianco is in effect destroyed—aged and rendered pitiable—by his public disgrace and humiliation. In the fourteenth and fifteenth centuries, the whole practice of *pittura infamante* (defamatory painting) in urban Italy, the large portrayal on public buildings of traitors and other criminals, often depicted hanging upside down and with their names in captions, was a special genre based upon the powerful sense of shame—the public sensitivity—of citizens.

Grasso's exchange with the judge, then, for all his wish to keep it secret, is an exchange with the world of elite learning, with the law, and somehow—given the jurisconsult's person as magistrate—with Florence as an organized political community. Brunelleschi may be the story's first Judas, but the second one is surely the judge, who will delight Grasso's old supper companions with descriptions of his (laughable) distress. In Grasso's mind—in his reading of signs, words, people, and occurrences—the entire Florentine community is arrayed against him as Grasso and for him as Matteo. His encounter with the judge validates and deepens this view. One thing alone is missing: the complicity of that powerful institution, the Church. But this is now introduced—Brunelleschi has thought of everything—in the form of a priest, the rector of Santa Felicita, the parish church of the Mannini (Matteo's) family. If the judge's entry into Grasso's disgrace is the work of chance, the entry of the rector is pure calculation. Having seemed to rally the state against Grasso in his arrest and imprisonment, the conspirators now enlist the spiritual arm of the community. Matteo's brothers are, in any case, consummate actors. Put up to the mischief by Brunelleschi, one of them easily hoodwinks the priest, drawing him into their proceedings. The innocent man then steps in to counsel and comfort one of his supposed parishioners. Although the scene of his interview with Grasso speaks for itself, two points about it deserve emphasis. First, the priest's essential message is social, not religious. Like Matteo's brothers, he works on Grasso's sense of shame and urges him to be concerned, above all, about his and his family's honor. Public name and face seem to be all. Secondly, whereas the judge is tricky and accepting, the parish priest will have none of the woodcarver's imaginings or reservations. He simply insists that Grasso stop his nonsense and keep to the matter-of-fact world of Matteo. But where the judge, as literary intellectual, enters into Grasso's discourse and is complex, the priest is peremptory and bureaucratic. That he is confronted, as a minister of God, by a strange phenomenon is a fact that never crosses his mind. The matter for him is perfectly mundane: either Grasso *is* Matteo, or he belongs to that everyday occurrence of children laughing and jeering at fools and madmen in the streets of Florence ("you run the risk of having the children taunt you in the streets," etc.). Revealingly, too, as far as we can tell, it never occurs to Grasso—so terrestrial is his crisis—to seek the assistance of a man of the cloth. If there is anything truly religious in him, no trace of it appears in the story, apart from a single ritual outburst, "God help me."

The Mannini brothers live on the far side of the river (Arno), just a short distance from the Ponte Vecchio. When, therefore, the woodcarver is drugged and "Matteo" is, as it were, killed off, though "snoring like a pig" (in a parodic echo of the Circe allusion), he is carried back in the dark, some 750 meters, to his old haunts and house hard by the cathedral. Here, in the morning, his first act of consciousness as the returned Grasso is his recognition of that most public sound, the ringing of the cathedral bell. Next, in a reversal for us of Descartes' "cogito-ergo-sum" proposition, he recognizes his bedroom, his house, his bed; and these establish that he is Grasso. They are, therefore I am: that is, they are Grasso's, and they are all around me and under me, therefore I am Grasso. We see here, as he also touches his own arms and chest, a quite material view of the world, with the objects there both constituting it and circumscribing personal identity. But the public world too is already there: first, in the pealing of the great cathedral bell, a distinctive urban sound, marking the liturgical and social hours of the day with unfailing regularity; and secondly, at the very moment when he is repossessing his undivided self, in the use of a striking noun, as he "realized that he was in his own house, and his heart was suddenly filled with great joy, for it seemed he had become Grasso again and was master (*in signoria*) of all his possessions." We shall never know whether the word *signoria* was Grasso's, Brunelleschi's in his retelling of the story, or was added by others and filtered to the author through the oral tradition. No matter. The point is that it is perfectly consistent, in its pivotal position, with the deconstruction and reconstitution of Grasso. For the act of his refinding and taking hold of himself is metaphorically envisaged in political and public terms. *Signoria* was the term for dominion, rule, command, lordship, or fullness of political power and authority. In Florence, it was the routine word for the republic's supreme executive body, the Priors and Standard-bearer of Justice. These public officials were "the lords" (*signori*); collectively they were the *signoria*; they also exercised *signoria*. Lawyers and political thinkers held forth on the subject. But in our story, where it turns up only once, the word and metaphor occur just as Grasso's heart is brimming with such joy that he almost weeps. At this most private moment—emotion here revealing the man—he suddenly goes, or is seen to go, public: he again becomes the political lord of himself and of all his things (*ritornato . . . in signoria di ogni sua cosa*).

From the moment when the reborn Grasso leaves home for his shop, to find additional solidity and identity in his tools and workplace, he is being carefully watched by his friends, the pranksters. They fail to realize, however, that his material world, now that he has been returned to it, is giving him the strength to confront them: first those exceptional actors, the Mannini brothers, whom he handles with aplomb, then Brunelleschi and Donatello in the cathedral, and finally Matteo himself. Hanging between private wonder, bafflement, and dismay on the one side and public derision on the other, Grasso maintains his self-possession and refuses to fall into the new trap, as Brunelleschi and Matteo perfidiously recapitulate the whole course of events. In the course of what must have been a relatively long exchange, twice only—before and after Matteo's arrival—is Grasso trusting enough to expose himself and openly confess that "these are very strange things"; and the second time he at once concludes his part, at least, of the proceedings in the cathedral. There

is more, however, in the woodcarver's self-control than just the vital-
izing contact with his material world.

After the swift departure from his shop of the Mannini brothers,
Grasso feels the need to reflect on things. But instead of going
home to sort out his thoughts in private, he makes for that great
public forum, Santa Maria del Fiore, the cathedral. Why? Evidently
because he feels at home there too and because instinct tells him
that the way to his salvation, at least at this point, does not lie in
private retreat. Like his tools, bed, house, and shop keys, the community or public dimensions of social space must also help to put
an end to his self-division. The story itself rather says this at just
that point, for he goes to the cathedral the better to certify whether
he is Grasso or Matteo in the recognition of other men. Just as the
communal world, counterfeited by a conspiracy of his friends, had
verged on turning him into Matteo, so now it must also reconfirm
him as Grasso. Brunelleschi had drawn no fewer than twenty-two
men into his plot: Donatello, the young chaser of debtors, the six
guardsmen and the official from the Mercanzia, the clerk-attorney
and bursar (*notaio*) at the front desk of the court and prison, the
three Mannini brothers, the parish priest, Pecori, Rucellai,
Brunelleschi himself, and the six dinner companions (possibly
including Donatello) who carried Grasso back to his house on the
night of his drugging. On top of these there were the other co-prisoners and the judge, all innocently drawn into the world arrayed
against Grasso. Now, on his return to himself and his material
surroundings, Grasso—what shall we say?—knows in his bones
that this alienated world must be neutralized or won back by a
counter-validating *public* world. This explains the uncanny propri-
ety of the final setting in the most public of spaces, the cathedral:
Grasso's doing. Here, even as Brunelleschi and company toil to

trammel him in their new round of lies, they also accept him as Grasso the Woodcarver. The whole scene is a fusion of private and public worlds, of clear and ambiguous intentions. Indeed, my distinction between "private" and "public" may now be seen as a useful notion—but little more—for the purposes of analysis and description. For the truth is, it seems to me, that in some profound respect public and private were one in Renaissance Italy; that there was so much more of the public forum in private experience then, as to make for a mode of consciousness quite different from our own. The easy, semiotic combining of the sacred and secular also followed. Thus, as Brunelleschi and Matteo rise to the peak of their perfidy in Matteo's mendacious account of his dreaming, and a few people begin to collect around them, Brunelleschi, taking Grasso by the hand, moves his party to the church choir, where they sit down and ironically conclude their utterly secular business. Like St. Paul's cathedral in London circa 1600, Santa Maria del Fiore, some two centuries earlier, was also a place of gossip and a rendezvous for conducting worldly affairs.

Place and identity went together. At the point where Grasso was most Matteo, he was also farthest from his daily stomping ground, across the river in the house of the Mannini brothers. In the early fifteenth century, their parish church, Santa Felicita, stood on a small, quiet site by comparison with the spaces around the Baptistery and cathedral, where building and decorative work went on for years on a magnificent scale. This was the city's artistic-artisanal heart: the venue for Ghiberti's bronze doors, for the life-size statues of Nanni di Banco, Donatello, and others, and for Brunelleschi's great cathedral dome. All these men, as well as Grasso and many others, drew energy and identity from that vast public site and from Florence's civic commitments of those years. Teams

of workmen, scaffolding, great hammerblows, shouts, and the cart-
ing of large quantities of stone, brick, and timber all featured in the
lives of skilled artisans from the vicinity. Understandably, therefore, master craftsmen such as Ghiberti and the others come
through to us, both in their works and in more conventional historical documentation, as strong and vigorous personalities.

Despite the fierce assault on his identity, the fat woodcarver
was no pushover. Arguably and paradoxically, his determined
character and distinctive personality were the very traits by which
he was borne to the brink of madness. In order to achieve outstanding success in the busy Baptistery and cathedral areas of a
city that teemed with first-class artisans, a craftsman had to have
all the requisite public and street-wise qualities, in addition to
skills and talent, to overcome competitors and attract commissions. Here too was the secret enemy: for in the elaborate deception staged by Brunelleschi, the very workshops, streets, and
squares that had fashioned Grasso suddenly appear to turn against
him, because they are essential parts of *his* public world, a world
both friendly and hostile. But now the hostility wins out and the
work of his hands, like the evidence of the shop key, is denied, as
he is "arrested" by the Mercanzia guardsmen within the sight of
the Baptistery and cathedral. Thus, in a certain sense, his own
vigor and alertness—rifled in some measure from the impinging
world—go to undo him. In this connection, it is most important to
point out that despite any eccentricities in his personality, Grasso
is a man who conforms; he fully accepts his world; which is why
he is ready to be Matteo, if his social world so insists; and why,
after Rucellai's visit to the jail, he is moved to lamentation, since
he had always sought, as he says, to avoid debt, sticky situations,
"and a thousand other dangerous mistakes." The terror, then, of

his situation is that in having his small universe ranged against him—a universe already *in* him—he is thereby turned against himself. The particulars of this mode of self-division or alienation would be impossible, I suspect, in the cities of the modern world, because our social structures are too mobile, not nearly so sharp, solid, finite, and community-oriented; nor are they circumscribed by massive city walls within the sight of all inhabitants. We may go crazy or see our personalities eroded, but on other grounds and for other reasons than those connected with Grasso's thirty-six hours of consternation.

Owing to the details and length of this analysis, I risk obscuring the fact that Grasso's experience *as* Matteo is so traumatic that it changes his life fundamentally. Given the keen emotional attachment to city and neighborhood space in fifteenth-century Italy, for a Florentine craftsman of his sort to abandon Florence for Hungary is in some ritual sense to die and to be born again as a different man. Grasso's devastating shame suddenly renders his beloved city absolutely intolerable. He does not see how he can ever again live there with dignity. Toward the end of the story, a glancing and mysterious remark of his indicates something about his rage in reaction to the social pain (humiliation and shame) which had been inflicted upon him. He says to *maestro* Pellegrino ("wanderer"): "You have often talked to me about going with you to Hungary, and I've always said no. Now, on account of something that's happened to me and a disagreement I've had with my mother (*per certa differenza ch'io avuta con mia madre*) . . . I've decided to come away with you." And since, early in the story, we hear Brunelleschi, the friend who knew Grasso's ways perfectly, impersonating him and pretending to scold Monna Giovanna for getting back late from the country and for not having his supper ready, we

may assume that Grasso occasionally bullied her. I take it, therefore, that after the charade in the cathedral, he hurried out to
Polverosa, as the story tells us, to find out whether or not his
mother had been in Florence on the ill-fated night. Finding that
she had been at their country place all along, the full horror of the
prank strikes him, and suddenly he vents his anger on her for
delaying her return to the city. There ensues an ugly scene
between mother and son—demography would put her, Giovanna,
in her early to mid-forties at most—and Grasso rushes back into
Florence, only to flee from it, leaving little more than a curt letter
for her.

But apart from any possible rudeness with his mother, it is
worth observing, historically, that throughout the story our craftsman is a near model of social correctness: he is unfailingly civil,
even at the most distressing moments, and always uses the appropriate status terms and pronouns. Stretching back for more than
two hundred years, an intense and enclosed urban life, with its
myriad guilds and rich political culture, had taught Florentines
the necessity of civility in everyday give-and-take, all the more so,
evidently, where there was a high degree of rivalry, suspicion,
malice, and envy. We may therefore see Grasso as an exemplar of
civility among Florentine craftsmen and in this respect, too, as a
man who conformed fully to the established and expected ways of
his community.

At the close of the story, in fairness to Grasso, and having noted that luck (*fortuna*) had favored the plotters, the judge shrewdly
remarks that Brunelleschi employed such "forethought and
finesse" in unfolding the conspiracy (*tanta era stata la cautela e
l'ordine di Filippo*), "that no one could have seen through the
trick." To *fortuna* and social structure we must also ascribe the

fact that Grasso was a single man who—like Brunelleschi and Donatello—lived with his mother. If she or a wife or other relatives had been at home on the fatal night, the use of other and more difficult snares for trapping Grasso would have been necessary. Moved by his failure to return home, wife or relatives would have raised the alarm and made a search for the woodcarver that night, even "up in the stars."

Grasso's unmarried state returns us to our original questions: why the dinner party rounded on him and how they could have regarded the plot as humorous. The fact that he was single and lived with his mother made him no more vulnerable on this score than Brunelleschi, Donatello, and perhaps others in their circle. But as it happens, he combined this possible point of fragility with his youth (naiveté?), bulk, craftsman's dress, humble social circumstances, a touch of the upstart, and a shy or contemplative bent in upper-class company. From everything we know and can gather about the ambitious and show-offish Brunelleschi, Grasso was thus a sitting duck for him. Moreover, and quite remarkably, although they seem to be peers, since both are craftsmen and close friends, with only some six to eight years between them at most (Brunelleschi being the elder), there is a definite social gap between them. For late in the story, in their few direct exchanges, Brunelleschi uses the familiar form of the pronoun in address with Grasso, who replies instead with the respectful *voi*. Now either this was so, or the oral tradition made it so, seeing something here that we, in modern times, do not easily see. At any rate, there was a relationship here *de haut en bas*; and this again goes to indicate the woodcarver's social vulnerability in that shifty dinner pack of his. Brunelleschi's education, father, financial means, social contacts, Spini relatives, wit, and—I suppose—general bearing put

him socially above Grasso. In 1425 he even served in the Florentine republic's highest ruling council, the *Signoria*. Did he wear
the garments of a craftsman? I suspect that he dressed both up
and down, depending upon his tasks and the occasion.

In view of Grasso's dramatic flight from Florence, Brunelleschi
must have felt some guilt or uneasiness afterward. In time, however, the great Florentine soldier of fortune up in Hungary, Pippo
Spano (Filippo Scolari: 1369–1426), would save the day for both
of them. Taking the woodcarver into his train as a master craftsman, he raised him in due course to the role of military "engineer," and in the fashion of many adventuresome Florentine merchants, Grasso returned to the banks of the Arno a changed man,
a rich artisan loaded down with social success. Only thus could he
face Florence, and now Brunelleschi could begin to joke and
boast about his having made the woodcarver rich, famous (even in
a hundred years' time), and one who, thanks to a virtuoso deception, had also got to know "the emperor of the world" (the Holy
Roman Emperor, Sigismund), Filippo Scolari, "and many other
great princes and lords." In his visits to Florence, Grasso made a
point of seeking out Brunelleschi. Did he avoid and now truly
snub the others? Perhaps so. In one of those intricate but common
psychological twists, he could transfer to Brunelleschi, his aggressor, the glow and good feeling of his foreign success, while still
resenting all the others, and especially the Mannini brothers (up a
good social notch from him), who had made such an ass of him.

That the joke was seen in all its particulars as being uproari-
ously funny is indisputable. The story itself provides the evidence.
In the late eighteenth century, one of its earliest commentators,
Domenico Maria Manni, still saw the story as comical and regarded
Grasso as a simpleton. This view persisted until the second half of

the nineteenth century and then began to break down, with the advent of bourgeois democracy, the "rise of the common man," and the cult of the individual. But if we are to understand the time and place of the story, and the story itself, we must strive to penetrate its humor.

The Italian reputation for cruelty in Renaissance Europe, as noted for instance by the French, has to be charged to an urban folk, because foreign traffic with Italians was overwhelmingly with men from Venice, Genoa, Milan, Florence, Rome, Bologna, Padua, Naples, and perhaps Lucca or Siena. These were a city people for whom success lay in bearing the best possible name and face into the public places of their urban clusters. To be strong morally and psychologically was to be strong in the daily glare of streets and communal life. This was especially so in Florence, city of astute merchants, clever politicians, ingenious fiscal strategems, golden words, meticulous accounting procedures, and devious string-pulling for favor, place, and office. Into this world came big, fat, ungainly Grasso, a brilliant craftsman but still a man who lived from the work of his hands. And there he was, the dinner associate of well-connected figures like Tomaso Pecori (twice a member of the *Signoria*) and Giovanni Rucellai, and the companion of one of the keenest minds in Florence, Brunelleschi, who also wrote some rather polished verse. Should Grasso not be proud to frequent the likes of such men? Surely, therefore, he knew who he was and what he was. How could he not know, unless he was odd or even simple? And if he was odd, would it not be a good thing to straighten him out?

Not practical jokes, which after all did no bodily or material harm, but rather bankruptcy, poverty, disease, crushing lawsuits, or death and damnation: these were the serious matters in a city

whose population had plummeted by nearly two-thirds over the
course of the previous sixty years (1348–1408), dropping from
about 110,000 people to something like a mere 45,000—the result
of plagues and other deadly epidemics, which occasionally exter-
minated whole households in the space of a few months. In such
circumstances, in a society keenly watchful of all public action, a
burly artisan must know who he was, whatever the tricks deployed
against him. His tongue must be able to distinguish mellifluously
between Manetto Ammannatini (Grasso) and Matteo Mannini, for
all their deceitful sound similarities. And he must not turn the
question of identity into a tricky or metaphysical business, as
Grasso had verged on doing. Identity was a thing of the here and
now: of my house, my room, my bed, my flesh, my tools, my workshop, my keys, my friends (?), plus the streets and familiar spaces
of my neighborhood. If you could not be one and indivisible in
the midst of so much tangible reality, then you must be a pro-
foundly comic figure, fit to be chased down the streets by laughing and baying children. At that point too, children—and Grasso's
dinner company—came together as a merry group, their collective good spirits recharged and renewed.

BIBLIOGRAPHIC COMMENTARY

Unless otherwise indicated, all the studies referred to below are listed in the bibliography which follows immediately after this commentary. I shall therefore cite only the last names of authors, followed by a date. Example: Rochon (1975), or in some cases, depending upon the sentence, (Rochon, 1975).

Amid so much talk, from me too (Martines, 1985), about "narrative," "representation," and "the linguistic turn" in current historical practice, I want to say first of all that some aspects of my reasoning in the six essays carry the marks of an American *maître à penser*, Kenneth Burke, with whom I studied many years ago. Three of his books are seminal: *Language as Symbolic Action* (1966), *A Grammar of Motives* (1969), and *A Rhetoric of Motives* (1969). They do not appear in the bibliography.

The best and most detailed general study of fifteenth-century Italian fiction is still a rich old inquiry: Di Francia (1924). Strict emphasis on the "greats" in the long tradition of Italian literary scholarship has tended to keep scholars away from study of the so-called minor writers and poets. Gentile Sermini and Piero

Veneziano, for example, do not even merit an entry in the *Dizionario critico* (1986), though the former just makes it into the *Dizionario enciclopedico* (1966–70). The ancient prejudice against the *minori* now seems, however, to be on its way out.

ONE

The Real in the Imaginary: *Ricciarda*

The text of *Ricciarda* appears in several editions. I used Gherardi (1867 and 1975) and Ferrero and Doglio (1975).

Owing to the passage of time and place, this tale has lapsed partly into code for us. The central figure, Ricciarda, can be fully understood only through a grasp of the evolving love poetry in the Petrarchan line: see Martines (1993), and the love poetry in Lanza (1973–75), Frati (1908), and Boiardo (1962). *Ricciarda* should be studied in the context of the history of women, on which see Klapisch-Zuber (1990a).

Gender relations in Renaissance Florence: on this topic see mainly Klapisch-Zuber (1985), which includes most but not all of the studies in her more recent collection (1990). There is also much material in Fiorato (1980), King (1991), Kirshner (1978), Kuehn (1991), La Roncière (1988), Martines (1974), Mazzi (1991), Migiel and Schiesari (1991), and Strocchia (1989). The fascinating letters of Datini (1977) and Strozzi (1877) bring us face to face with two Tuscan women. Where are their epistolary equivalents in, say, Siena, Milan, or Venice? The sheer wealth of Florentine documentation may continue to overshadow our view of gender relations elsewhere in Italy, even perhaps Venice, where Chojnacki (1988), Migiel and Schiesari (1991), Romano (1988), and especially Ruggiero (1985) are drawing away the veils.

The obedience of women and children is broached by Alberti (1969) Certaldo (1945), Klapisch-Zuber (1985), La Roncière (1988), and Ross (1975).

The following discuss the family and marriage from various viewpoints: again Alberti (1969), Bellomo (1970), Brucker (1971), Herlihy and Klapisch-Zuber (1978), Klapisch-Zuber (1985), Kuehn (1991), La Roncière (1977), Molho (1993), and Pandimiglio (1985).

On the chastity of women: Kirshner (1978), also Bk. IV of the *Decor Puellarum* (1461), which has directions and admonitions regarding the passivity, comportment, and bodily movement of girls.

Family honor and reputation, basic themes, are examined in Alberti (1969), Bec (1967), Kirshner (1978), Kuehn (1985), Martines (1963), Tenenti (1987), and Weissman (1982).

Average age at marriage: Herlihy and Klapisch-Zuber (1978).

Feud and vendetta: particularly relevant here is the article by John Larner in Martines (1972); also Brucker (1971), Kent and Kent (1981), and Kuehn (1991), all of which have case material on family feuding.

On the rural estates of wealthy Florentines: Herlihy and Klapisch-Zuber (1978).

The sexual experience of Florentine males may be inferred from a Venetian study (Ruggiero, 1985), from Bongi (1863) on the reasons for permissive attitudes towards prostitution in Lucca, and more directly from a recent Florentine inquiry (Mazzi, 1991). There is additional material on male sexuality and domestic servants in Klapisch-Zuber (1985) and Guarducci and Ottanelli (1982).

Florentine widows: Chabot (1988). The subject is to be treated in a dissertation by one of my doctoral students at U.C.L.A., J. E. Treble. There is a pertinent study of pious women in the fourteenth century: Papi (1990).

The essay's concluding views concerning Ricciarda, her masculine side, and the great gender divide, I take from my own current and forthcoming work on the love poetry of the Italian Renaissance: Martines (1993, and also "L'Amour et l'histoire").

TWO
Ceremonies of Identity: *Scopone*

I had recourse to several editions of this text: Sermini (1968), Borlenghi (1962) and Varese (1955).

In quantity, though not in quality, historical scholarship on Siena lags well behind work on Florence. Bowsky (1978, 1981) has given us excellent archive-based books on fourteenth-century Siena. For the thirteenth century, with its pointed inserts on the Buonsignori, Waley (1991) is certainly to be recommended. Ascheri (1985) deals with fifteenth-century Siena and has a useful bibliography, where I would single out the studies by A. K. Isaacs and the two articles in English by David Hicks. I should also call attention to the ambitious study by Cohn (1988) and the imaginative short synthesis by Hook (1979)

The Buonsignori claimed time-honored imperial privileges and were Siena's leading bankers in the thirteenth century, as noted by Waley (1991). See the entry in Repetti (1833–46) on the old fortress of Monteantico, a former feud of Siena's once-powerful Tolomei family.

Relations between city and country, *cittadini* (burghers) and *contadini* (rural folk), one of the most important of all topics in Italian history, has been increasingly studied in recent times. It would be pretentious here to cite the highly specialized and multi-volumed works by Elio Conti and Charles de la Roncière on parts of Tuscany. Instead, I adduce studies in a more accessible and generalizing mode: Balestracci (1984), Cherubini (1974), Mazzi and Ravezzi (1983), and Farolfi (1977) for the Bologna region. For the large lineaments, but for much detail too, Jones (1980) merits particular study, especially his book-length introducion.

Literary scholarship on relations between *cittadini* and *contadini* is also important and extremely revelatory. Here, interestingly, French scholarship rules the field: see Bec (1980, essay on *contadino*), Fiorato (1976), Plaisance (1985 and 1986), and Rochon (1976–77). These studies provide a detailed picture of urban attitudes toward the neighboring peasantry.

Courtly language: Martines (1993, and "Ritual Language," forthcoming).

Ritual activity in urban life has its best introduction and analysis in Trexler (1980).

Status pronouns: on this see my note in the bibliographic commentary for the essay on *The Fat Woodcarver*.

Surnames among rural Tuscans: Klapisch-Zuber (1985).

My information about the spear-throwing Florentine nobleman comes from Mazzi (1991), pp. 124-26. Exceptionally here I give the page references because this fascinating study does not have an index.

THREE
A Ritual Cleansing: *Friar and Priest*

Here, as with the five other stories in this book, I had no idea at all of what my analysis would reveal. I selected this tale, as I did the others, because it seemed to me intriguing and resonant. Only as I worked on it did I come to realize how uncannily it expresses some of the sexual and social-structural tensions of the day.

In working on the essay, I used the following editions of the text: Arienti (1981), Borlenghi (1962), Chiarini (1982), and Ferrero and Doglio (1975).

Giovanni Sabadino degli Arienti, the author of this tale, is accorded ample discussion in *Dizionario* (1960); see also *Dizionario enciclopedico* (1966–70). Gundersheimer (1973) has the information on Arienti's patronage contacts at Ferrara. The condition and general situation of the writer in Renaissance Italy is most convincingly sketched out in French scholarship: Bec (1986), and Fiorato and Margolin (1989).

Monte San Savino gets a brief history in Repetti (1833–46).

On country people (*forenses*) and the question of urban citizenship, see Kirshner (1973) and just about any major collection of municipal statutes of the period, of which I list two: Caggese (1921) and *Statuta* (1778–83).

The clergy, clerical misconduct, and anti-clerical feeling. This major topic has a good point of departure in Bizzocchi (1987), whose masterly analysis of lay patronage and the close social links between the Church and temporal power reveal the profound worldliness of the ecclesiastical order. In this perspective, clerical hypocrisy and delinquency suddenly seem to be almost inevitable and a part of the routine order of things. For additional material

see Brucker (1991), Hay (1977), and *Storia* (1986). A virulent
contemporary attack on mendicant friars is contained in Bracciolini (1946). A scatter of incidents, centering on clerical misconduct, may be found in the anecdotes concerning a fifteenth-
century parish priest: Folena (1953).

Florentine homosexuality has been studied at length in an outstanding doctoral dissertation: Rocke (1989), and one hears that it
is forthcoming as a book. Ruggiero (1985) has an important chap-
ter on sodomy in Venice. We need equivalent studies for say
Rome, Genoa, Ferrara, Bologna, and even Perugia, where in the
fourteenth century there was a group or school of homosexual
poets. Bernardino da Siena (1880) noted approvingly that the
Genoese were hard on homosexuals. My remarks on Lucca are
based on the annotations in Bongi (1863).

Patronage in the Bentivoglio circle at Bologna has an interest-
ing collection of studies: Basile (1984). An important old book,
Frati (1908), provides considerable information on poets, literary
activity, and literary friendships in Bologna, in addition of course
to its invaluable verse texts. See Malinowska (1966) on political
organization in fifteenth-century Bologna.

On love and courtly language: Martines (1993, and forthcoming, "L'Amour et l'histoire"). The Boiardo verse quotations are in
Boiardo (1962), pp. 3, 8, 11.

FOUR
The Wages of Social Sin: *Bianco Alfani*

The adaptability of this story may be gauged from the fact that the
Sienese writer, Gentile Sermini (1968), author of *Scopone*, has a

tale in his collection (no. 25) about the son of a rich peasant, the pushy Mattano of Siena, who is tricked into believing that he has been elected to Siena's highest office. In fact, he is despised by those who dupe him, a party of well-connected young men from Siena.

In working on *Bianco Alfani*, I employed the following editions: Manni (1782), *Novelle* (1804), Borlenghi (1962), and Ferrero and Doglio (1975). Short but trenchant, the basic study of the text and its authorship is still Di Francia (1924), who, basing himself on a fifteenth-century copyist, assigns a date of 1433 to the story. Colleagues in the historical profession may ask why I did not myself consult the appropriate manuscripts in Florence. The same question could also be raised about three other tales in this book. The short answer is that I am not a philologist and that I have other things to do as a historian.

Pullini (1958) and Lanza (1989) serve as creditable literary introductions to the whole spirit of the practical joke in the fifteenth century, at all events in Florence.

The fundamental study, referred to in my text, and accounting for the reality of all the Florentines in the story, is Rossi (1930), originally published in 1901; but see also Manni (1762a). Rossi draws on a variety of archival sources, chiefly the *Catasto*.

The play of antagonism and distrust in the everyday consciousness of republican Florence is astutely caught by Weissman (1982), the first historian, I believe, to verge on talking about an out-and-out culture of quotidian animosity in Florence.

The oral features of Florentine social life get some treatment but no analysis in Beccherini (1948), Branciforte (1990), Flamini (1891), Lanza (1981), Levi (1914), and Rochon (1975). The subject deserves a dissertation.

Pronouns in fifteenth-century address and conversation: I have looked in vain for studies on this theme, though at one point Weissman (1982) grazes it.

Some technical terms, administrative and political, are defined in Guidi (1981) and Rezasco (1881).

On members of the Alfani lineage as leading Guelf bankers in the later thirteenth century, see Davidsohn (1956–68), Vol. IV.

Sources on particular *personaggi*, apart from Rossi (1930), are the following: on Ser Martino Martini, see Marzi (1910); on Niccolò Tinucci, see Tinucci (1974); on the poet-herald, *messer* Antonio, see Branciforte (1990); on Isaù Martellini, see Archivio di stato di Firenze, *Catasto*, 67, fols. 63r-69r. Public thanks are due here to Dr. Gino Corti for checking the last of these items for me.

The insult, "to be a Bianco Alfani," is documented by Rossi (1930).

Debtors and debtors' prison: here is a topic which awaits sustained, large-scale study. Legal norms governing debtors and bankruptcy are spelled out in *Statuta* (1778–83), I, Bk. 3. See Fanti (1978) on charitable assistance provided to imprisoned debtors in Bologna.

Regarding prostitution, I refer readers to my bibliographic commentary on the sources for the *Giacoppo* essay.

On the *Catasto*, see Conti (1984).

On average age at marriage, see the commentaries for the *Ricciarda* and *Giacoppo* essays.

On feud and vendetta, see the commentary for the *Ricciarda* essay.

Political wheeling and dealing in quattrocento Florence gets sustained analysis in Kent (1978) and Molho (1979).

On the importance of secrecy in personal and family affairs, see Weissman (1982), Alberti (1969), plus Certaldo and Morelli in Branca (1986).

Regarding investment in the *Monte*, see Conti (1984), Martines (1988a), and especially Molho (1994).

FIVE
A Patriotic Prank: *Giacoppo*

The text of this tale appears in Borlenghi (1962), Chiarini (1982), Del Lungo (1923), Fatini (1929), Ferrero and Doglio (1975), and Medici (1965). Del Lungo was the first to publish it in his original edition of 1865. Fatini still assumed the tale to be anonymous.

In view of the well-known element of *campanilismo* in Italian history, the patriotic undercurrent in this tale seems to me self-evident.

The notion of religious credulity as an unworthy or base *forma mentis* appears everywhere in early Renaissance literature, in fiction as in verse, ranging from Boccaccio to Piovano Arlotto, Luigi Pulci, and Lorenzo de' Medici. But it has yet to be grasped as historical subject matter, where the aim would be to see whether or not the "simple-minded" faith under attack is usually and hence ideologically assigned to "inferior" folk such as women, peasants, lowly tradesmen, or the enemy (e.g., the Sienese).

The current of strong feeling against friars was often directed against Franciscans, but all the regular orders were subject to sharp criticism. See my bibliographical commentary for the essay on *Friar and Priest*, under "The clergy [and] clerical misconduct."

On age and aging in Renaissance Florence, see Herlihy (1969).

The incidence of adultery among women in Renaissance Italy is unstudied and likely to remain so as a serial enterprise, owing to spotty source material. How can we generalize from occasional instances of female adultery? But because they were watched by relatives, friends, and neighbors, and stood to forfeit their dowries, adultery among women of the propertied classes must have been exceptional. For them at least it was far too risky. Even Ruggiero (1985), in a systematic study of police and court records at Venice, found relatively few cases of adulterous women from the middle and upper classes.

The character Meina introduces the subject of prostitution, on which see Bongi (1863), Brucker (1971), Larivaille (1975), Lawner (1987), Masson (1975), Mazzi (1991), Ruggiero (1985), and Trexler (1981). Mazzi is now the most detailed study for Florence.

The social significance of the period's grand amatory language is examined in Martines (1993 and 1994).

The intellectual and social world of Lorenzo de' Medici's youthful years has been closely studied by Rochon (1963).

Whether or not sacrilege was ever seen in Renaissance Italy on the scale and in the manner of Friar Antonio's misconduct must remain a matter of pure speculation. My concern, however, is not with sacrilegious actions as such but rather with Lorenzo de' Medici's imaginative countenancing of the friar's astonishing cynicism.

SIX
Who Does He Think He Is? *The Fat Woodcarver*

Truth *is* stranger than fiction. In French scholarship on Italian Renaissance literature, one of the two leading gurus, André Rochon, holds that we shall not know whether the plot against Grasso ever really took place until we have "external" documentation for it. He is thus skeptical of Manetti's external claim in his *Vita di Filippo Brunelleschi.* Since we have more accounts of the Grasso story than we do of a thousand historical incidents, I hold that the story is the account of a real incident, until we find external documentation to the contrary.

The *Novella del Grasso Legnaiuolo (The Story of the Fat Woodcarver)* reaches us in at least five versions and fourteen different manuscripts: these include ten variant copies of a shorter account (one-third the length of Manetti's), an edited example different from the ten, two versions in verse, and the Manetti redaction, here offered in translation. I relied chiefly on the Tanturli and De Robertis edition (Manetti, 1976), but also used Contini (Manetti, 1976a), Borlenghi (1962), Chiarini (1982), and Varese (1955). See also Barbi (1893). The short version appears in an early English translation by Thomas Roscoe (Pettoello, 1930). There have been two recent English translations of the Manetti text, Martone (Manetti, 1991) and Smarr (Manetti, 1983), but I must enter a strong recommendation against use of the Martone translation.

I could find no analysis of this story by a historian. Grasso's plight has seemed unworthy of qualifying for any historical dignity. The best and longest study by far is Rochon (1975), though the first half is tenaciously philological. Two short pieces are rather suggestive: Di Blasi (1985) and the article by Borsellino (1989). Di Blasi usefully employs the metaphor of the mirror: Grasso *is* what he sees himself being in the reactions of others, hence society in quattrocento Florence is mirror-like.

Dennett (1991), in line with current materialist thought, has made a cogent attack on the self as a continuous and central quiddity.

The contours of Florentine feeling and thinking may be gleaned from the following sources and studies: Alberti (1969), Bec (1967 and 1981), Branca (1986), Brucker (1967, 1971, and 1983), Da Bisticci (1926), Klapisch-Zuber (1985) Kuehn (1991), Lanza (1973–75), Martines (1963), Molho (1993), Molho and Sznura (1986), Sapori (1945), Trexler (1980), and Weissman (1982).

The world of the Florentine artisan may in part be pieced together from Wackernagel (1981), Saalman (1970), and Goldthwaite (1980); but my general interpretation is already in Martines (1988, first ed., 1979). Najemy (1983) deals with guild life.

Brunelleschi's life is set forth of course in Manetti (1976). On Pecori and Rucellai, see Rochon (1975). On Donatello, see *Dizionario biografico* (1960–).

Regarding the nature and importance of the merchants' high court (the *Mercanzia*), there is Bonolis (1901); but he neglects entirely the Mercanzia's strong political presence and, through its six *consoli*, the court's active participation in government. In this connection, consult Guidi (1981). Proper study of the Mercanzia is one of the great lacunae in Florentine historical scholarship.

Pronouns in address are, as far as I can tell, completely unstudied in Florentine social history. Herein lies a tale. The same may be said about the semiotics of dress, particularly as regards the dress of petty tradesmen and the lower orders generally. One of my doctoral students, C. C. Frick, is currently completing a dissertation on dress in fifteenth-century Florence, but her focus is the upper class.

The addenda and marginal notes of two manuscripts indicate that the unnamed judge was Giovanni Gherardi da Prato, the author of *Ricciarda*. Manetti's text also refers to him as *dottore*, meaning a doctor of law. The odd thing is, however, that he never turns up in any of the documentary sources that would throw some light on his activity as a judge or jurisconsult: see Martines (1968).

Urban, neighborhood, and political space is a complex system of signification. Study of this historical phenomenon is a recent development. There is nothing on Florence to compare with a new Venetian inquiry, Elisabeth Crouzet-Pavan's *"Sopra le Acque Salse": espaces, pouvoir, et société à Venise à la fin du Moyen Âge*, 2 vols., Rome (1992). But see a rich scatter of material in Kent and Kent (1982), Muir and Weissman (1989), Trexler (1980), Weissman (1982), an old but still very suggestive book on Bologna (Frati, 1900), and a superb introduction to the publicity of Florentine streets and squares (Molho and Sznura, 1986). The question of urban space is linked, inseparably in my view, with the problem of private versus public—another theme insufficiently broached by historical scholarship, though for the early communal period in Bologna see Heers (1984). As Waley (1991, p. 158) has rightly remarked of thirteenth-century Siena, "Nothing was so private a matter that it lay beyond the reach of the commune." As an assault on individuals, revealing the anxious fear of public humiliation, defamatory mural painting has been treated by Edgerton (1985). The public-private tandem and puzzle may be couched thus: since honor, name, and reputation were so important—and by definition public—for Grasso's Florence, when these were wholly lost, such as by some dreadful disgrace, how much or what aspect of the person remained intact? Was it the case, in short, that to lose public face was to lose some part—and perhaps the major part —of identity, essence, and being? In his pitch to Grasso, the priest of Santa Felicita is looking above all to the public-social person; the woodcarver's "soul" does not seem to be on the line. Weissman (1982) has some substantive points on the laity's relations with parish priests.

The figures I provide regarding distances within Florence—e.g. 750 meters from Santa Felicita to the cathedral—are my own approximate calculations.

On the matter of Grasso's relations with his mother, one manuscript, as cited by Rochon (1975), suggests that Monna Giovanna was having sexual relations with the parish priest at Polverosa and that this delayed her return to Florence. If so, and Grasso knew of the affair, we can imagine his disgust and fury—in that time and place—in the light of what happened to him. But then why does Manetti's narrative, by far the most complete account of the story, pass this tidbit over in silence? Fifteenth-century Florentines, schooled in their "agonistic" society (Weissman, 1982), did not suppress such matters out of delicacy or kindness; they reserved fine feeling for amatory verse in the Petrarchan line. In view of his scathing humiliation, Grasso's rage needs no explanation based upon his mother's sexual appetite. This tantalizing detail was, I reckon, a mischievous invention. Or do we want to believe that his mother's "chastity" would have obviated Grasso's flight from Florence?

This brings me to the woodcarver's remarkable civility. Short of adducing stories, tales, letters, poetry, primers of advice, chronicle material, sermons, certain *ricordanze* (family logbooks), court records, and legislation on insult and assault, I do not see how we might go about establishing my claim regarding the *civil vivere* or polite conduct of the class of highly skilled craftsmen in Italian Renaissance cities. This is matter for yet another doctoral dissertation.

The Italian reputation for cruelty is noted, for instance, in a couple of tales in *The Heptameron*, Navarre (1984). The consequences of bankruptcy, not of big banking firms but of small men like Grasso, need to be studied, and this would include imprisonment for tax defaulting, on which Conti (1984) has some revealing pages.

On plagues and epidemics, finally, there is Carmichael (1986).

BIBLIOGRAPHY

Ady, Cecilia M. (1937) *The Bentivoglio of Bologna: A Study in Despotism*, Bologna.

Alberti, Leon Battista (1969) *The Family in Renaissance Florence*, trans. Renée N. Watkins, Columbia, So. Carolina.

Arienti, Giovanni Sabadino degli (1981) *Le Porretane*, ed. Bruno Basile, Rome.

Ascheri, Mario (1985) *Siena nel rinascimento: istituzioni e sistema politico*, Siena.

Asor Rosa, Alberto, general editor (1982–89) *Letteratura italiana*. 7 vols., some of which in separate tomes, Turin.

Balestracci, Duccio (1984) *La zappa e la retorica: Memorie familiari di un contadino toscano del Quattrocento*, Florence.

Barbi, Michele (1893) *Antonio Manetti e la Novella del Grasso Legnaiuolo*, Florence.

—— (1927) "Una versione inedita della Novella del Grasso Legnaiuolo," *Studi di filologia italiana* 1: 134-144.

Basile, Bruno, ed. (1984) *Bentivolorum Magnificentia: principe e cultura a Bologna nel Rinascimento*, Rome.

Bec, Christian (1967) *Les marchands écrivains. Affaires et humanisme à Florence, 1375–1434*, Paris.

—— (1981) *Cultura e società a Firenze nell'età della Rinascenza*, Rome.

—— (1986) *Florence 1300–1600: Histoire et culture*, Nancy.

Beccherini, Bianca (1948) "Un canta in banca fiorentino: Antonio di Guido," *Rivista musicale italiana*, 50: 241–247

Bellomo, Manlio (1970) *La condizione giuridica della donna in Italia. Vicende antiche e moderne*, Torino.

Bernardino da Siena (1880–1888) *Le prediche volgari dette nella Piazza del Campo l'anno MCCCCXXVII*, 3 vols., ed. L. Bianchi, Siena.

Bizzocchi, Roberto (1987) *Chiesa e potere nella Toscana del Quattrocento*, Bologna.

Boccaccio, Giovanni (1972) *The Decameron*, tr. G.H. McWilliam, London and New York.

Boiardo, Matteo Maria (1962) *Opere volgari*, ed. Pier Vincenzo Mengaldo, Bari.

Bongi, Salvatore, ed. (1863) *Bandi lucchesi del secolo decimoquarto*, Bologna.

Bonolis, Guido (1901) *La giurisdizione della Mercanzia in Firenze nel secolo XIV*, Florence.

Borlenghi, Aldo, ed. (1962), *Novelle del Quattrocento*, Milan.

Borsellino, Nino (1989) *La Tradizione del Comico: l'eros l'osceno la beffa nella letteratura italiana da Dante a Belli*, Milan.

Bowsky, William (1978) *The Finance of the Commune of Siena, 1287–1355*, Oxford.

—— (1981) *A Medieval Italian Commune: Siena under the Nine, 1287–1355*, Berkeley.

Bracciolini, Poggio (1946) *Contro l'ipocrisia (i frati ipocriti)*, ed. Giulio Vallese, Naples.

Branca, Vittore, ed. (1986) *Mercanti scrittori: ricordi nella Firenze tra Medioevo e Rinascimento*, Milan.

Branciforte, Suzanne (1990) *Ars poetica rei publicae: The Herald of the Florentine Signoria* (doctoral dissertation in the Italian Department, University of California, Los Angeles).

Brucker, Gene A., ed. (1967) *Two Memoirs of Renaissance Florence*, trans. Julia Martines, New York and London.

—— (1971) *The Society of Renaissance Florence: A Documentary Study*, New York.

—— (1983) *Renaissance Florence*, Berkeley.

—— (1986) *Giovanni and Lusanna*, Berkeley and Los Angeles.

—— (1991) "Ecclesiastical Courts in Fifteenth-Century Florence and Fiesole," *Medieval Studies*, 33: 229-257.

Caggese, Romolo, ed. (1918–21) *Statuti della repubblica Fiorentina*, 2 vols., Florence.

Carmichael, Ann G. (1986) *Plagues and the Poor in Renaissance Florence*, Cambridge-London-New York.

Certaldo, Paolo da (1945) *Libro di buoni costumi: documento di vita trecentesca*, ed. Alfredo Schiaffini, Florence.

Chabot, Isabelle (1988) "Widowhood and poverty in late medieval Florence," *Continuity and Change*, 3(2): 291-311.

Cherubini, Giovanni (1974) *Signori, Contadini, Borghesi: Ricerche sulla società italiana del basso medioevo*, Florence.

Chiarini, Gioachino, ed. (1982) *Novelle italiane: il Quattrocento*, Milan.

Chojnacki, Stanley (1988) "The Power of Love: Wives and Husbands in Late Medieval Venice," in *Women and Power in the Middle Ages*, eds. Mary Erler and Maryanne Kowaleski, Athens (Georgia) and London.

Cohn, Samuel (1980) *The Laboring Classes in Renaissance Florence*, New York.

—— (1988) *Death and Property in Siena, 1205–1800: Strategies for the Afterlife*, Baltimore.

Conti, Elio (1984) *L'imposta diretta a Firenze nel quattrocento (1427–1494)*, Florence.

Da Bisticci, Vespasiano (1926) *The Vespasiano Memoirs*, trans. by William George and Emily Waters, New York.

Datini, Margherita (1977) *Le lettere di Margherita Datini a Francesco di Marco, 1384–1410*, ed. Valeria Rosati, Prato.

Davidsohn, Roberto (1956–68) *Storia di Firenze*, trans. G.B. Klein and E. Dupré-Theseider, 8 vols., Florence.

De Robertis, Domenico and Duro, A., eds. (1968) *Novella del Grasso legnaiuolo nella redazione del codice Palatino 200*, Florence.

Decor Puellarum (1461) Anonymous, Venice.

Del Lungo, Isidoro (1923) *Gli amori del Magnifico Lorenzo*, Bologna.

Dennet, Daniel Clement (1991) *Consciousness Explained*, Boston.

Di Blasi, Patrizia (1985) "Gusto della burla e mito dell'onore, oralità e scrittura nella novella del Grasso Legnaiuolo," in *Metamorfosi della novella*, ed. Giorgio Bàrberi Squarotti, Foggia.

Di Francia, Letterio (1924) *Novellestica, Vol. I, Dalle origini al Bandello*, Milan.

Dizionario biografico degli italiani (1960–), Rome.

Dizionario critico della letteratura italiana (1986), 3 vols. ed. Vittore Branca, Turin.

Dizionario enciclopedico della letteratura italiana (1966–70) 6 vols., Rome-Bari.

Edgerton, Samuel Y. (1985) *Pictures and Punishment: Art and Criminal Prosecution During the Florentine Renaissance*, Ithaca.

Edler, Florence (1934) *Glossary of Mediaeval Terms of Business, Italian Series: 1200–1600*, Cambridge, Massachusetts.

Fanti, Mario (1978) "La Confraternità di S. Maria della Morte e la conforteria dei condannati in Bologna nei secoli XIV e XV," *Quaderni del Centro di Ricerca di Studio sul movimento dei disciplinati*, 20: 17-34.

Farolfi, Bernardino (1977) *Strutture agrarie e crisi cittadina nel primo cinquecento bolognese*, Bologna.

Fatini, Giuseppe, ed. (1929) *Novelle del Quattrocento*, Torino.

Ferrero, Giuseppe G. and Doglio, Maria Luisa, eds. (1975) *Novelle del Quattrocento*, Torino.

Fiorato, Charles A. (1976), "Rustres et citadins dans les nouvelles de Bandello," in *Ville et campagne dans la littérature italienne de la Renaissance*, ed. André Rochon, 2 vols., Paris, I: 77-138.

—— (1980) "L'image et la condition de la femme dans les Nouvelles de Matteo Bandello," in *Images de la femme dans la littérature italienne de la Renaissance*, ed. A. Rochon, pp. 167-286, Paris.

—— and Margolin, Jean-Claude, eds. (1989), *L'écrivain face à son public en France et en Italie à la Renaissance: Actes du colloque international de Tours (4–6 Dec. 1986)*, Paris.

Flamini, Francesco (1891) *La lirica toscana del Rinascimento anteriore ai tempi del Magnifico*, Pisa.

Folena, Gianfranco, ed. (1953) *Motti e facezie del Piovano Arlotto*, Milan.

Frati, Lodovico (1900) *La vita privata in Bologna dal secolo xiii al xvii*, Bologna.

—— ed. (1908) *Rimatori bolognesi del Quattrocento*, Bologna.

Gherardi da Prato, Giovanni (1975) *Il Paradiso degli Alberti*, ed. Antonio Lanza, Roma.

—— (1867) *Il Paradiso degli Alberti*, ed. Alessandro Wesselofsky, Bologna.

Giusti, Giuseppe and Capponi, Gino, eds. (1956) *Dizionario dei proverbi italiani*, Milan. Original edition, 1852.

Goldthwaite, Richard A. (1980) *The Building of Renaissance Florence*, Baltimore.

Guarducci, Piero and Ottanelli, Valeria (1982) *I servitori domestici della casa borghese toscana nel basso Medioevo*, Florence.

Guidi, Guidobaldo (1981) *Il governo della città-repubblica di Firenze del primo Quattrocento*, 3 vols., Florence.

Gundersheimer, Werner L. (1973) *Ferrara: The Style of a Renaissance Despotism*, Princeton.

Hay, Dennis (1977) *The Church in Italy in the Fifteenth Century*, Cambridge, London, New York.

—— and Law, John (1989) *Italy in the Age of the Renaissance, 1380–1530*, London and New York.

Heers, Jacques (1984) *Espaces publics, espaces privés dans la ville: Le liber terminorum de Bologne (1294)*, Paris.

Herlihy, David (1969) "Vieillir à Florence au Quattrocento," *Annales ESC* 24: 1338-1352.

—— and Klapisch-Zuber, Christiane (1978) *Les Toscans et leurs familles. Une étude du catasto florentin de 1427*, Paris.

Hook, Judith (1979) *Siena: A City and its History*, London.

Jones, Philip (1980) *Economia e società nell'Italia medievale*, Turin

Kent, Dale V. (1978) *The Rise of the Medici: Faction in Florence 1426–1434*, Oxford.

—— and Kent, Francis W. (1981) "A Self-discipling Pact Made By the Peruzzi Family of Florence (June 1433)," *Renaissance Quarterly*, 34, 3: 337-355.

—— (1982) *Neighbours and Neighbourhood in Renaissance Florence: The District of the Red Lion in the Fifteenth Century*, Locust Valley, New York.

King, Margaret L. (1991) *Women of the Renaissance*, Chicago and London.

Kirshner, Julius (1973) "Civitas sibi faciat civem": Bartolus of Sassoferrato's Doctrine on the Making of a Citizen," *Speculum: A Journal of Medieval Studies*, XLVIII, 4: 694-713.

—— (1978) *Pursuing Honor While Avoiding Sin: The Monte delle Doti of Florence*, Milan. Originally in *Studi senesi*, LXXIX (1977): 177-258.

—— (1985) "Wives' Claims Against Insolvent Husbands in Late Medieval Italy," in Julius Kirshner and Suzanne Wemple, eds., *Women of the Medieval World*, pp. 256-303, Oxford and New York.

Klapisch-Zuber, Christiane (1985) *Women, Family, and Ritual in Renaissance Italy*, trans. Lydia Cochrane, Chicago.

—— (1990) *La maison et le nom: Stratégies et rituels dans l'Italie de la Renaissance*, Paris.

—— ed. (1990a) *Storia delle donne: il Medioevo*, Rome-Bari.

Kuehn, Thomas (1985) "Reading Between the Patrilines: Leon Battista Alberti's *Della Famiglia* in Light of His Illegitimacy," *I Tatti Studies*, 1: 161-187.

—— (1991) *Law, Family, and Women: Toward a Legal Anthropology of Renaissance Italy*, Chicago.

Lanza, Antonio (1971 and 1989) *Polemiche e berte letterarie nella Firenze del primo Rinascimento (1375–1449)*, 1st and 2nd eds., Rome.

—— ed. (1973–1975), *Lirici toscani del Quattrocento*, 2 vols., Rome.

Larivaille, Paul (1975) *La vie quotidienne des courtisanes en Italie au temps de la Renaissance: Rome et Venise XVe et XVIe siècles*, Paris.

La Roncière, Charles de (1977) "Une famille florentine au XIVe siècle: les Velluti," in *Famille et parenté dans l'Occident médieval*, eds. Georges Duby and Jacques Le Goff, pp. 227-248, Paris.

—— (1988) "Tuscan Notables on the Eve of the Renaissance," in *A History of Private Life: Revelations of Medieval World*, ed. Georges Duby, trans. A. Goldhammer, II: 157-309, Cambridge (Mass.) and London.

Lawner, Lynne (1987) *Lives of the Courtesans: Portraits of the Renaissance*, New York.

Levi, Ezio (1914) *I Cantari leggendari del popolo italiano nei secoli XIV e XV,* supplement 16 of the *Giornale storico della letteratura italiana.*

Malinowska, Irena (1966) "L'ordinamento del Comune di Bologna nel '400," *Archivio della Fondazione per la storia amministrativa*, Bologna.

Manetti, Antonio (1976) *Vita di Filippo Brunelleschi preceduta da La Novella del Grasso*, eds. Domenico de Robertis and Giuliano Tanturli, Milan.

—— (1970) *The Life of Brunelleschi*, see Saalman, Howard.

—— (1976a) "La novella del Grasso legnaiuolo," ed. Gianfranco Contini, in *Letteratura italiana del Quattrocento*, pp. 470-500, Florence.

—— (1983) "Fatso the Carpenter," in *Italian Renaissance Tales*, ed. and trans. by Janet L. Smarr, Rochester, Michigan.

—— (1991) *The Fat Woodworker*, trans. Robert L. and Valerie Martone, New York.

Manni, Domenico M. (1762) "Notizie di Manetto Ammannatini, detto Il Grasso Legnaiuolo," *Le veglie piacevoli*, 4 vols., Venice, III: 36-50.

—— (1762a), Pages on Bianco Alfani in "Burchiello," *Le veglie piacevoli*, I: 44-47.

—— ed. (1782) *Libro di novelle e di bel parlare gentile*, Florence.

Martines, Lauro (1963) *The Social World of the Florentine Humanists, 1390–1460*, Princeton.

—— (1968) *Lawyers and Statecraft in Renaissance Florence*, Princeton.

—— ed. (1972) *Violence and Civil Disorder in Italian Cities: 1200–1500*, Berkeley and Los Angeles.

—— (1974) "A Way of Looking at Women in Renaissance Florence," *The Journal of Medieval and Renaissance Studies*, 4, 1: 15-28.

—— (1985) *Society and History in English Renaissance Verse*, Oxford and New York.

—— (1988) *Power and Imagination: City-States in Renaissance Italy*, 2nd ed., Baltimore.

—— (1988a) "Forced Loans: Political and Social Strain in Quattrocento Florence," *Journal of Modern History*, 60: 300-311.

—— (1993) "The Politics of Italian Renaissance Love Poetry," in *Historical Criticism and the Challenge of Theory*, ed. Janet Smarr, Urbana-Champagne and Chicago.

—— "Ritual Language in Renaissance Italy," to appear in *Rites et Rituels dans les sociétés médiévales (XIIIe-XVIe s.)* eds. Agostino Paravicini Bagliani and Jean-Claude Maire Vigueur.

—— (1994) "L'Amour et l'histoire: carrefour de la renaissance italienne," forthcoming in *Annales ESC* (1994).

Marzi, Demetrio (1910) *La cancelleria della repubblica fiorentina*, Rocca S. Casciano.

Masson, Giorgina (1975) *Courtesans of the Italian Renaissance*, London.

Mazzi, Maria Serena (1991) *Prostituti e lenoni nella Firenze del Quattrocento*, Florence.

—— and Ravezzi, Sergio (1983) *Gli uomini e le cose nelle campagne fiorentine del Quattrocento*, Florence.

Medici, Lorenzo de' (1965) *Scritti scelti di Lorenzo de' Medici*, ed. Emilio Bigi, 2nd ed., Turin.

Migiel, Marilyn and Schiesari, Juliana, eds. (1991) *Refiguring Woman: Perspectives on Gender and the Italian Renaissance*, Ithaca and London.

Molho, Anthony (1979) "Cosimo de' Medici: Pater Patriae or Padrino?," *Stanford Italian Review*, 1: 5-33.

—— (1994) *Marriage Alliance in Late Medieval Florence: A Study of Ruling Class Endogamy Based on the Records of the Monte delle Doti*, Cambridge, Massachusetts.

—— and Sznura, Franek, eds. (1986) *Alle bocche della piazza: Diario di anonimo fiorentino 1382–1401*, Florence.

Morelli, Giovanni di Pagolo (1956) *Ricordi*, ed. Vittore Branca, Florence.

Muir, Edward and Weissman, Ronald E. (1989) "Social and Symbolic Places in Renaissance Venice and Florence," in *The Power of Place*, pp. 81-105, eds. John A. Agnew and James S. Duncan, Boston.

Najemy, John (1982) *Corporatism and Consensus in Florentine Electoral Politics, 1280–1400*, Chapel Hill.

Navarre, Marguerite de (1984), *The Heptameron*, trans. Paul A. Chilton, New York.

Novelle di vari autori (1804), Milan.

Pandimiglio, Leonida (1985) "Casa e famiglia a Firenze nel basso Medio Evo," *Cultura*, 23, 3: 304-327.

Papi, Anna Benvenuti (1990) *In Castro Poenitentiae*, Rome.

Pettoello, Decio (1930) *Great Italian Short Stories*, London.

Piccolomini, Enea Silvio (1985) *Storia di due amanti*, Palermo.

Plaisance, Michel (1985) "Les rapports ville-campagne dans les nouvelles de Sacchetti, Sercambi et Sermini," in *Culture et société en Italie du Moyen-Age à la Renaissance: hommage à André Rochon*, pp. 61-73, Paris.

—— (1986) "Città e campagna (XIII–XVII secolo)," in *Letteratura italiana*, V: 583-634, ed. Alberto Asor Rosa, Turin.

Poliziano, Angelo (1983) *Detti piacevoli*, ed. Tiziano Zanato, Rome.

Pullini, Giorgio (1958) *Burle e facezie del Quattrocento*, Pisa.

Repetti, Emanuele (1833–1846) *Dizionario geografico, fisico, storico della Toscana*, 6 vols., Florence.

Rezasco, Giulio (1881) *Dizionario del linguaggio italiano storico e amministrativo*, Florence.

Rochon, André (1963) *La jeunesse de Laurent de Médicis (1449–1478)*, Paris.

—— (1975) "Une date importante dans l'histoire de la *beffa*: La nouvelle du Grasso Legnaiuolo," in *Formes et Significations de la "Beffa" dans la littérature italienne de la Renaissance (Deuxième série)*, Paris.

—— ed. (1976–77) *Ville et campagne dans la littérature italienne de la Renaissance*, 2 vols., Paris.

Rocke, Michael J. (1989) *Male Homosexuality and its Regulation in Late Medieval Florence*, 2 vols. (doctoral dissertation in the History Department, State University of New York at Binghamton).

Romano, Dennis (1987) *Patricians and Popolani: The Social Foundations of the Venetian Renaissance State*, Baltimore and London.

Roscoe, Thomas (1825) *Italian Novelists*, 4 vols., London.

Ross, James B. (1975) "The Middle-Class Child in Urban Italy, 14th to early 16th Century," in *The History of Childhood*, ed. Lloyd de Mause, pp. 183-228, New York.

Rossi, Vittorio (1930) "Sulla novella del Bianco Alfani," in his *Scritti di critica letteraria*, 3 vols., Florence, II: 371-400.

Rubinstein, Nicolai (1966) *The Government of Florence Under the Medici (1434–1494)*, Oxford.

Ruggiero, Guido (1985) *The Boundaries of Eros: Sex Crime and Sexuality in Renaissance Venice*, New York and Oxford.

Saalman, Howard, ed. (1970) *The Life of Brunelleschi by Antonio di Tuccio Manetti*, trans. Catherine Enggass, University Park and London.

Sacchetti, Franco (1984) *Il Trecentonovelle*, ed. Antonio Lanza, Florence.

Sapori, Armando (1946) "La cultura del mercante medievale italiano," in *Studi di storia economica, secc. XIII-XV*, vol. I: 9-62, Florence.

Sermini, Gentile (1968) *Novelle*, 2 vols., ed. Giusepe Vettori, Rome.

Smarr, Janet L. (1983) ed. and trans., *Italian Renaissance Tales*, Rochester, Michigan.

Statuta populi et communis Florentiae anno salutis MCCCCXV (1778–83), 3 vols., Freiburg.

Storia d'Italia: Annali 9 (1986) ed. Giorgio Chittolini and Giovanni Miccoli, Turin.

Strocchia, Sharon T. (1989) "Death Rites and the Ritual Family in Renaissance Florence," in *Life and Death in Fifteenth-Century Florence*, ed. Marcel Tetel, Ronald G. Witt, and Rona Goffen, Durham, N.C. and London.

Strozzi, Alessandra (1877) *Lettere di una gentildonna fiorentina del secolo XV ai figli esuli*, ed. Cesare Guasti, Florence.

Tartaro, Achille and Tateo, Francesco (1971) *Il Quattrocento: l'età dell'umanesimo*, vol. III, 1 of *La letteratura italiana storia e testi*, ed. Carlo Muscetta, Bari.

Tenenti, Alberto (1987) *Stato: un'idea, una logica*, Bologna.

Tinucci, Niccolò (1974) *Rime*, ed. Clemente Mazzotta, Bologna.

Trexler, Richard C. (1980) *Public Life in Renaissance Florence*, New York.

—— (1981) "La prostitution florentine au XVe siecle: patronages et clientèles," *Annales ESC*, 36: 983-1015.

Varese, Claudio (1955), *Prosatori volgari del Quattrocento*, Milan and Naples.

Wacknernagel, Martin (1981) *The World of the Florentine Renaissance Artist: Project and Patrons, Workshop and Art Market*, trans. Alison Luchs, Princeton.

Waley, Daniel (1991) *Siena and the Sienese in the Thirteenth Century*, Cambridge.

Weissman, Ronald F. E. (1982) *Ritual Brotherhood in Renaissance Florence*, New York.

Wolfgang, Marvin E. (1960) "A Florentine Prison: Le carceri delle Stinche," *Studies in the Renaissance*, 7: 148-166.

—— (1990) "Crime and Punishment in Renaissance Florence," *Journal of Criminal Law and Criminology*, 81, 3: 567-584.

Of publications since the first edition of the book, but also including others that should have been listed in my original bibliography, I have selected the following titles on the basis of their direct bearing on, proximity to, or resonance with Italian Renaissance fiction.

Alberti, Leon Battista (1987) *Dinner Pieces*, trans. David Marsh, Binghamton.

Brand, Peter, and Lino Pertile, eds. (1999, revised ed.) *The Cambridge History of Italian Literature*, Cambridge.

Chojnacki, Stanley (2000) *Women and Men in Renaissance Venice: Twelve Essays on Patrician Society*, Baltimore and London.

Connell, William J., ed. (2002) *Society and Individual in Renaissance Florence*, Berkeley, Los Angeles, London.

Crouzet-Pavan, Élisabeth (2002) *Venice Triumphant: The Horizons of a Myth*, trans. Lydia G. Cochrane, Chicago.

Dean, Trevor, and K.J.P. Lowe, eds. (1998) *Marriage in Italy: 1300–1650*, Cambridge.

Fabbri, Lorenzo (1991) *Alleanza matrimoniale e patriziato nella Firenze del '400*, Florence.

Malato, Enrico, ed. (1989) *La novella italiana: Atti del Convegno di Caprarola 19–24 settembre 1988*, 2 vols., Rome.

Martelli, Mario (1996) *Letteratura fiorentina del Quattrocento: Il filtro degli anni sessanta*, Florence.

Martines, Lauro (2001) *Strong Words: Writing and Social Strain in the Italian Renaissance*, Baltimore and London.

——— (2003) *April Blood: Florence and the Plot against the Medici*, London and New York.

Najemy, John M. (1993) *Between Friends: Discourses of Power and Desire in the Machiavelli–Vettori Letters of 1513–1515*, Princeton.

Panizza, Letizia, ed. (2000) *Women in Italian Renaissance Culture and Society*, Oxford.

Rocke, Michael (1996) *Forbidden Friendships: Homosexuality and Male Culture in Renaissance Florence*, New York.

INDEX

An index of the essayistic parts only

public vs. private, 233-34, 256. *See also* space, public
Pucci, Dionigi, 160
Pulci, Luigi, 160

rectors (magistrates), 126
Remole, 64
revenge, 133. *See also* feud
Ricasoli, Galeotto da, 122
Ricciarda, 25-35, 132, 161, 229
ritual, 57, 59, 61-62
"rock star," 31
Rome, 240
Rossi, Vittorio, 124, 128, 129
Rucellai, Bernardo, 160
Rucellai, Giovanni di Messer Francesco, 221, 222, 225-26, 229, 233, 235, 240

Sacchetti, Franco, 14, 31
sacrilege, 253
Salimbeni family, 56
St. John the Baptist, patron saint of Florence, 228
St. Paul's Cathedral, London, 234
Salutati, Coluccio, 227
San Bernardino of Siena, 33, 159
San Gallo, via, 128
San Marco (Florence), church of, 120, 121, 128, 130
Santa Croce quarter, 127
Santa Felicita, church of, 230, 234
Santa Maria degli Angeli, convent of, 118
Santa Maria del Fiore, Florence cathedral, 233, 234, 235
Santa Maria Novella quarter, 127
Santa Maria Nuova, hospital of, 129
Santi (Santo), Giovanni di, 121, 124, 126, 128, 129
Santo Spirito quarter, 126
self-identity, 214. *See also* identity and society
Sercambi, Giovanni, 14, 31
Sermini, Gentile, 14, 57, 67-68, 156
Siena, 27, 55-68 *passim*, 81, 153-67 *passim*, 215, 240; population of, 55
Sigismund, Emperor, 239
Signoria, Florence ruling council, 219, 239, 240
signoria, meaning of, 231-32

Other Books by Lauro Martines

The Social World of the Florentine Humanists

Lawyers and Statecraft in Renaissance Florence

Violence and Civil Disorder in Italian Cities: 1200–1500

*Not in God's Image: Women in History from the Greeks
to the Victorians*, with Julia O'Faolain

Power and Imagination: City-States in Renaissance Italy

Society and History in English Renaissance Verse

*Strong Words: Writing and Social Strain
in the Italian Renaissance*

April Blood: Florence and the Plot against the Medici